THE
BUSINESS

THE BUSINESS

BUSINESS

DICK HOBBS

JB

First published in the UK by John Blake Publishing
an imprint of Bonnier Books UK
The Plaza,
535 Kings Road,
London SW10 0SZ
Owned by Bonnier Books
Sveavägen 56, Stockholm, Sweden

www.facebook.com/johnblakebooks
twitter.com/jblakebooks

First published in paperback in 2021

Paperback ISBN: 978-1-78946-414-6
Ebook ISBN: 978-1-78946-416-0
Audiobook ISBN: 978-1-78946-415-3

Design by www.envydesign.co.uk

Printed and bound in Great Britain by Clays Ltd, Elcograf S.p.A

1 3 5 7 9 10 8 6 4 2

Text copyright © Dick Hobbs

The right of Dick Hobbs to be identified as the author of this work has been asserted
by him in accordance with the Copyright, Designs and Patents Act 1988.

MIX
Paper from
responsible sources
FSC® C018072

John Blake Publishing is an imprint of Bonnier Books UK
www.bonnierbooks.co.uk

Dedicated to:
Sue, our sons Pat and Nik, and our grandson
Alfie Jack Hobbs.

And to skulduggery

CONTENTS

INTRODUCTION:
RESEARCHING SKULDUGGERY

'You fucking come and see me, fucking write about me you fucking long streak of fucking useless . . . Come and put this in a fucking book, fucking Professor fucking Thunderbirds Brains.'

TEDDY

This book is about criminal lives and how they have changed over time. I have used the words of thieves, gangsters and dealers along with my observations to present a nuanced view of a complex world that is usually misrepresented and too often glamourised. While a few big name historical figures do make an appearance, I have always been far more interested in people near the bottom of the food chain, 'the poor bloody infantry', who do the hard work and serve most of the hard time.

Much of the research was done on the villains' home ground, in pubs, cafes, pie and mash shops, workshops, garages and warehouses, as well as in front rooms and kitchens. I also attended birthdays, weddings and funerals, and become acquainted with some of their spouses, girlfriends, boyfriends, children, grandchildren, and great-grandchildren. Since I started studying crime in the early 1980s, many changes have taken place and most of the venues where I conducted my early research have now been demolished, while the neighbourhoods in which they stood have been infected by gentrification, the original occupants either fleeing to the suburbs or retreating to the sofa with a bottle of supermarket spirits and a few ounces of bootlegged tobacco.

I also spoke to a few writers, barristers, drug rehab professionals, local council officials, Customs officers, civil servants, police officers, and, around the turn of the 21st century, during that fascinating period between the end of the Cold War and 9/11, to members of the security services. However, while I have benefited from off-the-record chats with pissed off police officers, I found that official information was geared towards the agenda of whatever police agency had passed it on and that generally, police case files or intelligence reports, even when they were not redacted to the extent of being worthless, told me more about police work than they did about criminal life. This is due to the fact that the ultimate aim of the police is to gain convictions, whereas my job is to understand criminal life, and seldom the twain meet. Indeed, in the mid-1990s, when a confidential report that I had written on the policing of organised crime was leaked and made front page headlines next to an account of the final day's proceedings at the Conservative Party annual conference, the head of the National Criminal Intelligence Service threatened me with a visit from the security services.[1] However, if MI5 did visit my office, I must have been in the pub at the time

---

1 'Leak reveals contempt for British "FBI"' *Independent*, 10 October 1996.

and I continued to operate as a researcher publishing books, papers and reports for an academic readership.

I am not an investigative journalist intent on exposing crime, criminals or criminal groups, and I have never had to work undercover – that would have been ridiculous. I just talked to a lot of people who have been involved in crime and kept my ears and eyes open, while simultaneously reading everything I could lay my hands on that has been written about crime and criminal life. I had no interest in putting any of the people that I have studied into prison. Consequently, with a few obvious exceptions, all of the individuals and many of the places mentioned in this book have been anonymised, and some incriminating details have been altered or omitted in order to protect the guilty. Indeed, many, perhaps most, of the people featured in this book are dead, living in the suburbs, or both, and I can state with total confidence that no animals or villains were harmed in the writing of *The Business*.

Part one of this book is based largely in and around London and covers the post-Second World War criminal era that was dominated by extortion and theft. Part two has a wider geographical scope and is concerned with the impact of the drug trade and the other unlicensed enterprises that have replaced the old underworld and now dominate large portions of the overworld. Much of my career has been spent decrying the tendency since the early 1990s for both the police and their friends in the mass media to present serious crime in terms of 'Mr Bigs' and the infiltration of British life by foreign villains, mafias, cartels and other cliches of organised crime. The truth is far more mundane. Throughout *The Business*, whenever possible, I let ordinary criminals talk about ordinary crime.

I first went to university in my early thirties and then

embarked on an academic career researching criminal life. I am now retired as a full-time academic and, looking back, I realise that I was fortunate to work in higher education when I did: I was given a lot of freedom and I had a really good time. Researching various aspects of crime enabled me to make a living from what became an obsession but, as I explain in chapter one, my exposure to the world of skulduggery did not begin at university.

PART ONE

Chapter 1

ONCE UPON A TIME IN PLAISTOW: A STROLL DOWN FELONY LANE

'And when at last I made into the East End, I was gratified to find that the fear of the crowd no longer haunted me. I had become a part of it. The vast and malodorous sea had welled up and over me, or I had slipped gently into it, and there was nothing fearsome about it.'

JACK LONDON, *INTO THE ABYSS*

THE SMOG OF WAR

Mum was in trouble. She had newborn twin boys in the pram and was dragging a two-year-old me by the hand through another killer London smog. We were all coughing. She had survived the Blitz despite working night shifts in a munitions factory, stepping over fire hoses and crunching over broken glass as she returned home in the early morning, through smouldering piles of rubble and dust and past billowing curtains and splashes of torn wallpaper. A few doors down from her home in Plaistow, three generations of one family died in their Anderson shelter at the bottom of the garden. Bomb blast had broken their necks and when my grandfather found the bodies they looked as if they were sleeping. One night, the river itself was alight. Then South Hallsville school, which was being used as an evacuation centre, received a direct hit, killing an estimated 600 sheltering civilians. Many of the bodies were not recovered and after the war, the bombsite was bulldozed and tarmacked over.

But although the war was over, there was now another airborne threat. While it was quieter, more insidious than the bombs, like the Blitz it hit East London particularly hard. Smog. This thick, yellow, polluted air had killed up to 12,000 Londoners the previous year. I could taste the sulphuric threat in the back of my throat as I was half dragged the last couple of hundred yards past clanking trolley buses and newspaper sellers spluttering out headlines about this deadly miasma. Mum's anger, terror and resentment at a world that continually produced new horrors vibrated down her arm as she tugged me along. We stumbled home, into a damp passageway lined with brown wallpaper the colour of dark shit. The front door was slammed shut and, while Mum tended to the babies in the living room, I stayed in the hallway on the bottom step of the stairs, watching the yellowish grey smog seep in under the door and along the floor towards my feet. I stayed very still, entranced by this swirling silent entity that inspired so much fear among adults. Gradually, it rose up my legs and enveloped my body. My clothes were already imbued with its rotten-egg stench but if I kept my mouth shut and my nose above the smog I could breathe.

My parents were part of a bomb-damaged generation who had experienced poverty, war, chaos and insecurity.

The population that had fought fascism for six years was encouraged to keep their heads down, enjoy the spam, and wait for rationing to end. Despite the immediate benefits that the welfare state delivered, the fear of unrestrained chaos remained very real for my parents and a steady job, along with avoiding any risk, was vital if they were to quarantine their family from impending disaster.

My parents had difficulty in coping with three children born so close together, so, soon after I learnt to breathe above the smog line, I was taken in by my maternal grandparents, in whose home I spent most of the next few years. While I was only a few minutes' walk from my parents', I may as well have been on another planet.

Most days, my grandfather would take me out for leisurely walks, usually to the local street market. He knew a lot of people and he would stop and talk to many of them, including a group of men who congregated at the top of the market outside Upton Park station. They were different from the other men who populated my small 1950s world. Unlike the ex-servicemen who nervously smoked and drank tea through tense evenings of heavily edited reminiscences in my parents' home, these market men were relaxed, but wary. Of what, I wasn't certain. They were very well dressed, in trilby hats and overcoats over dark suits, though they seemed to talk in code, and my grandfather always politely refused the coins that they offered to me.

Over half a century on, I know now that the men were thieves and bookies' runners. Although my grandfather was a working man and no villain, he was at ease in their company and they held him in some respect. He and the men he spoke to shared something that had been acquired the hard way: a street wisdom and a willingness to do what was necessary in the face of constant grinding poverty and unemployment.

Glimpses of the quasi-Dickensian lives of older relations peppered my childhood and I pieced together fragments of conversations concerning booth boxing at Mile End Waste, fights in Victoria Park, knuckledusters and pickpockets, 'Jackie Spot' and coin-tossing rings, dodgy bookmakers at the races, the police horses at Cable Street, rat-baiting in Brick Lane, 'coming off worst' in a fight with two pimps during the war and a detective's unsuccessful attempt at blackmail. There was clearly something going on outside the gratefully received oppression of a respectable job and not everybody kept their heads down.

In many ways, the 1950s were the beginning of the East End's golden age. For generations it had been associated with poverty, filth, disease, ignorance, racism and violent depravity. But as the post-war years moved into the modern era, the gloom that had settled upon the East End appeared to be lifting. Rehousing, although it destroyed established neighbourhood networks, improved the lives of families. 'Getting a council place' with a bathroom, indoor toilet and perhaps central heating, was a highpoint for those who, both literally and figuratively, had dug themselves out of the insanitary rubble of the Blitz.

And there was work, and plenty of it. As ships queued up along the Thames to unload in the East End's booming docks, dockwork – once a job that only pariahs would do – became a desirable occupation, in part due to the strength of the trade unions. Numerous other industries reliant on the docks – factories, processing plants and the like – also prospered and as London's bomb sites were turned into construction sites, building trades and crafts blossomed. Men had money in their pockets, many of the women who had experienced paid labour during the war years never went back to full-time domestic toil and East London was no longer a place defined by poverty.

Yet it was clear to anyone involved in dockwork that the good times could not last. Cargo was becoming increasingly containerised, which mechanised dockwork and reduced the need for labour, while the ships themselves were rapidly outgrowing the narrow confines of the London Docks. But for the time being, the pubs, clubs and many of the streets of East London took on a vibrancy that inspired an irresistible cocktail of hedonism, anti-authoritarianism and embrace of skulduggery that would have been recognisable in the Wild West or the Caribbean pirate havens of the 18th century.

However, co-existing with this vivacious world was an alternative universe where working-class families such as mine lived in terror of their children getting into trouble with the authorities. If you took liberties, you got caught, and if you got caught, the police would ruin you. For a relatively timid kid such as myself, this could be terrifying. And yet the rules of engagement were confusing: while the direction to keep your head down was commonly enforced at home with levels of violence that are difficult to explain to contemporary youth, it was clear to me that other people were taking liberties and nobody seemed to get caught.

Much of the liberty-taking had its origins in London's docks, and every level of theft – from petty to professional, from handfuls to lorry loads – was nurtured in the neighbourhoods that serviced the world's largest port. Local pubs were alternatives to the corner shop and few people failed to spice their lives with the odd roll of cloth, box of shirts or leg of lamb. And it was all so normal. Once I was at a friend's house when his dad, a docker, came home from work looking as if he had put on a lot of weight. He took off his donkey jacket and then removed a sweater, and another sweater and another – all in all he wore eight sweaters under his work clothes after plundering a shipment from the Far East. One famous tale from the 1960s involved a man who was staggering down the street apparently the worse for drink. When he collapsed onto the pavement, concerned bystanders rushed to help the stricken pale-faced man, who was shivering and incoherent. Eventually, he was taken by ambulance to the casualty department at the local hospital, where nurses discovered six large frozen steaks inside the patient's trousers, secured by clips attached to a scaffolder's belt. The meat, which had been liberated from the nearby Royal Docks, was resting against the docker's bare skin, causing hypothermia.

As a child, I was already learning about hypocrisy and the usefulness of denial – on occasion from inside the four walls of my respectable, law-abiding family home. It was always late at night after I had gone to bed when Mickey called. He was a docker and the brother of a close neighbour. When my mum answered the door a familiar, and somewhat reassuring, pantomime would commence.

> Mickey: Hello Mary, I have got a lovely roll of material for you.
> Mum: It's not knocked off, is it?
> Mickey: No, of course not, I got it from the auctions like the last lot.
> Mum: All right, let's have a look.

Even the most virtuous could be seduced by the lure of a bargain, their conscience salved by a throwaway enquiry as to the legal status of the goods on offer before the swag was unloaded into the front room of the now absolved grateful punter. However, most people did not bother with such niceties and considerable prestige was often attached to being involved in these 'little earners'. Just like the contemporary drugs trade, goods were regularly sold on several times before reaching the eventual consumer. Everybody was at it.

Normal punters, despite whatever 'little earners' they were on, didn't see themselves as criminals. No, 'real' criminals 'thought the world owed them a living', took the little earners and fiddles 'too far' and worst of all, they got caught. This opened the door to the police – not the fictional avuncular *Dixon of Dock Green* types but big ex-military men who didn't wipe their feet when they came in, who wanted information on neighbours and workmates and who would 'knock you about' if they didn't get what they came for. My parents did not hate the police but they were realists and, as they knew all too well what the police were capable of, they told me they were to be avoided.

At the age of 15, I was knocked down by a car on the way home from watching West Ham lose to Stoke and a police constable brought me home from hospital. My mother answered the front door to be confronted by my battered face accompanied by a large smiling policeman and, assuming that my injuries were the responsibility of the young PC, she violently berated the bewildered officer. Such was the state of distrust of police by ordinary working folk that they were guilty until proven innocent.

Violence was an ever-present fact of life. Working-class

men of my father's generation had taken to boxing in the same way that modern-day kids play computer games. Violence had been hardwired to their sense of self and these mild-mannered but war-damaged men who had experienced extreme violence in Europe, Africa and Asia would instinctively 'raise their hands' to anybody threatening their home, their family or their self-respect. If there was a problem, a police officer was the last person you would call on, that was merely inviting more trouble. When one late evening my father heard breaking glass and rushed to the front door to find a man breaking in, he opened the door and knocked the would-be intruder spark out. However, this was no burglar but a neighbour who had returned from the pub drunk and could not understand why the key to number 13 did not fit the lock to number 9. Next day, without a word from either combatant, our hungover neighbour fixed a new pane of glass to the front door. Calling the police was not an option.

CRIMINAL LESSONS

Street fights at pub closing time were a nightly occurrence, two policeman were once shot dead a mile from where we lived and when on the way to school I found a small sheath knife in the gutter, a bewildered elderly uncle exclaimed, 'In our day, we only used bike chains.' Thankfully, my secondary school had a culture that prized verbal dexterity above violence and produced a high proportion of self-employed and entrepreneurially minded individuals. However, in my neighbourhood there were members of large feral families who could turn a minor scuffle or an unwise glance into a visit to casualty. If they didn't get you, an older brother, cousin or uncle would oblige. Easing uncertainly into adulthood, I observed some of these playground warriors evolve into weapon-wielding crews/mobs/firms, and I devised a strategy for dealing with the realities of night life, and hostile neighbourhoods both by working on my social skills and developing a remarkable turn of speed from a standing start. While not every boy was part of a youth mafia, there was sufficient violent skulduggery to keep most kids watching, listening and generally on their toes, and, by my mid-teens, everyday life and the crime that was integral to it was starting to get more serious.

MAY 1968

St Philip's church and a handful of other local religious and charitable institutions provided some of the few non-sporting leisure outlets for youths too young or too skint to spend an evening in the pub. The monthly dances at St Philip's church hall were run by a group of Franciscan monks who appeared to have been handpicked to spread the Lord's word via their physical rather than spiritual attributes. A fight followed swiftly by the violent intervention of two or three of the brothers was the norm and added an edge for most of the 14 to 17-year-olds who had paid their entrance fee to a large scowling monk in brown robe and sandals.

On this particular evening, a group of five youths gathered in the church's foyer to eyeball new arrivals. Three of them wore newly fashionable Harrington jackets. Jay, who wore a V-necked sweater and sharply creased formal trousers, was a particularly dangerous young man, while his brother Don, resplendent in a camel-coloured Crombie overcoat, beige mohair trousers and red leather steel-capped boots – was equally violent. This group, who relished going toe to shiny toe with individual police officers on the football terraces, occasionally came together with other mobs to make up a formidable local alliance capable of contesting cafes, parties, parks, streets and clubs across East London. My friends and I made sure to publicly acknowledge Jay and his attack squad. It was the politically astute thing to do and showed that we were no threat.

Don left soon after and the evening played itself out in familiar fashion with around a hundred teenagers congregating inside, dancing and laughing, each one of us fuelled by little more than a bottle of beer bought at a local off-licence and drunk surreptitiously in the shadow of the dustbin sheds of a nearby block of flats. At one point, one of the monks dragged a young man wearing a suit and a Fred Perry shirt out of the hall by his skinny lapels while his muscular colleagues patrolled the periphery, concentrating their missionary zeal upon the prevention of heavy petting.

The St Philip's dances were renowned for the music that was played, which always featured tasteful selections of Tamla Motown and Stax, and it was during a slow ballad that the evening erupted in an all-too-familiar way. As couples slow-danced, voices were raised and boys stumbled in the dark. As the music stopped and the lights came up, Jay and a large teenager with a split lip squared up to each other. In time-honoured fashion, the crowd cleared to form an impromptu arena. Then a female voice rang out, 'He's got a gun!' There was now panic as some people tried to get out of the hall, screams and voices were raised, punches exchanged and the monks waded in with slaps and cuffs to clear the hall.

From outside there came the sound of fighting but the three in Harrington jackets remained in the hall. They calmly reached to the inside pockets of their tartan-lined jackets, taking out long thin cases perhaps six inches in length from which they removed open razors. They calmly placed the cases back in their pockets, opened the razors and, holding the weapons at shoulder height, joined the huddle of bodies who were fleeing the hall. Outside was chaos and above the heads of spectators and combatants, the razors could be seen slashing down onto faces and protective hands. In the doorway of some flats, a dark bundle received a vigorous kicking and a running fight took Jay, his compatriots and their prey towards the main road, while the remainder of the St Philip's congregation rapidly dispersed to back streets, bus stops and chip shops at the end of another Saturday night.

Violence was commonplace on the street and most young men became involved, albeit in a minor way. But the St Philip's incident was different, it was a unique opportunity to watch violence being choreographed through its various stages. I found it fascinating, and for a kid such as myself, who was as intent on avoiding injury as he was on embedding himself in environments where violence was an inevitability, understanding how violent situations evolved was vital and I became ever watchful and sensitive to the possibility of it 'going off'.

As working-class Londoners, we were largely untouched by the attempts to overturn capitalism taking place in Paris – that was for an alien breed called 'students'. As for those branded by Otis Redding as 'the love crowd', the middle-class posturing of hippies was rare and risky in the East End of 1968. The St Philip's incident took place in the same month that the

Kray twins were arrested and over the days and nights that followed, my friends and I made connections with the adult gangsterism that was part of the East End's brand and the battle in the Franciscans' backyard. Life was getting serious, and interesting.

WRONG AND WRONGER

Around the time I left school, I began to glimpse what could happen when skulduggery backfired. I was on nodding terms with one youth who bled to death on the floor of a pub when a sliver of glass pierced his jugular. After several years robbing his employers and emerging as a successful dealer in stolen goods, a neighbour in his twenties was imprisoned for theft. A close friend found himself charged with theft and was in danger of losing his apprenticeship before his father intervened with an envelope full of used notes for the desk sergeant. A classmate from secondary school was convicted for being a violent pimp. A schoolfriend from primary school was convicted of armed robbery and a friend waiting at a bus stop was hit by shotgun pellets fired by robbers fleeing a bank. When I was in my early twenties, a workmate was stabbed in a pub (by the landlord) and later woke up in hospital while being given the last rites. He told the priest to 'fuck off' and, after many weeks in hospital, got married and stopped going out on a Friday night.

With warehouses and lorry parks still clogging the pre-gentrified East End, opportunity was always knocking and as we were quickly absorbed into the well-established local culture of theft, either as thieves, fences or consumers, buying and selling 'hookey gear' was a normal part of life. There was a ready market for all kinds of goods, but particularly for clothes, which were often bought and sold several times before they arrived on the backs of grateful consumers. Entering into any new situation, the only questions were 'What's the swindle and where's the coup?' Stealing, fiddling and dealing was a way of life and part of a flash, self-confident style that flourished in an environment where competence as a ducker and diver was a highly desirable attribute.

Working on building sites, I watched as workmates diverted lorry loads of bricks and copper piping to projects being run by friends and relations. This was insolent, upfront and imaginative, and the only question anybody asked was, 'Do I get a drink out of it?' I worked for a time in a warehouse and I was regularly asked to come on Saturday mornings to 'clear a backlog of orders'. Along with two other young men, I would load up lorries and vans, for which we were paid cash in hand by a grateful foreman. I left the firm but about a year later the foreman was convicted for stealing hundreds of thousands of pounds worth of goods and redirecting them to a well-known high street chain of shops. Management promptly installed close circuit TV cameras and plain clothes security men throughout the premises. As a colleague of the convicted man lamented, 'They always get greedy, somebody gets nicked and then they have a clamp down. Spoils it for everybody.'

Everybody was on an earner. There was joy to be gleaned from being 'at it' – it showed that no matter how lowly you were, how many layers there were above you, by living on your wits you were making a mark, carving a personal niche in a predatory world where mere wage slaves were not expected to exhibit intelligence, imagination or creativity. Labourers would supply goods damaged to order at a massive discount, along with a tidy backhander, and if you walked around with an official looking document and a straight face it was easy to load a van with goods before meeting up with the grateful customer in a local cafe for a cup of tea and a ten pound note.

Negotiating deals and exploring business opportunities required sensitivity and social skills, as care needed to be taken at all times. As Nob, a warehouse labourer, explained, 'Usually they are a friend of a friend, they want something so they see me, they say they want it and I usually say, "Fuck me though, they're expensive." They say, "Are they?" So I say, "Yeah, about 50 notes." So they say, "Well, can't you find some damaged or old stock then?" Then you know.'

Once the customer was committed, profit became the name of the game and sometimes deception rather than theft was the preferred method.

'Sometimes I say to them, you know, "It's expensive, 50 quid." I sell it to them for 30 and it's only worth 20.'

Meanwhile on other occasions, Nob would revert to theft while employing deception to maximise his profit, stealing goods but claiming that he had to buy them.

'My brother-in-law wants a set of taps so I get him one and charge him £60. I said, "Now, Ken, I'm not earning out of you, I wouldn't, would I? But the geezer I work with wants £60." But that was all bollocks. The wife had some shoes, the boy needed some trousers and I had a nice drink, so it all goes.'

I left school shortly before my 17th birthday and worked for two years in a succession of junior clerical jobs, before taking on various labouring jobs both in the East End and beyond. I was able to observe at close quarters these ingenious scams that, despite gleaning little monetary return, were nonetheless important in terms of self-respect and independence. In short, crime could make life worth living and this everyday entrepreneurship was apparent in the most unlikely settings.

For a few weeks in the early 1970s I worked with Lee, who drove a small truck collecting waste paper for recycling from homes and businesses. Lee, who could not read or write, lived close to the depot and after filling the truck with paper, we would park outside of his house, wedge a garden hose into the top of the load and turn the tap full on. Meanwhile, we stood outside of the house drinking tea. Long experience had taught my new friend that in the time it took to make a pot of tea and drink one cup, the water had soaked almost, but not quite, through the load. At this point, we would remove the hose, jump into the cab and drive at breakneck speed back to the depot and onto the weighbridge. The discerning reader will have guessed by now that we were being paid a productivity bonus and the heavier the load, the weightier our pay packets. The trick was to get off the weighbridge just before water started pouring out of the bottom of the truck.

In my late twenties, I saw a man buy a car in the saloon bar of a pub for £200. No money changed hands but he told the vendor that he would be paid in cash by the end of the evening. He took the car keys into the adjacent public bar, sold the car for £250 cash, gave the keys to the new owner and walked the 15 feet back in to the saloon bar and delivered £200 to the grateful vendor. I watched the entire process. That was for me a truly educational experience.

Crime was burnt onto the walls of the post-war East End. With the street wisdom of my grandfather lurking somewhere in my subconscious, I became drawn to a vantage point at the edge of skulduggery. All of the whispers of violence, business, anger, police and thieves had started to make sense; my parents' mantra of 'be good' had morphed into 'be lucky' – advice that I suspect would have made perfect sense to my grandfather. For me, this world was always within touching distance and, as I learnt as a toddler, if you watched carefully, keeping very still with your nose just above trouble, you could observe this occasionally toxic but always fascinating world of skulduggery without choking on its fumes.

Chapter 2

THE CITY ARMS: EAST END IN MINIATURE

'I graduated to the billiards hall and public house, and as I established myself on the fringe of this kind of world, I became both fascinated and challenged by it, their rakishness, their flamboyant clothes, their tough, self-reliant manners, their rejection of conventional attitudes to sex and money – such things forced me and mesmerised me into conquering the mysteries of the world they lived in. I unconsciously modelled myself on the more successful representatives of this new society.'

JOHN MCVICAR

In every big city in England during the 1970s and 1980s there were pubs and clubs where ducking, diving and general skulduggery were a way of life. Some of these drinking palaces were venues where detectives, pros, cons and a few respectable people could socialise, where information was exchanged and blind eyes were turned. These were not exclusive underworld haunts but well-kept working-class pubs with smart bar staff and a wide-ranging, usually immaculately behaved clientele: the good, the bad and the salaried.

I started drinking in The City Arms in the late 1970s and throughout most the eighties it was a valuable place to watch the East End at work and play. It was a classic backstreet Victorian boozer that had undergone umpteen serious renovations during its lifetime, the most significant of which was its conversion from its original two-bar and a snug layout into one large drinking space located around an oval bar. With mobile phones yet to conquer the world and no juke box or piped music to pollute the airwaves, The City Arms was alive with multiple conversations, some of which tended to increase in volume as the clock edged closer to closing time, while the more enticingly conspiratorial remained hushed. With a sticky carpet around the immediate bar area, and just a few cheap hunting prints adorning the flock wallpapered walls, The City was nonetheless one of the smarter pubs in the area. It was spotlessly clean, despite this being an era when most of its clientele felt obliged to smoke. Empty glasses and full ash trays were quickly cleared by the staff of smartly dressed middle-aged local men and women who were on first-name terms with most of the drinkers.

When the husband-and-wife team who ran The City Arms emerged from their private quarters on the first floor and floated behind the bar to serve, there was a shift in the air as drinkers shifted their gaze from their co-conspirators to take in a bronzed and bejewelled couple whose overwhelming glow of health and well-being was completely at odds with the nicotine-stained reality of both the pub and its patrons.

While male customers plotted their sorties to the bar in order to be served by the 'lady of the house', who led the bar team with grace and humour, the landlord never seemed that interested in actually serving people. He used every opportunity to pose; even the pulling of a warm pint of soapy bitter was a chance to flex his bulging biceps and ridged forearms. However, in case a honed-to-near-perfection tendon might pop, a less glamorous member of the bar team was tasked with making back-breaking trips down to the cellar to bring up crates of bottles, leaving *mein host* to chat with his exclusive coterie of drinkers, blaggers and bullshitters.

The City Arms' clientele regularly featured a number of professional thieves and several armed robbers. There were also fraudsters, small businessmen, fantasists, school teachers, clerks, jump-up merchants, dabblers, ex-boxers, a number of well-paid workers from the local container depot, builders – and me. This motley crew was joined most nights by a few detectives who worked locally, along with a number of cops based at CID offices a few miles westward dropping in for a swift half-dozen on the way back to their semis in the suburbs. Importantly, this was a boozer for regulars, with each section of the pub servicing a subtly different clientele who knew their place.

Both of the pub's doors could be seen from the exclusive standing space at the far side of the pub where the landlord's drinking group convened. This was reserved for serious villains, businessmen, CID officers and 'their company'. To join this elite, you had to make your way past various other individuals and groups, all doing the business. The search for bargains dominated most of the conversations in The City Arms and the closer you drank to the elite section, the better the deal and the bigger the bargain. But before you could make the long journey across 15 metres of an East End pub, the local wildlife had to be negotiated.

CLIENTS

There were a few tables and chairs for occasional drinkers and more secluded spots for couples, but the loosely defined space away from the bar was informally reserved for the saddest category of drinker. 'The client' did a 'bit of business', assumed nonchalant attitudes in stay-press slacks and casual but smart shirts and wore too much gold on their wrists, fingers and necks. When it came to entrepreneurial imaginations, the clients had few parameters and some of their schemes and dreams, particularly when lubricated by half a dozen pints of cooking lager, were staggering. For instance, Bert, a self-employed car mechanic with perpetually oily hands, pontificated one night on his intention to open an old people's home: 'Take their pensions, give 'em a bed and some grub and you're doing everyone a favour.' I risked catching a right hander by laughing hysterically at the prospect of this dreamer in oily overalls doing the morning rounds at 'Bert's Rest Home for the Elderly', wiping a greasy screwdriver and consoling a concerned relative with such soothing patter as, 'Sorry darling, the bodywork's kosher but she's going to need a new big end.' Of course, this was 40 years ago, before the care home crisis created such a ripe market for predatory businessmen to exploit. Back then, the ramblings of greasy Bert seemed just another example of comical magical thinking. But what did I know?

Clients tended to be barely on nodding terms with the drinkers in the elite section, most of whom were entirely unaware of their existence, primarily because they had nothing to sell, nothing to offer. Even the relatively respectable punters in The City were immune to the offers and deals that oozed around the clients as they went through the ritual motions of buying and selling, conspiring to set up vacuous schemes that could never come to fruition. Night after night, the clients mimicked the wheeler-dealer world of business with plots, plans and deals that had little attachment to reality. One client, Keith, had once worked as a builder and considered himself to be comfortable working at heights. Over six too many lagers, he and another fantasist declared themselves tree surgeons and spent a couple of days plying their new-found profession in a nearby suburb. The result was £50 to put over the bar of The City and a pile of tree branches dumped over the fence of a local school.

Things started to come to a head when, after a close relative suddenly died, Keith became a heavy drinker and even the residents of the more exclusive regions of The City Arms were sympathetic. Drinks would arrive at his table from unexpected places and his drunken crying jags resulted in him being carried home and put safely to bed by men who had looked down in contempt on clients like Keith. Suddenly, he was no longer excluded from conversations taking part in sections of the pub that had previously been closed to him and Keith moved across the pub floor to be enveloped in the racy tales and wheeler-dealer blag speak of 'the chaps'. Trouble came when he tried to join in.

Keith began missing work, spending all day and most of the night in The City Arms. He borrowed money from the chaps in order to finance his drinking and his lunchtime sessions in particular brought him into contact with the elite who lived in a close-knit world of entrepreneurs, heavy villains and detectives. Some of these men were highly knowledgeable regarding how social security and welfare agencies could be manipulated and they always had things to sell which Keith might be able to move on for a slight profit.

A group of accomplished local thieves paid Keith for the use of his lock-up garage to store stolen goods. Keith, who by now was permanently pissed, told anyone who would listen about the arrangement and within a month, the lock-up was burgled and the entire contents were stolen. As a result, several of the original crooks toured local pubs advising prospective punters not to buy from thieves who steal from thieves.

Two of the more prominent denizens of the elite section hired Keith to dismantle and steal some scaffolding that had been erected in the City of London. Keith hired two young men to assist him and the trio were intercepted by the police as they travelled to the drop-off point with a full load of scaffolding. However, due to the unique community policing connections with prominent City Arms drinkers, over the weekend Keith and his two helpers were allowed to re-erect the scaffolding under the supervision of passing patrol cars.

Eventually, Keith landed a regular 'cash-in-hand' job working as a driver for Billy D, a builder who owned two white Daimler limousines that he hired out for weddings. Banned from driving, Billy, who was a well-respected City Arms drinker, hired Keith to drive one of the wedding cars. Soon Keith was talking about 'our partnership', which quickly became 'my business'. While Billy sat in the chair at the hairdresser's, the barber snipped away, telling Billy about Keith's lucrative business and what a kind, generous man he was. Billy then went into The City Arms, looking for Keith.

When he made enquiries, the barmaid replied, 'He'll definitely be in later cos he's taking me for a driving lesson. He lets me drive his big Daimler. He's a lovely man. He's got a good business, doing very well.'

Eventually, Bill caught up with Keith and pinned him to the wall of The City, while forcefully telling him what he thought of him. He then handed the keys of the Daimler to his friend Terry Jackson who enjoyed driving for Billy for the next few months.

Keith had proved himself to be incompetent and unreliable. He had discussed the whereabouts of stolen goods, ruined a lucrative deal in stolen scaffolding, deluded himself into believing that he owned a business and in doing so had treated the actual proprietor with disrespect. Keith had to be put back in his box and Billy D loudly and very publicly threatened him in The City Arms, an episode that effectively banished Keith. However, after a couple of weeks' absence, Keith quietly returned and was soon back drinking, scheming and dreaming with the other clients, no longer trying to break into the elite's ranks. The social order of The City Arms had been restored.

LITTLE EARNERS

Away from the clients' draughty badlands, close to the front door and a just little closer to the exclusive zone of the elite, reside the little earners who, although they were legitimately employed, would nonetheless pursue ways of generating 'little earners' on the side. Their contact with the elite was tenuous but the Little Earners seldom aspired to the elite status that comes with full-time villainy. For them, crime was a means of supplementing meagre wages and low status, not forgetting the little boost that comes from making something from nothing.

Charlie Nails was a little earner. For decades, he lurked in the basement of a wholesale builders' supply company studying the racing papers. Charlie's job was to weigh out the orders for nails and screws on an old-fashioned weighing machine, box them, seal the box and take them by barrow up the steep slope of the delivery bay and unload it. Then, just as rapidly, he'd be off down the slope and back into his burrow to study form for the 3:30 at Kempton Park.

He worked on his own in a cold damp cellar running alive with rats. He never wore anything other than an ancient faded suit jacket, a pair of faded jeans, a cloth cap and muffler. You couldn't really tell what Charlie was thinking, behind the Benson & Hedges affixed to his bottom lip and heavy black-framed spectacles. However, Charlie did have one thing on his mind other than the 3:30 at Kempton Park: his own personal little earner, a swindle that was genius in its pure simplicity.

Spillage was the name of the game. Every time Charlie weighed out a quantity of nails and screws some would fall to the floor and within a few weeks, he would be ankle-deep in shrapnel. Charlie's boss insisted that he swept up the detritus once a month, which would then be handed over to a local scrap metal dealer who would pay a tiny fee to the company. Eventually, the scrapper did a deal with the company enabling him to sort the nails and screws into various sizes and sell them back to the company at a massive discount.

Charlie Nails decided to cut out the middle man entirely and sold fresh unopened boxes of screws and nails to the scrapper, who sold them directly to the company. Over the decades, Charlie kept the boxes circulating, the company felt prudent, the scrapper was earning and Charlie Nails could regularly put a few quid on the 3:30 at Kempton.

Charlie Nails is now in the celestial bookies and the beautiful mid-19th-century building where he worked was demolished in 2019 to make way for yet more office space. After the apocalypse, archaeologists sifting through the rubble of Shoreditch will find a pair of National Health glasses held together with Sellotape, an empty Benson & Hedges packet, a betting slip and a box of nails, all indicating that a great man had once laboured here.

In contrast to Charlie's inscrutability, George was a wiry, physically powerful man, with a loud voice and quick temper and his love of a little earner oozed out of every pore. George had been employed by a building supply company all of his working life and his knowledge of the trade was vast. He was also a very proud man, only willing to share the benefit of his experience with those who'd acknowledge his competence as a wheeler and dealer. I worked with George for a time and was able to observe him operating at close quarters.

After unlocking the warehouse at 7am, George would retire to the cafe (no one actually saw him pay his bill) where he would conduct some business before returning to work at 7:50. All day long, George received his own personal 'customers', many of whom were long-standing acquaintances whose legitimate businesses had benefited from George's mastery of his trade. Rather than seeking out a besuited member of the office staff, they often queued up to consult with George, who regarded himself on a par with these men.

Their subsequent transactions were carried out with decorum and discretion. George did not become involved in direct theft; rather he utilised his knowledge of the trade, the company and its employees to contrive alternative strategies to thieving. For instance, in collaboration with one of the office staff, he arranged special discounts or reserved damaged stock – which sometimes involved also arranging for the stock to be damaged in a manner that was beneficial to its end user. Soon-to-be obsolete goods were also tucked away in the warehouse's labyrinthine outer reaches to await a call from one of George's favoured customers.

George usually received 'a drink' in return for this preferential treatment but more significantly for him, he also obtained favours or goods rather than cash. For instance, a regular client of George's was a local garage owner and George's car was indeed an immaculately turned out, highly tuned machine. Every Friday lunchtime George would visit other regular clients of his – a butcher and a fruit and vegetable wholesaler – and by the end of the working day, his tiny 'office', which consisted of a small table, two ancient chairs and an ash tray, would be crammed with punnets of strawberries, trays of peaches and a large bag of choice cuts of meat. Sometimes his customers would deliver to him at the firm and we labourers would unload the foodstuffs, plundering fruit despite George's watchful eye.

Sally Shirt was another little earner, once dubbed by the pub's landlord as 'Stratford's Liz Taylor' on account of her jet-black hair and extravagant jewellery,. She worked for a clothing manufacturer and loved a gin and tonic. Her family had stalls in a number of the local street markets and she was always able to mix up stolen shirts and blouses with legitimate market stock. Sitting in a cloud of cigarette smoke with her friends from the factory, she would take orders, usually for school uniforms or maybe a carton of clothing to be sold on at a small profit, and the multiple G & Ts that crowded Sally's table were testament to the gratitude of the many parents who drank in the City. Sally had friends, status and a few pounds in her pocket, and was no different from any number of locals who could provide cheap goods at a fair price. No customer would ever enquire of the goods' legality; to them, it was just another bargain and to Sally Shirt, a little earner.

ON THE CORNER

Before anyone could breach the elite enclave, they would have to brush shoulders with the cornermen who resided on the edge of the elite. The 'corner game' was a craft which involved selling goods that did not exist to buyers who, after handing over their money, would find cigarette cartons full of old newspaper and vans crammed with fresh air. As the buyer usually believed that the goods were stolen, calling the police was out of the question.

Teddy worked the corner game and was always exceptionally easy to find, leaving in his wake a powerful and all-pervasive reek of cheap, sweet aftershave that clung to your clothes and entered every pore of your skin. A not very well preserved man in his late forties, Teddy was also notable because of his hair, a carefully coiffured busby of blond highlights, that had its origins in an early sixties centre parting, siphoned through a seventies shaggy working-class hippy, before running to ground with an eighties professional footballer's demi-perm. His hair was always immaculate and the sideburns densely Edwardian. They framed a face that resembled a map of the British Empire circa 1920: red irregular-shaped blotches ranged across a visage of uncompromising crags, peaks and valleys, dominated by a pitted and carelessly off-centre nose.

Teddy always wore a suit – invariably beige or light grey, tight of beam and wide of lapel. A dark polo-necked shirt emphasised his bulbous neck. Teddy was known as someone who would steal anything. He had once stolen a bus from a local depot when late one night he experienced some trouble hailing a cab. Similarly, he had once entered an off licence with the intention of buying some lager, only to emerge some minutes later with a case of vodka on his shoulder, pilfered while the shop's owner toiled in the stockroom. But that was just for fun.

As a youth, Teddy had worked on the 'find the lady' card scam in London's West End. He worked with friends and family as a lookout, while punters were relieved of their money under the misapprehension that they were gambling. In this working environment, Teddy met pickpockets, prostitutes and gangsters, and became acquainted with a varied range of money-making opportunities. He sold fake gold and jewellery, worked on long frauds and plundered lorries, warehouses and offices. The reputation of Teddy's family, a sprawling brood of fighting alcoholics, was insurance against complaints from dissatisfied customers.

Despite his decades of unremitting skulduggery, Teddy was never able to retire to a villa on the Costa Del Sol. Instead, he rented a flat stumbling distance from The City Arms and the betting shop. One day, that accumulator at Sandown, York or Kempton Park might come off, but until then there were always mug punters looking for a bargain.

An everyday scam for Teddy involved a shopper browsing in premises selling white goods, who would be surreptitiously approached by Teddy wearing a warehouseman's coat. Teddy would offer to provide an illegal staff discount for a very reasonable amount of money, that would then change hands in a nearby cafe. A meeting place arranged for 30 minutes' time would be agreed upon. At which point, Teddy's warehouseman became a phantom.

Teddy regularly offered publicans van loads of spirits, which turned out to be water, or cartons of cigarettes consisting of one layer of the legitimate product followed by a lot of waste paper. These transactions were carried out quickly with plenty of diversionary chat and action, often involving multiple locations.

Dressed in slacks, a double-breasted navy-blue blazer, white shirt, college tie and discreetly expensive loafers, Chester would not have looked out of place in any yacht club bar or exclusive gentlemen's club. He described himself as: 'Casual but smart, that's me. Some people reckon I am flash, but I am not, not really. It's a matter of self-respect.' Yet this vision of conservative decorum was undermined by what appeared to be several hundredweight of gold around his neck, fingers and wrists: 'The Tom,[2] well, it's me. I do like a bit of gold. I can't resist stopping to have a look in a gold shop window. It's a good investment.'

The City was Chester's place of business, which was central heating installation, double glazing, cavity wall insulation, carpet fitting, furniture removal, building work – and so much more. Chester would arrive at The City shortly after lunchtime opening and receive a free drink. If the pub's payphone was busy, Chester's excellent relationship with the landlord meant

2   Jewellery

he could dominate the pub's private phone behind the bar for hours on end. A gin and tonic or a bottle of premium lager by his side, when Chester was not on the phone, he was usually personally receiving 'clients', 'business partners', 'customers' and potential collaborators. This went on throughout the day and negotiations often continued long after closing time. He networked, wheeled, dealed, passed the business cards and took a slice of whatever was available. Chester knew a man who knew a man. He could 'produce the goods', as a freelance broker of cut price barbecues and discounted toiletries; he could also operate as an agent for the services of a fully qualified tree surgeon. Smart, sharp and game for a ten-pound note, his presentational skills were applied to both legal and illegal activities, and everything in between.

There were many like Chester around at this time – smartly dressed, well-groomed and personable, masters of a predatory scheming that merged seamlessly with the actions of others armed with business cards so that the gap between legal and illegal, and indeed real and unreal, was blurred. They wanted your money but they also wanted to be respected as smart, competent operators who were 'in the know'. They were entrepreneurs, taking a commission in exchange for connecting duckers and divers with legitimate tradesman, and connecting needy people to people in need of their money.

And then there were the elite players, the ones who everyone else always had half an eye on.

THE ELITE

If you managed to break into the elite section of The City Arms it was of utmost importance not to look pleased about it.

For if you had any insecurities about your membership to this peculiar congregation of laconic, dangerous, conspiratorial, self-congratulatory, entitled villains – cops and robbers alike – perhaps you shouldn't be there.

Peter was a lorry thief whose presence in the exclusive elite section was due more to past glories than to current achievements. An amiable man, his contacts in the transport industry had dried up a couple of years earlier and he had been getting by on scraps ever since. One evening in The City, he told me that he had purchased some 'old books' from a relation.

'I couldn't resist it,' he told me. 'He's only done a museum. Course everything's belled up[3] and he's creeping about all these fucking statues and that in the middle of the night. His bottle's starting to go. He never knew what to do. I mean, what do you fucking have in a museum full of belled-up old shit?'

Out of desperation, Peter's relation forced open a cupboard that did not appear to be connected to an alarm, grabbed the contents and left. On his safe return home, profoundly disappointed with the dozen antiquarian books he had procured, he attempted to offload them onto his friends and relations. Peter bought the lot for £25 and embarked on a course of self-education in the antiquarian books market. Over about six months, he succeeded in selling all of the books but one.

'It's my fucking enigma, Dick. The others were easy. Just went out to Cheltenham or somewhere and knocked 'em out to a local bookseller. You don't get top price but it's a drink. I

---

3   Alarmed.

was getting 25, 40 quid for a book worth a ton[4] in an auction, no questions asked. But this little fucker's years old. It's the real deal. Comes to more than a drink, a take-away and a piss up the wall on the way home. This is the big one, this is the fucking enigma.'

Peter turned to his cousin Max to help him deal with his enigma.

Max's career break came when the police captured him shortly after he had taken receipt of a lorry-load of menswear originally destined for a well-known gents outfitters. During his 18 months in an open prison, he struck up a relationship with a much older man, a professional criminal, who on his release from prison employed Max to manage a business. Max was now a wheeler-dealer entrepreneur whose well-cut suit stood out in contrast from the regimented leisurewear of most of the c lientele of The City. He did not often choose to sup his Perrier there but when he did, he effortlessly graced the pub's elite section. All of which reminded Peter that it was he who had stolen the ill-fated consignment of menswear in the first place.

'I thought I was lucky to get away with it, I felt sorry for the bastard,' he told me ruefully. 'When he got put away, I was gutted. Now he got a house, two motors, a gaff in Spain, pound notes. All cos I was prick enough to park a hookey lorry outside his lock-up.'

Peter could not risk approaching a specialist dealer or auction house with his enigma for fear of detection, so went reluctantly to Max. Max showed some interest in purchasing the book on behalf of a well-connected contact in the art world and suggested meeting at The City.

---

4 £100.

The two men caught up over a pint and a mineral water but the business of the evening was not broached until Doug, a stranger to Peter, arrived at around ten o'clock. Apart from his taste in heavy gold jewellery, Doug shared Max's understated style and blended into the elite section of The City Arms comfortably for the next 20 minutes, when at last Max brought up the subject of 'our bit of business'. He explained to Peter that while his contact in the art world was happy with the price, there remained the issue of possible detection.

'It's not like a load of shirts, is it, Pete?' he told him. 'I mean, you cut out the labels and knock 'em out anywhere, on a stall, and there's no way of tracing them. And who's going to bother? But when this went missing it must have brought a lot of attention on the thieves. It's a bit iffy.'

Peter saw Max bringing up stolen menswear as a dig at him and it seemed that the evening was about to end abruptly. At this point, Doug intervened, saying that if Peter would care to write down the details of the book, he would check to see if it had appeared on any stolen lists. Aghast, Peter looked to Max who smiled benignly and assured his cousin that it was a good idea. As the colour drained from his face, Peter scribbled the details on a scrap of paper and handed the note to Doug who left the pub saying that he wouldn't be long.

'Why didn't you say he was Old Bill?' Peter asked his cousin. 'You winding me up?'

Max insisted that Doug was 'as good as gold' and that he owed him several favours.

But Peter wasn't having it. 'You should have said. He don't owe me fuck all.'

The next 40 minutes were spent in virtual silence as Peter switched from lager to whisky. When Doug returned, he smilingly announced that the book was not on any list. Max was pleased, Peter was still wary, but the deal was agreed.

To my knowledge, Doug received no money for this service. Max went into property development and Peter, still unmolested by the forces of law and order, invested in a consignment of ladies' blouses.

Historically, the CID, particularly in London's Metropolitan Police, had been a separate high-status organisation distinct from the uniform branch. Independence and autonomy was the name of their game and detectives were expected to go forth and get their own work, collecting intelligence and manipulating both the criminal community and the criminal justice system in order to get the job done. And they liked a drink. When I was researching my PhD in the mid-1980s, they were in the office by 9am, in the pub by 11, back in the office for 2pm and, as the sun disappeared 'over the yardarm' at about 5pm, a bottle of Johnnie Walker would appear from a filing cabinet. Back in the boozer by 6pm. I once saw a young detective become so drunk that he fell asleep standing up before throwing up over a colleague's trouser leg and picking a fight with a superior officer who he accused of having an affair with his girlfriend. Eventually he lay down asleep in the corner before he was carried to a cab and taken home. The next morning he was giving evidence at the Old Bailey. Still, it was a Christmas party. I returned from this party as dawn was breaking and as I threw up in the gutter outside of my house, my neighbour, a hard-working man, was emerging from his home on the way to grind out another eight hours. He looked at me with disdain and asked, 'You been doing that research again?'

Detectives were, like everyone else, always looking for a

bargain and one night a detective negotiated a sweet price for an otherwise expensive bathroom suite that was to be liberated from the building trade by a City Arms' regular and occasional drinker in the elite section. When this regular and his friend delivered the goods a few days later, they were halfway up the stairs carrying a six-foot avocado-coloured cast-iron bath when the man at the lower end, who was admiring the decoration and suburban ambience of this fine semi-detached home, asked what the owner did for a living. When his colleague who was walking backwards up the stairs silently mouthed 'Old Bill', the friend loudly uttered, 'Fuck me!' and the heavy bath slid loudly and dangerously to the bottom of the stairs, taking the skin from the man's shins along the way.

This was not corruption, it was merely doing the business. A few drinks, a box of snide[5] Lacoste shirts or a cast iron bath and, 'Good night, my cab has arrived'. Perhaps the cop would learn something that was useful, and if he could still remember it in the morning then so much the better. For instance, 'I saw Kev trying to sell tickets for this bout in Finsbury Park. Silly cunt has only printed them himself'. Which may or may not prove to be useful information when 300 angry holders of bogus tickets are intent on tracking Kev down.

If pressed, detectives could always justify spending time in the pub by invoking time-honoured clichés such as, 'You don't catch villains in church,' or 'Villains don't work nine to five'. Through a haze of booze and bullshit, they could rapidly switch into professional mode. 'He phoned me up and wanted help but he had nothing for me, nothing to tell me. So I says,

---

5   Fake.

"Jacko, you come back to me when you've got something to deal." For me, it's business.' As another experienced officer explained, 'Profit, I want profit, want to do a deal. You can't just have your way in this world. I want to trade, compromise, give and take. Just like any business, if they don't want to trade then they are competition. I shit on 'em, put 'em out of business.'

On one occasion, I was having a drink with Benny and a detective. Benny always had a seat among the elite and his reputation was based on his ability to make trailers, lorries and 40-foot containers disappear into a vortex of transport yards and industrial estates across East London and Essex. He was respected as an amiable thief who would also buy whole loads of stolen goods at a decent price. He was very much part of the local neighbourhood and his multi-scarred face and forearms were reminders of both work-related disputes and recreational rucks. We were deep into a discussion about the merits of various high-performance cars, a subject of which I know nothing, when we were interrupted by a shell-suited man insisting on off-loading a van load of CDs onto Benny. Without realising that our drinking partner was a cop, Shell-suit delivered an aggressive sales pitch that brought a staunch refusal from Benny, while the detective turned his back on the conversation and struck up a conversation with a fringe member of the group. It was clear that Shell-suit was a regular supplier of hookey gear to Benny – 'What the fuck's the matter? It's the same gear from the same place. Good stuff, no rubbish. Dolly Parton and that.'

At this point, the zealous shell-suited salesman was physically taken aside by Benny and informed of the detective's identity. Shell-suit retreated and gathered himself, the detective returned to his original position at the bar and we hesitantly resumed our conversation. Shell-suit stepped up to the bar and bought us all a drink, claiming, as he collected his change, that, 'Course, they aint all iffy really. I bought them at the auctions.'

By choosing to turn a blind ear and ignoring the van load outside, the cop had gained some credit and 'showed his class', perhaps in the expectation of better-quality information to come in the future. He was clearly a man to be trusted, a man who understood how to do a deal. Or maybe he just couldn't be bothered nicking some hapless chancer with a van load of hookey country and western CDs.

While there are limits to these relationships, with a bit of care and craft, even when the police organisation makes its demands, there are still bargains to be made. I got to know DC Simon beyond the context of The City Arms via our interest in football. We both drank in the pub, he more enthusiastically than me, and when I started to study detective work he was always available to help me with my research. In the confines of his comfortable suburban living room, he explained how deals were struck.

'Bodies, bodies[6] is what it is, what the brass want and that is the name of the game. You might be well acquainted with a good class villain. You do each other little favours, little trades, have a drink, no problem. Then his name comes up for something and he just has to go. A bit of co-operation from him and you can trade down so robbery turns into receiving, that sort of thing. I got a body, he gets six months instead of six years, the governor's figures look a bit sweeter, so everybody earns.'

---

6   Prisoners.

These bargains depend on everyone acknowledging that deal-making is the name of the game. 'Put it this way, out there you got the punters, taxpayers and regular civilians; they pay my wages and they want a service from me. Then there's villains. To provide a service to the punters, I nick the villains. But if I do deals with some villains I can nick those that really need nicking. So I do a deal here, a trade there, somebody goes down and I keep paying my mortgage.'

But not all of the detectives were smart professionals, adept at manipulating the ebbs and flows of unlicensed capitalism that washed around London's backstreets. Most were on the piss in The City because they enjoyed the ambience and, like many mere civilians, they got a buzz from proximity to the dark side. Some of them were as comically delusional as Keith the client, the big difference being that the cops had warrant cards. There was also a fair proportion of fantasists among the boozy Old Bill and some of the 'gangsters' they fawned over were more Benny Hill than Billy Hill. As for the so-called 'armed robbers', some of them could barely hold their trousers up. But this hardly mattered as the bullshit blended with the real deal in this boys' only game of charades. In many ways, the detectives had more in common with the ducking and diving entrepreneurship of East Enders than with the rigid hierarchy and legalistic rule-based practices of mainstream policing.

During the seventies, eighties and much of the nineties, The City Arms was the East End in miniature. It was one of a number of magical old boozers where cops, robbers, pros, cons and civilians came together in a maelstrom of crime, business and entrepreneurial fantasy. Some of its customers were smart, some stupid, some were legal, others illegal, but everybody was doing the business.

Chapter 3

DUCKING, DIVING AND JUMPING UP: TERRY JACKSON

'You just can't explain what it's like to "do one". It's unbelievable to be in a gaff full of gear and it's yours to do what you like with. You are the boss, no questions.'

TERRY JACKSON

Terry is old school, a throwback to a time when East Enders, impoverished by the insecurities of casual work, were forced to make money from nothing. The only difference was that Terry jumped into an old van, instead of a horse and cart to go scavenging as they had done in my grandfather's day. Terry Jackson is now in his early seventies, about five feet seven and 16 stone with ancient fading tattoos on both forearms, a scar under his left eye and multiple indentations on his forehead. For most of his adult life, he has roamed the East End like a cross between Arthur Daley and Del Boy, but with a potential for violence that was absent in these cosy cockney stereotypes.

We met about 40 years ago, when I was briefly a schoolteacher before going to university and the most mischievous boy in the school was Terry's son Marshall. One day, while I was busy reprimanding young Marshall in the corridor for some misdemeanour or another, Terry came bowling through the school on an urgent parental errand, heard me bollocking his son and, without missing a beat, breezed past with a 'Don't bother talking to him, Mr Hobbs, give him a clump.' The other children roared with laughter. As far as the local kids were concerned, Terry was a winner. He was central to the local community. When the football team that I ran needed transport, he bought an old van, hand-painted it in the team's colours, threw some cushions in the back and the kids had a bespoke coach.

From day one, we got on famously. I had been away from the area for a while and the East End was starting to change. The docks had closed and there had been a shift of the local population to Essex, where home ownership and competitive consumption became the new priorities for escapees from the old neighbourhoods. But Terry was old school, a throwback to simpler times when scavengers like him were commonplace and loyalty to friends and family, independence and the ability to make something from nothing were attributes valued above all else. Religiously self-employed, he declared himself to be 'too expensive for wages' and thrived for decades on his motto: 'Never turn down a pound note.'

I've got to know Terry's son Marshall and daughter Terri over the years, especially Marshall, who gave me his perspective on his father's work ethic:

'What you gotta understand about the old man is he's always said, "Earn money, don't be a ponce, earn." And he's always grafted, so that's what you see when you're a kid. That's what I fucking want, bit of graft, some money, fuck it.'

Terry has been a driver, a labourer, handler of stolen goods, thief, publican, counterfeiter and much more, shunning a 'job on the cards' in favour of a rich and varied life ducking and diving, where the line between legal and illegal money-making is so blurred as to be non-existent.

JUMP-UP

Terry described himself as a 'jump-up merchant', which refers to the practice of following a delivery vehicle until the driver stops to unload, then 'jumping up' onto the van or lorry and grabbing its contents – or even the vehicle itself.

When it came to stealing the entire vehicle, Terry had some big successes, although the major problem was, of course, not knowing what was inside and he often ended up with worthless or unmarketable goods. Sometimes he got lucky. During one particularly dry period, he decided to take a legitimate job coordinating the drivers and loads for a transport firm. On his first day, he discovered that the company would often leave fully laden trucks that were due to be picked up very early in the morning outside of the depot with the keys hidden under the front wheel, which meant that the depot did not need to be opened up at 3 or 4am, allowing staff to spend longer in bed.

'I saw it straight away and told them that this was out of order and they were bound to get nicked by someone. But I was just the new bloke and they said that they'd been doing it for years. But I never let up, I used to go on and on about it being out of order. Then one night there was a lorry load of men's clothing.'

Terry made some phone calls, arranged a slaughter[7] for the load and lined up buyers. He then stole the lorry, the goods were unloaded and sold and the lorry dumped. When he arrived for work at his usual time, police officers were taking statements. 'I said, "What's going on? What's happened?" Nobody would even look at me, they all turned away. "Oh, for fuck's sake, don't tell me they've had the lorry. I fucking told you this would happen." I went totally garrity, shouting and hollering and shaking my head. They couldn't calm me down.'

The empty lorry was soon found and when a television crew needed a driver to be filmed driving it around the block as part of a popular crime reconstruction programme, guess who volunteered? So there was Terry smiling out of my TV screen while the presenter of the programme solemnly appealed for witnesses.

But pillaging lorries was merely one option for a man who roamed the streets day or night free to plunder and prosper without the hindrance of HMRC, social security or any other branch of the state. 'What I do like is to dabble. Oh, I do like a dabble. I have a little mooch, and there's so much building going on round here. Well, I have a look round and the fore-man on the house next door, he's well at it. He likes to dabble; he's like me. I said to him, "Anything going cheap? Cos I want what you got." So he said, "Come back about three o'clock." You know me, Dick, I'd have been there at three o'clock in the morning. So I've had bricks, wood, everything.' He was, above all, game. 'If I get known as a wheeler-dealer, a right grafter, then when another job comes up, they're going to say, "We want Jacko. We want him on this. Where is he?"'

---

7   A place to store and process stolen goods.

ESKIMO TEL

Terry's family background is classic East End. His paternal grandfather was a Ceylonese seaman who came to East London in 1909. A decorated veteran of the First World War, he married an East End woman of Portuguese heritage. 'When people look at me, they say: Are you Pakistani? Greek? Turkish? I tell them I like the cold so I must be a fucking Eskimo.'

Terry's father, Marshall, fought in the Second World War and, in 1947, married Florence. 'My old man was without a doubt a diamond. Everybody knew him. In those days, they took a lot of racist stick when they were out together in the street. He was a black man out with a white woman and it wasn't the thing back then. He was a great character. He had a good voice and used to sing in the Aunt Sally pub in Burdett Road. He used to pretend that he was singing in Italian – he couldn't, he just made the words up. Dad would have a row with anybody, like anybody, but he wasn't what you would call a hard man. He was a singer. On a Sunday morning, he would do the breakfast and I would lay in bed waiting, and he would just make up these songs. I dunno, [sings] "Get out of bed and getta your double egg, bacon, bubble and two fried slices." He was a good old boy, my dad.'

Terry's father died at the tragically young age of just 29. When Florence remarried a few years later, Terry rejected his stepdad. 'I wasn't having it. He said, "I'm your new dad," so I said, "No, you aint, and you never will be." When Mum got married to him he would try to make me do things but I just used to go missing.'

Meanwhile, the racism continued. 'It was blackie this and blackie that, your dad's a blackie. I had to look after myself.' Which he did to great effect. He gained a local reputation for fighting as well as for ducking and diving and although Terry changed jobs many times between the ages of 15 and 17, minor villainy took up an increasing amount of his social and working life. 'The word got around that I was up for one and I was earning.'

An inevitable ten-week spell in a detention centre followed for breaching a probation order after being found guilty of stealing a car.

'Best thing that ever happened to me. In there, you have to learn you can't just do what you like, you learn, "Yes sir, no sir." You wash the floor and when the screws tread over it you just wash it, don't fucking moan, just do it. Because that's the game. It don't get to you. You just hold it back. Some of the screws were gentlemen, they call you mister and you called them sir and it was all right. There was a couple of nasty bastards, like fucking Hitlers, give you a little dig, shout and scream. Just go, "Yes sir, no sir," and then spit on their backs so they never knew. Walk around with a nice flob running down their back.'

At the age of 21, Terry married Sylvie and worked as a self-employed lorry driver, moving effortlessly between hard physical graft and 'buying and selling'. He made deliveries, cleared gardens, anything to make a living. He also continued his criminal activities, particularly commercial burglaries from lorries, factories and warehouses.

'We were doing well. We had holidays, the lot. I bought a caravan, put it on a site in Clacton. Then later when I got the HGV, I really started to earn. I was doing lorry loads, moving anything. We made thousands, fucking thousands.'

LEISUREWEAR

However, by the time Terry was in his mid-thirties times had become tough.

'I had about five really good years but I pissed it up the wall. I had motors, a couple of lock-ups, spent money boozing like it was yours. I was at it like a good 'un, always at it. Straight and hookey, if there was any dough, the carbuncle on the hip,[8] that is what it all was. I got into some debt with a new unit lorry but I never thought nothing of it, I was earning so well. Then there was the 1980 steel strike, we was doing steel all over the country but it dried up.'

Terry had invested time and money in his haulage business but in addition to the impact of the strike, he was sure that he had been ripped off by his partner. This was a big blow: Terry had been on a roll, his young family were living well, and then suddenly it all came to an end.

'We had all this gear for the unit it went missing. Tools, covers, ropes. I was well stitched up. He did me like a kipper.'

There was only one thing for it: a visit to the pawn shop to hock his huge gold chain with a prominent J at the front, an elaborate chunky gold bracelet and gold ring with his initials studded in diamonds. As soon as he'd done a bit of thieving or a deal had landed, he'd be straight back to the pawn shop to retrieve his finery.

Throughout the 1980s, Terry was a regular visitor to my home and I always knew that his life was on an upward trajectory when he arrived on my doorstep looking like a cross between the Pope and Liberace. On one occasion, he stood in my living room, spread his arms and pronounced, 'I've had it

---

8   Roll of paper money in your pocket.

off. It was an inside job. Easter weekend, great big warehouse. Bobby set it up with the manager. Drove in, locked the doors behind us and took our time.'

But the manager needed Terry and his merry band to fake a break-in.

'We loaded up and the manager says, "What about the hole in the wall?" I says, "What fucking hole?" He says, "There aint one." So I says, "Out the way, I'll give you a fucking hole in the wall." So I jumps in the fork lift and goes bosh: "There's your fucking hole." They just pull the bricks through and make it look like we come in through the wall.'

The loot was a large quantity of branded Italian leisurewear, and while some buyers purchased large quantities, Terry enthusiastically sold individual items to a voracious local clientele. 'It was easy cos it's good gear – Bonetti, everybody wants it, don't they? Some people was having a few hundred in a parcel. I knocked most of it out myself. I went to work punting the same day I got it.'

Not for the first time, Terry became a local hero, selling individual items at less than half the retail price with a negotiated discount for larger quantities. All over that part of East London, sweatshirts, shirts and sweaters were being resold at a small mark up in pubs and workplaces, and Terry's local pub became the centre of the operation.

THE STEAMSHIP

A bog-standard Victorian pub, the most notable characteristic of The Steamship was that it sat at the end of two cul-de-sacs connected by a narrow pedestrian walkway. It had no passing trade, which meant you could not end up in this boozer by accident, and it became a destination where those in the know would gather for a proper drink. The clientele did not include police officers; they were drinking down the road at The City Arms, although the rare stranger who ventured into The Steamship was always suspected of being Old Bill and was served politely and given the right change before being studiously ignored until they left. This was a pub for locals and local rules applied.

During the Bonetti episode, Terry and anyone in his company had free drinks sent to them from every corner of the pub, and one night, having been deep in conversation with Terry and now even deeper in drink, I surveyed the crowded pub to find that every male from 12 to 80, many of the female customers and all of the bar staff were wearing sweatshirts in various colours all emblazoned with the Bonetti logo.

Over the years, Terry had become the mainstay of the pub. He had made money in there and put most of it straight back over the bar. He played in the darts team with his teenage son, was at the centre of any party and was always available to enforce the rules of the house. When the lease for The Steamship came up in 1984 it was inevitable that Terry would be a contender. 'Let's face it, that had to be mine. It had a bad reputation, rough pub sort of. But I knew I could turn it round, turn it into a family house.' When the new owners took over they asked Terry to run it for them. 'Nothing on the books because you can't be a licensee if you have a criminal record. And I had one of them.'

The Steamship did have a dodgy reputation. In the 1970s, a routine row over nothing in particular led to a customer dragging a barman over the bar by his collar. The young man collided with a piece of ornate wrought iron that framed the bar. The spike went through his eye into his brain. The barman's death, along with the subsequent manslaughter conviction, made the old boozer infamous and it consequently went into a slow decline.

However, under Terry's new regime, The Steamship returned to its former glory as a community pub and there was never any trouble. Apart from when one angry customer intent on murder turned up with a gun. 'I just had a word, talked him round and he went outside, put it in his motor and came back and had a drink with me,' Terry explained. With him in charge, The Steamship became a wonderful boozer, and Terry was totally at home. His repertoire of strategies for dealing with awkward customers included kind words as well as two large fists, and he was well known and liked by a wide range of villains, would-be entrepreneurs and captains of industry who valued the pub as a discreet place to socialise or plan a coup.

One night, Danny, an infamous and unpredictable man of violence, came into the pub, ordered a drink and refused to pay. Terry was in the adjacent saloon bar and the barmaid called him in and explained the situation. Terry came from behind the bar and sat on a barstool next to Danny who claimed, 'I aint got no money.' Terry explained that it was out of order to come out for a drink with no money and, with a stroke of genius, offered to buy him a drink. They drank together exchanging pleasantries and when Danny had finished his drinks he shook Terry's hand, thanked him for his hospitality and left. Next time this extremely dangerous man visited The Steamship, his generosity to his new friend Terry could not be faulted. It was a great loss to the local community when the pub was sold.

WELL AT IT

Terry was part of that generation of thieves who thrived during an era when technology such as security cameras was a rarity. Terry had an inbuilt urban radar that was acutely sensitive to legal and illegal money-making opportunities, all of which merged into something called business. He was interested in anything that offered money, autonomy and freedom from the emasculating grind of the nine-to-five. He was a highly adaptable predator and any excursion with him was turned into a reconnaissance for a possible foray into felony. Up at dawn, Terry would breakfast in a nearby kitchen and enjoy watching the police, who were creatures of habit, making a dawn raid on his house. Then, with a beer mat in place of his road tax, he would tour the manor in his old transit van. He might clear a garden for a tenner, check out a local lorry park for vulnerabilities or splash some undercoat over the inside of a newly acquired shop for a fellow businessman. On one occasion, we parked up while Terry surreptitiously checked out the alarm system of an electrical store. While I waited outside the shop, a sales rep gave me a couple of quid to carry a heavy box inside and that paid for breakfast.

By the time I eventually went to university, I had developed a taste for shelter and hot food and was keen to pay my bills. Consequently, I briefly went back into schools as a supply teacher and took various part-time and temporary labouring jobs, which, along with buying and selling the flotsam and jetsam of various jump-up merchants' forays into the backs of lorries, helped to keep the wolf from the door.

At one time, Terry and I decided to pool our resources and run a Sunday morning market stall selling toiletries but we were immediately stymied by not having a VAT number and were therefore buying our stock at a price that promised little profit. After we failed to bribe the market inspector into taking us off of the waiting list and giving us a pitch for our stall, we decided to cut our losses and Terry did nothing to discourage customers from The Steamship and beyond from believing that these legitimate goods were stolen. Consequently, the toiletries sold out in two days, despite being more expensive than in some legitimate high street shops.

If Terry arrived at my house minus the gold but with the addition of a few fresh facial scars I knew that he was having a bad day. But the stitches and the odd magistrate's court fine could never keep him down for long and, looking like Bob Hoskins on steroids, he always bounced back with a new scheme and a van load of hookey gear.

When a friend of his took over the lease on a small shop, Terry agreed to clear out the detritus left by the previous owners who had cleared off in a hurry. But when he realised that a significant amount of stock had been left behind, he negotiated to clean up the premises for nothing, as long as he could keep the remaining stock. After several days' work, he was the proud owner of several hundred bottles of fake tan, some tea chests of assorted zips and buttons, and a few hundred large reels of cotton. He had also acquired four large rolls of sleeping bag material, and six pairs of platform-soled 'Gary Glitter shoes'. However, the real prize was two gross of pregnancy testing kits, of which Terry had especially high hopes.

'Worth a fortune, Dick, if I can only find a buyer. Jimmy's gone in the chemist's on the bridge all covered in cement dirt and shit, and gone, bosh! On the counter. "Want to buy some of these, pal?" Fucking wally. I'm going in suited and booted and do it right, they must sell.'

But Terry's usual outlets who were accustomed to a few boxes of clothing or the odd case of booze were not at all enthusiastic. At one point, he tried to involve me as a middleman for the pregnancy testing kits. 'All those students, there must be a fair bit of that going on. We could clean up.' Terry sold the zips, buttons, cotton and sleeping bag material to market traders. Though unfortunately the fake tan cream had burnt his son's face and Terry had to pay for the toxic lotion to be disposed of at the local council dump as chemical waste. As for the pregnancy testing kits, he left one at my home and my heavily pregnant wife registered a negative result. The Gary Glitter shoes were, until recently, stored in a lock-up awaiting a fashion revival. You win some and you lose some, but for Terry the buzz of operating as an entrepreneur was more important. If it didn't work out and the streets paved with gold all turned to shit, so be it. Terry always bounced back with another scheme, often involving a set of borrowed retractable ladders and a pair of bolt cutters.

A BIBLICAL COUP

In the build-up to Christmas, warehouses become prime targets for predators such as Terry. One year, after a relatively quiet summer, he planned to take his time over selecting the plumpest target offering the greatest return. Along with his partner, Tom, a drunk who had once been an outstanding schoolboy athlete, they traversed the East End in a transit van wearing brown overalls, arriving at premises with 'delivery orders' in their hands, before wandering the site while checking out stock, security and general layout. Eventually, someone would challenge them, and they would wave their papers and mention the name of a nearby transport firm to which they would be redirected.

Eventually, they found a likely target. They only needed to recruit another man to position himself at the base of the ladder and load goods into the van. Henry, they decided, was the man for the job.

Regarded as 'a good worker with no bottle', Henry was a large man in early middle age whose reputation as a steady, small-time thief had been seriously damaged when he ventured into armed robbery. He was appointed the driver of the getaway vehicle but unfortunately a wave of hysteria and a bout of diarrhoea on a hot summer's day cost him his reputation. Consequently, Terry got him cheap. Tom, on the other hand, was an established thief; the only drawback to working with him was his tendency to drink beforehand. However, this often resulted in some spectacular athletic feats: fences, walls and windows proved no obstacle for a pissed-up Tom, whose party piece was to perform a backflip onto a pub's bar, earning the nickname 'Cat'.

In the early hours of the morning about a month before Christmas, Terry, Tom and Henry parked outside of the gates of a secluded warehouse on the edge of what is now known as Docklands. Terry wielded his long-handled bolt cutters, the gates swung open and Henry drove the box van into the yard before Terry closed the gates and attached his own expensive Swiss padlock to them, enabling the three thieves to plunder the warehouse undisturbed by passing police or security. A ladder was taken out of the truck and placed on to the roof of the large pre-fabricated building. While Henry stayed on the ground, Terry and Tom went up the ladder and got to work on the roof with the bolt cutters.

Once a decent-sized hole had been cut, the pissed-up Cat, who had sung football songs all the way from the pub to the target, fell through it. When Terry eventually shone a torch down into the warehouse, instead of a corpse he saw Tom lying on his back just ten feet from the hole, his fall broken by imported paper decorations packed in cardboard boxes stacked about 20 feet high. A now more sober Tom prowled the floor and quickly found a stock of small electrical goods such as hair dryers, curling tongs, personal stereos and other easily transported goods that were highly desirable and easily marketed at any time of the year. But at Christmas this really was a coup, the big one, and for Terry this was an opportunity to purchase a truck and set himself up as a self-employed contractor. All that was required was a couple of hours of hard graft and a golden future beckoned.

After a few minutes of Tom prowling the floor shouting out 'hair dryers', 'tongs', etc. up to Jack, the Cat was silent. Terry became concerned and shone his torch down, eventually locating Tom who was crouched by some tea chests. 'Whisky,' he mumbled. 'What?' said Terry. 'Whisky!' screamed the Cat. This really was a bonanza. Fuck the curling tongs and electric carving knives, whisky and Christmas was a cocktail that promised big money. What's more, the tea chests were stamped and bonded as miniature bottles. Nothing could be easier to knock out in the season of goodwill to all good people seeking a bargain.

Terry lay over the hole and hauled the tea chests by rope onto the roof and then slid them down the ladder to Henry. 'My fucking arms felt like they were bursting. But all I could think of was the fantastic fucking result we were going to get.' When the tea chests were packed away, Tom climbed up the rope, and the team drove away – 'Feeling like we was leaving Wembley with the fucking cup.' The cases were transported to several lock-ups before Henry was dropped off at his home and, as dawn broke, Terry and Tom retired to Tom's flat and replayed the night's action. 'You just can't explain what it's like to "do one". It's unbelievable to be in a gaff full of gear and it's yours to do what you like with. You are the boss, no questions.'

Eventually, they decided to return to one of the lock-ups to sample the loot. 'Just to make us feel good.' Tom broke the steel bands on the first case and slowly prised open the lid. He stood in horrified shock before lifting one of the items out. It was not whisky but a book. The good book. 'Bibles, fucking Bibles,' he cursed. Another case was opened, then another, all revealing stacks of blue-bound Bibles. 'Tom was still pissed so he sat down and grinned. I didn't know whether to laugh or cry. We dropped them in the river but first I took one each for the kids, you know, to put next to their beds on Christmas morning. I thought under the circumstances like it was the right thing. Trouble was, Christmas morning, when they opened them they was written in fucking Polish.'

I still have one of these Bibles on my bookshelf.

Pregnancy-testing kits, Polish Bibles, right handers, heavy lifting and back street boozers, for good or for bad Terry Jackson is his own man. He's lived his life in a cavalier fashion, always open to cash in hand opportunities, operating just under the radar of any serious police attention. However, in his late fifties, Terry's life took a number of unexpected turns that afforded him global notoriety.

TERRY THE FOILER

Over the years, Terry always drew the line at 'doing anything that you could really get nicked for'. He was a good and reliable earner, thieving was part of his repertoire and although he had offers to engage in heavier crime, Terry stuck to what he knew. He enjoyed being in control of his own fate and liked being everybody's favourite local pirate. However, the East End was changing fast and opportunities for thieving were seriously reduced. The docks had long gone, the warehouses disappeared, cameras were everywhere, cheap imports flooded the high street and the neighbourhood networks and outlets for hookey gear became part of the nostalgia fest that was *Only Fools and Horses*.

Terry's personal life was in turmoil and he kept hours that would have felled a man 20 years his junior. He then suffered a series of heart attacks before eventually succumbing to a temptation that a few years earlier would have been unthinkable: he got a job as a driver. He enjoyed driving a van and stayed sharp with the odd dabble if an opportunity came up; I think that he would have continued with this lifestyle if he had not been offered good money to perform a simple, somewhat repetitive task that was better paid than his daily battle with London's traffic.

In 2006, Terry was convicted for his part in a major counterfeiting case, which, according to the judge threatened, 'the fiscal well-being of the British state'. The firm of counterfeiters had been active for several years and had tried to recruit Terry on numerous occasions before he eventually accepted their offer and became involved in 'foiling' and 'finishing' – heat-pressing holograms and metal strips onto fake £20 notes. Terry operated the 'foiler' for four months – 'I doubt that I made four grand out of it in the end,' he reflected later.

The police had commenced their surveillance of the operation long before Terry had even started work for the counterfeiters. When his home was raided by 'the biggest Old Bill you have seen', he was found bang to rights with a foiling machine and a large quantity of forged notes. 'They confiscated my motor; it was 12 years old. They took my caravan, which was worth about three grand and a few bits of gold that I bought. They wanted to put a confiscation order on me of £1.3m and I have got a 12-year-old motor and a caravan!'

Ten men and women were convicted for up to seven years, for their role in 'Britain's biggest ever counterfeiting operation'. As tends to happen in complex cases, the police and prosecution simplified things as much as possible and while it was clear that this was a long established counterfeiting operation, the case concentrated not upon the complex, probably international distribution networks or the whereabouts of the printing plates, both of which would have tied up police resources for many years if fully investigated, but upon a single node of the network that was concerned solely with production. Consequently, the case featured a few usual suspects padded out with 'lever pullers' such as Terry, who, while they were undoubtedly guilty, had their role in this multi-site conspiracy exaggerated by the prosecution's use of language more appropriate to the *Godfather*. For instance Terry was branded by the prosecution as a 'lieutenant'.

The story captured the imagination of the global mass media who concentrated on the seriousness of this 'organised crime' and the vast amount of money that was involved, which was estimated at the trial to be £14m and later assessed by the police at £27m. Consequently, for Terry, 'When we walked onto the wing in Pentonville everybody clapped and cheered.' Terry was 58 when he commenced his five-year sentence and due to his age and the fact that this was his first prison sentence, inmates assumed, 'that I was some sort of mastermind, that I had plenty of dough stashed away and that I had been at it for years and hadn't been nicked. Instead, I had just been involved for a few months and never had a pot to piss in. I got offered up all sorts of deals while I was inside. Geezer comes in, a forger, says he wants to meet me and comes on like we was best of pals. Says that I am the business and that he wants to make one with me when I get out. I tells him no fucking chance.'

Although he 'spent the first month crying', he buckled down and was trained by the Samaritans as a 'listener', working with suicide risks and helping troubled prisoners come to terms with their plight. He became trusted by both inmates and the prison authorities, was able to move around the prison at will and was eventually freed with an exemplary prison record. On his release, Terry went back to live with Sylvie, who had remained as loyal throughout his prison sentence as she had through his years as a ducker and diver.

Despite being very candid concerning his role in the crime and the small amount of money that he made from it, his brief period as a threat to global capitalism prompted many local people to regard him as a success. 'The kids think I am some gangster, and the older ones wish they could have made all the money that I am supposed to have made. I get people saying, "Terry, why didn't you give me some? I would have had some." But they don't understand they were being sold in batches of a thousand; you couldn't say I will have five or ten, you had to take a big batch and even then only certain people would be allowed to buy. But anyway, all of that was nothing to do with me, I just had a little job and got on with it. But fuck 'em, if they want to think I am some mastermind that is up to them.'

Terry has not been beaten by the experience of prison and there are times when he conjures up the same confrontational style that earned him such a formidable reputation during his younger days. For instance, I saw him go out of his way to walk through the midst of a large group of local youths who were blocking a narrow pavement. As he swayed purposefully through the young men they either avoided his still menacing gaze or acknowledged him with a nod and a grunt. One hot summer afternoon, Terry and I drove past a playground and one of the same group of youths screamed something unintelligible at the car. When Terry hit the brakes and wound down the window, the young men stopped playing basketball and watched expectantly. Terry stared at the youth, who took a step forward and politely explained that he was merely informing Terry that one of his brake lights was not working. Terry politely thanked the boy and, looking at the road ahead, smiled and said, 'Good as gold', before driving away.

Terry's son is unable to work due to health problems, his grandson has been up to his neck in the criminal justice system for a number of years and his son-in law is serving a long sentence for a serious violent offence. Terry acknowledges that his family suffered during his time in prison and he is now dedicated to helping them deal with their multifarious problems. He is immensely proud of his Samaritans qualification and uses his skills to provide informal support to local people, regularly representing them at tribunals. He coaches table tennis, chairs the patient liaison group at his local health centre and visits an old people's home, chatting to the residents and singing some of the songs taught to him by his father.

Terry is nursing Sylvie, who has cancer. Her bed has been set up in the living room where she will die within a few days. When I arrived at his house, a nurse was showing him how to administer pain relief to his wife and explaining to Terry that hallucinations are common among terminal patients. While friends and neighbours visited Sylvie, we sat in the kitchen drinking tea and talking about people who had been 'good grafters', the plight of various relatives and who was making money and how, as well as reflecting on his colourful life. 'Over the years, I have taken a lot out of the local community, one way or another, and I want to put something back. I'm not a bad man.'

Chapter 4

BIG BEASTS

'When people go to the circus, they don't want to see clowns. They want to see lions and tigers, and that's what we are.'

JOHN GOTTI

Over the past 30 years, there has been a vibrant industry at work producing books about big-name London crime firms of the post-Second World War era. Alongside the volumes covering the deeds of the famous faces sit others, concerning their associates, their victims, their mother's hairdresser, or penned by the many police officers who have supplemented their pensions by documenting their role in notable cases. In this way, a small number of criminal firms have, via numerous books, films and TV series, become symbols of British organised crime and benchmarks for subsequent generations of villains.

Although the focus of this book is upon the 'poor bloody infantry' of crime, they operated in a milieu that was inhabited, and to an extent constructed by, these notorious crime firms.

The public's perception of 'organised crime' and the villains behind it was of course hugely influenced by the way these famous underworld histories were reported. In contrast to the anonymity necessary for most modern criminals to operate, many of the big characters from previous eras actively encouraged notoriety, hiring their own biographers. The next four chapters will provide some context for the fascination and entertainment that they continue to provide for villains and non-villains alike.

RACING CERTAINTIES

In the late 19th and early 20th centuries, groups of violent young men roamed London punching, kicking and cutting local rivals. For the most part, this violence was recreational but every now and then a group would emerge who could turn their violence into hard cash. The Titanics were an immaculately turned out group of English pickpockets and robbers based around Nile Street in Islington in the second decade of the 20th century. They enhanced their violent reputation by plundering local territories such as Clerkenwell, which had emerged as the centre of the Italian community in London.

The Sabinis, led by boxer and bouncer Darby, sprang up in opposition to the Titanics' attacks on Little Italy's clubs. The Anglo-Italian Sabinis were brutally effective and, as their reputations as efficient protectors grew, they were rewarded by Little Italy's businessmen, before extending their operations beyond the local neighbourhood to become instrumental figures in British crime.

By the start of the First World War, the Italian community

already had a strong presence in the West End, running clubs, pubs, cafes, restaurants and shops. The fierce reputation of the 'Italian firm' ensured that these businesses, along with illegal gambling and drinking clubs, were soon paying Sabini extortionists.

In the years after the First World War, an even more enticing market beckoned. Street gambling was illegal but if you wanted to place a bet there were ample legal opportunities at the racecourses, where bookmakers were allowed to set up shop. The bookies became targets for violent predators who controlled the best pitches in exchange for extortionate fees, and dominated the market in chalk, betting slips and other paraphernalia of on-course bookmaking.

The racecourses offered the richest prize to any group who could break out of the streets where they had forged their reputations. The dominant racecourse gang during the early part of the century came from Birmingham, the 'Brummagems', led by bookmaker Billy Kimber who, in collaboration with a number of North London-based groups and most notably with a powerful group from Elephant and Castle in South London, established dominance particularly over tracks in the north of England.

However, the Sabinis, assisted by a powerful group of Jewish bookmakers and criminals, were soon matching the Birmingham firm. The gangs were competing for big money – profits from Derby Day alone were estimated at £15,000–£20,000, the equivalent in 2021 of £858,000–£1,144,000 – and racetracks all over the country reported violent clashes, while racing-related stabbings, beatings and shootings also became commonplace in central and North London. This prompted uproar in the press and the intervention in 1925 of the Home

Secretary, which in turn led to joint action by the Flying Squad and the Jockey Club and a brief Sabini/Kimber truce. Having punched his way out of his local neighbourhood, Sabini's gang now dominated most major English racecourses, as well as the all-important honey pot of the West End of London.

Criminals had for generations regarded the centre of London as a prize and during the Second World War it became particularly valuable, as the West End played host to thousands of young servicemen in search of a good time, creating fantastic criminal opportunities that the Italians, particularly with their colonisation of Soho, were well set to exploit. The alcohol licensing laws of the day created a demand for illegal drinking venues, prostitution thrived and men with reputations acquired at the racetrack or as thieves and gangsters flocked to this booming marketplace.

However, in 1940, many of the Italian mob were interned as enemy aliens, including Darby, who, semi-retired, was now living in Brighton. Darby was released from internment in 1941 but in 1943 was sentenced to two years' hard labour for receiving stolen goods. His file in the National Archives contains material from MI5 as well as the police, describing him as a 'dangerous gangster and racketeer of the worst type', a man with fascist sympathies who was 'liable to lead internal insurrections against this country at the behest of an occupying power'. However, Darby Sabini had no allegiance to Mussolini; the Sabinis were Londoners who neither visited Italy nor spoke Italian. Indeed, Darby's only son was killed in action in Egypt aged 21 while serving in the Royal Air Force.

Also in Darby's National Archive file is a report from the chief constable of Brighton, claiming that he had not been a criminal force for 20 years – undoubtedly an example of the enduring relationships with the police that was a mark of the Sabinis' operation. In terms of dominance over his key criminal markets and the influence that he was able to wield, Darby Sabini was the most significant criminal of the first half of the 20th century. The racecourse era featured men who went on to become key players in the legal gambling industry, while descendants of both the Italian firm and their competitors went on to enjoy careers as legitimate businessmen.

TWO WELL CUT VILLAINS

Of the thieves and gangsters who converged upon the West End of London both during and immediately after the Second World War, two men in particular were of note, and while initially their relationship was collaborative, this changed as the post-war criminal world evolved.

Billy Hill was a violent thief and cardsharp from Camden Town via Seven Dials, who by the end of the war, had served a number of sentences amounting to 20 years in prison. A knife- and razor-wielding thief who had been taught safe-breaking by his brother-in-law, Hill forged his reputation in the black market of the Second World War, which, as Frank Fraser enthused in his autobiography, produced unprecedented opportunities for criminal entrepreneurs: 'Now, everyone was crooked. Mums, they'd want to buy extra eggs for their children and a bit of extra meat. Everyone was involved. It was wonderful.'

Shortages in a wide range of products, from building materials to food and clothing, alongside rationing, the blackout and a fragmented civilian population, created an environment in which theft and the trade in stolen goods was normalised. When I interviewed Fraser on the 50th anniversary of the end of the war in Europe, his face lit up and he became positively nostalgic: 'It was a wonderful time to be a thief. I will never forgive that Hitler for surrendering when he did.'

The nature of this new market place may have been unprecedented but it was quickly understood by professional villains, as Fraser explained. 'The war organised criminals. Before the war, thieving was safes, jewellery, furs. Now a whole new world opened up. There was so much money and stuff about – cigarettes, sugar, clothes, petrol coupons, clothing coupons, anything. It was a thieves' paradise.' Hill exploited many of these new opportunities by establishing a network of thieves and receivers from a base in a Hertfordshire barn as well as supplying forged documents for deserters. When the war came to an end, Hill struck up an alliance with Spot.

Like many other gangsters, Jewish gangster Jack 'Spot' Comer started out providing 'protection' for communities where a police presence was both rare and unwelcome – in his case, for Jewish shopkeepers and stallholders who were being abused and exploited by non-Jews. However, much of his reputation stems from his claim to have attacked and beaten the fascist leader Oswald Mosley's bodyguard at the Battle of Cable Street in 1936. Although there is not a scrap of evidence for this act of heroism, the wily Spot traded on the legend for the rest of his life. Discharged from the army in 1943, his heroic status enabled him to operate in a number of northern cities with sizable Jewish communities before returning to London in 1947.

Spot and Hill teamed up against the White family, former

allies and adversaries of the Sabinis, who had gained a considerable foothold in the West End. The armies and vast arsenals that Hill and Spot later claimed to have assembled in anticipation of a Hollywood-style gang war with the Whites were not needed after losing a battle with Spot in 1947 at the wonderfully named Nut-House club, the Whites left Soho for the relative tranquillity of the racecourses. Hill and Spot quickly became not only key figures on the racecourses but also a powerful force in Soho.

Hill and Spot shared Soho with the five Messina Brothers. Although labelled as Maltese, the Messinas were of mixed Egyptian, Sicilian and Maltese descent, and had operated brothels in Sicily, Malta, Egypt, Morocco and Spain, before turning their attention to London in the mid-1930s. While the police were keen to accuse the Messinas of 'controlling vice' and running a 'vice empire', the brothers were paying protection money to Hill and Spot, as well as to the police. Historian Stefan Slater's research shows that these 'emperors of a vice empire in the heart of London' had at the peak of their careers only 20 women working for them. However, the Messinas were dark skinned, very well dressed and looked like proper gangsters. In the late 1940s, a newspaper exposé by Hill's biographer and cohort Duncan Webb kicked off a series of prosecutions, deportations and fines, resulting in the fragmentation of the business interests of these exotic, highly photogenic brothers. Subsequently, other well-tailored pimps and extortioners moved into the West End, which remained synonymous with vice, while Hill and Spot diversified.

In 1948, while Hill was serving three years in prison for a warehouse burglary, Spot's status as main player in London's crime scene took a blow when he became involved in robbery.

Security was almost non-existent at the newly opened London Airport and it was proving to be a ripe target for all levels of villainy. A heist was planned by a loose collective of thieves and hard men known as the Upton Park mob and, while this experienced group had no need of a 'mastermind', legend has it that Spot was the financier. Bullion worth £250,000 was due to arrive at the airport from South America; it would be stored in a warehouse along with jewellery and other valuables that would double the total value of the haul.

An inside man was tasked with drugging the coffee of the three security guards at the warehouse and letting the robbers in. However, as is often the case in big robberies, the inside man lost his nerve and informed the head of security who promptly contacted the police. On the night of the robbery, the three guards were replaced by police officers who feigned unconsciousness, while Flying Squad officers secreted themselves in the warehouse and other officers hid inside an adjacent lorry.

When the 11 masked robbers entered, the police announced themselves, prompting a pitched battle which ended with most of the robbery team unconscious and a number of broken bones among the police. But four of the robbery team escaped, including Franny Daniels who suffered severe burns by clinging to the underside of a vehicle until it arrived at its destination at Harlington police station, when he dropped to the floor and walked away. Eight men received sentences of between five and ten years' imprisonment and although he was never charged, Spot's reputation took a big hit.

While Spot was an old-fashioned street gangster lacking the organisational qualities required of a serious robber, Hill had a talent for planning project crime, as he showed with the Eastcastle Street Robbery in 1952. The £287,000 (nearly £8.5m in 2021) taken from a post office van was at the time Britain's largest robbery and prompted questions in the House of Commons. In his somewhat florid ghostwritten autobiography, Hill describes the robbery:

> 'As the mail-van, on its way from Paddington, turned into Eastcastle Street both cars shot out from each mews simultaneously . . . Six men sprang out of the cars . . . The three Post Office employees were struck over their heads and left lying on the pavement . . . No robbery has ever taken place like it. No robbery has ever been carried out with such perfection, from split-second timing to the concealment of evidence.'

The 1954 hijack of a KLM bullion van carrying £45,000 (£1,250,000) in gold was also attributed to Hill's organisational skills. However, Spot remained rooted to old practices and arcane enmities and found himself rapidly losing power and influence. Tensions with Hill grew and, jealous of Hill's claim to be the 'boss of Britain's underworld', Spot broke the arm of Hill's biographer Duncan Webb and hired his own scribe, the pulp writer Stephen Francis, who under the name of Hank Jansen produced *Jack Spot: The Man of a Thousand Cuts*.

Hill astutely recruited many prominent members of the Italian firm whose careers had been delayed by internment and war service, notably 'Italian' Albert Dimes (Alberto Dimeno), who provided a key connection with a group of Italian bookmakers who would side with Hill against Spot.

In 1955, Dimes refused to pay racecourse protection to Spot's men and, as a result, Spot attacked Dimes with a knife.

The bloody fight culminated with a greengrocer beating both men about the head with a metal scoop from her shop's weighing scales. At the subsequent trial, the 88-year-old Reverend Basil Andrews testified that Spot had not wielded a knife and both men, despite being seriously injured with knife wounds, were acquitted. It later emerged that the reverend had perjured himself for £25.

When rumours spread in the mid-1950s that Spot had informed on three men in an assault case in 1937, retribution became inevitable. Spot's inability to reciprocate the loyalty that he demanded of his followers led to a shedding of what had once been a formidable backing and his power rapidly disintegrated. Key veterans of the 1948 London Airport fiasco had a cordial meeting with a pro-Dimes group and agreed not to intervene in the violence that was to come. However, Spot associate Bobby Ramsey, a boxer with 83 professional bouts to his name who had previously worked with Hill as a bodyguard, proved less open to gentle persuasion and was stabbed to assure his non-involvement. In the 1970s, Ramsey forged himself a new career in TV and film as a non-speaking extra and at the age of 75 was still working the doors at an Essex club.

In 1956, with his bodyguard Joey Cannon mysteriously absent, Spot was ambushed by five associates of Hill and Dimes, leaving the ex-Black Shirt basher requiring a blood transfusion. Although Spot played the underworld game and refused to give evidence, his wife Rita had no such compunction and the perpetrators were convicted for the attack.

Spot soon declared himself bankrupt and faded into obscurity. Dimes, along with fellow Anglo-Italian graduates of Little Italy Bert Marsh and Bert Rossi, was a valuable conduit for both Italian and American Italian criminal interests in London. More importantly, he became a key player in 1960s Soho, where his networking skills earning him the title of 'The League of Nations in Soho' and helped stymie the West End ambitions of the Krays.

Billy Hill meanwhile made a fortune from an elaborate gambling swindle in collaboration with the owners of London's Clermont Club, invested heavily in property – at one time he owned the old Earls Court Exhibition Building – and purchased Churchill's, an exclusive Tangier nightclub for his wife. His criminal imagination assured a peaceful and comfortable retirement in Spain and West London, while mentoring his successors with Machiavellian relish.

Chapter 5

MAD WORLD: FRANK FRASER AND THE RICHARDSON BROTHERS

'Villains then would dress the part, immaculate, and if you were around them you had to dress the same. I suppose what I am saying is they carried themselves, how should I say, like people should.'

COLIN, AN EX-THIEF

Nobody embodied what it was to be a professional criminal and esteemed member of the underworld more than Francis Davidson Fraser. I had seen Frankie ('call me "Mad"') Fraser at a number of events around London in the 1990s when, following an appearance in a BBC documentary series and a successful biography written in collaboration with James Morton, Frank had become something of a media celebrity. However, it was only when I met him personally that I fully realised what all the fuss was about.

Along with a BBC radio producer, I met him at the flat that he shared with Marilyn Wisbey, the daughter of Train Robber

Tommy Wisbey. The intimidation, which thankfully proved to be playful, started at the entry phone.

> Frank: Hello.
> BBC: Hello, Mr Fraser, this is Matt Thompson from the BBC.
> Frank: Hello.
> BBC: Hello, Mr Fraser, this is Matt Thompson from the BBC.
> Frank: Hello, this is John Major. (The then prime minister.)

At this point Fraser had us. Was he demented? Crazy? Well his name was Mad Frankie Fraser. After what seemed like a very long pause he put us out of our misery.

'Just joking boy, come on up.'

He buzzed us in and as we took the flight of stairs to his apartment, I looked up to see the tallest 5-foot-4-inch 72-year-old in the world. He was standing over us at the top of the stairs in a crisp white open-necked shirt tucked into a pair of black slacks with razor sharp creases. The light from the open door of his flat was behind him, giving his coal-black hair an unnatural sheen. He invited us into his kitchen where he made tea, and I found my eyes constantly drawn to the box of hair dye on a shelf.

Frank filled the kettle, turned to me and said, 'I know you, don't I?' I said that we had never met but he came back with, 'Yeah, Dick Hobbs, you were the hospital orderly in Wandsworth in '73.' His eyes drilled into mine as my jaw dropped and my bowels quaked. After what seemed like several hours, he broke into a strange smile: 'Just joking, boy, just joking.' He offered us biscuits and I gratefully took one; when my colleague politely refused, Frank loudly insisted, 'HAVE A BISCUIT!' So he did.

Frank was a proper gangster who knew all there was to know about the art of intimidation. With the ground rules now established, the next four hours in the company of this sharp, polite, incredibly knowledgeable man with an astonishing memory were invaluable.

Fraser's career touched every major crime figure of the pre- and post-Second World War era. Born in 1923 into a hard-working, law abiding, South London family of Irish, Norwegian and Native American ancestry, as a child young Frank established contacts not only among the fighting gangs of South London's riverside hamlets but also across the river in Clerkenwell's Little Italy. By the age of nine, he was working for Darby Sabini, who employed children to wipe down their blackboards at the end of each race.

From a Sabini 'bucket boy', Fraser commenced a career of theft. However, he was not very good at it, by his own assessment and that of the police. A conviction for shoplifting was quickly followed in 1939 by his first custodial sentence for warehouse breaking. However, he escaped from approved school[9] and on his recapture in 1941, was sent to Borstal, where he was subjected to hard labour and experienced the physical brutality that runs like a thread through his long prison career. He was conscripted into the Army in 1942 and promptly deserted, before launching a career as a professional thief.

Frank Fraser was first declared insane in 1945 when he tried to escape after being caught in a round-up of deserters.

---

9   A residential institution where young offenders were sent by a court.

He was sent to a psychiatric hospital, court marshalled in his absence and medically discharged from the Army. Now the convictions came thick and fast and in 1945, while serving 20 months' hard labour, Frank Fraser appears to have decided to take on the prison service single-handed.

He began by attacking the governor of Shrewsbury prison. He had already been given the birch[10] while in Borstal; this time, Fraser received 18 strokes with the cat o' nine tails. This deeply disturbing experience clearly still affected him a full half a century later. In his autobiography, he described receiving corporal punishment.

'The Governor would read out, "Francis Davidson Fraser, you've been sentenced to eighteen strokes of corporal punishment – in your case the cat". "Stroke One" Whoooosh, "Stroke Two" and so on . . .Your back was cut to ribbons and the thud knocked the air out of you. Some men ended up with consumption after they'd had the Cat . . . There were always plenty of screws watching you get the Cat. They didn't have to be there but they loved it, just hoping they would see you crying or showing you were hurt. No man worth his salt would let them have that satisfaction. That was the most important part – not to let them see hurt or fear.'

In 1948, while serving another sentence, this time two years for a raid on a jewellers, Fraser embarked upon his epic personal vendetta with Governor Lawton in Pentonville

---

10 A bundle of twigs bound together into an implement that was retained as a means of corporal punishment in British prisons for violent breaches of discipline until 1962.

prison. After clashing with officers in Wandsworth prison, Fraser was transferred to Pentonville and put in a punishment cell where he cut his forearms so badly that he required 78 stitches and was subsequently placed in a straitjacket. When the straitjacket was removed, Fraser deliberately opened up the stitches and assaulted Lawton, covering him in blood. After also covering Lawton with the contents of his toilet bucket, Fraser was again placed in a straitjacket, this time padded out with heavy blankets soaked in water, in what Fraser claimed was a deliberate attempt by Lawton to murder him.

After his transfer back to Wandsworth prison, he continued to match any violence meted out to him by prison staff, before faking madness, being certified insane and getting himself transferred to the comparatively liberal regime of Cane Hill psychiatric hospital where he spent the remainder of his sentence. But Frank Fraser could hold a grudge and in 1951 he stalked Governor Lawton as he walked his dog on Wandsworth Common, knocking him unconscious and hanging both Lawton and his pet by their necks from a tree limb. Lawton survived but the dog died.

Fraser became particularly partial to wage snatches and in 1953 he received a three-year sentence for burgling a cigarette factory in Edgware. Back in Wandsworth prison again, he attacked the hangman Albert Pierrepoint in the prelude to the execution of Derek Bentley and again clashed with Governor Lawton before being transferred to Durham prison. Here the war between Frank Fraser and the prison regime escalated further and he was again certified insane, spending the remainder of his sentence in Broadmoor before his release in 1955.

On his release from Broadmoor, Frank Fraser teamed up

with Billy Hill and became a key player in his conflict with Jack 'Spot' Comer to control the illegal markets that were booming in London's West End. This culminated in 1956 when Fraser received seven years for his part in the attack that effectively ended Jack Spot's criminal career. Back behind bars, Fraser continued to violently resist the prison authorities and was brutally beaten by teams of prison officers, spending most of his sentence in punishment blocks and on hospital wings as he was ghosted around the prison system.

THE RICHARDSONS

Like Darby Sabini and Billy Hill, the Richardson brothers appreciated Frank Fraser's talents. When he was recruited by Charlie and Eddie Richardson in the early 1960s, it was described by Mickey Bloom, an associate of North London's Nash Brothers: as 'like China getting the atom bomb'. Born into a traditional South London working-class family, after the insecurity and trauma of wartime evacuation, the brothers enjoyed the vibrant local street life and became talented boxers and prominent local street-fighters – Eddie in particular. The Richardson brothers also had a penchant for hard work and made good money from the post-war scrap metal trade by shrewdly plundering abandoned wartime airfields. They went on to establish themselves in a number of legitimate businesses and became adept at extortion and long firm fraud.[11]

---

11 A legitimate business creates good trading relationships with suppliers by initially paying bills on time. Once a good credit rating is established with a range of suppliers, large consignments of goods from multiple suppliers are purchased and the villains 'bust out', sell up and disappear. Sometimes the episode is concluded by a fire at the premises followed by a successful insurance claim.

NO CONTEST

Charlie Richardson had first met the Kray twins in Shepton Mallet military prison while they were all awaiting a dishonourable discharge from National Service; they were reacquainted years later by the allure of the West End. The Richardsons could boast among their associates some of London's most violent and feared men and did not take the Krays seriously. Despite the fact that the Krays' associates claimed to be preparing for gang warfare, and Ron Kray in particular fantasised about a Chicago-style conflict, Eddie was unconcerned: 'There was never any direct threat from them. They were playing at being gangsters, like you see in the movies.' The Richardsons were beyond territorial squabbling.

An ex-member of the Fraud Squad recently explained to me that when Charlie was beginning to see the benefits that limited companies and stock exchange shells could bring to his long-firm operations, he was often to be found socialising with members of the City of London Fraud Squad in various pubs off Lime Street in EC3, just over a mile from Vallance Road, the twins' Whitechapel base. Frank Fraser once said of Charlie Richardson: 'He was a genius, not like a professor who might know about art and paintings, but as a money maker.'

In addition to long firms, gaming machines, pornography, five scrap metal yards and a lucrative car-parking scam at Heathrow airport, Billy Hill, Eddie Richardson, Frank Fraser and Albert Dimes formed Atlantic Machines, supplying gaming machines to premises all over the UK. Charlie had become increasingly fascinated by South Africa – in particular, opportunities in the country's mineral industry. Bizarrely, he then became entangled with the South African security services, who offered him mining licences in exchange for Charlie arranging for the telephones of both Amnesty International and Prime Minister Harold Wilson to be tapped.

PLAUSIBLE ROGUES

Ex-professional boxer, pickpocket and cohort of Charles Kray senior, Jimmy Kensit was employed by Charlie Richardson for his skills as a long fraudster. Described to me by Eddie Richardson as a 'plausible rogue', in 1962, Kensit was invited by Charlie Richardson to invest £150 in a company specialising in 'hire purchase in boats' before becoming employed at Central Supplies, a Richardson-run wholesalers. It was during this period that he witnessed an associate being beaten after he had objected to Charlie Richardson plundering the stock.

Kensit was part of a small group sent to Milan to buy stockings directly from the manufacturers to be sold by mail order, but a mixture of chaos and outright larceny ensured that the Italians could not be paid. With the Italian creditors pressing, Charlie decided to simplify things. He told Kensit to ensure that he had an alibi for the following night, so Jimmy visited the cinema with his wife, making sure to retain the ticket stubs, before going on to the high-profile Astor Club. That night, Central Supplies burnt down.

Much of Jimmy Kensit's value to the Richardsons stemmed from his background as a pickpocket. His generation of 'dipper' was especially effective at mass events such as race meetings and their specialist skills afforded them a notoriety that made them easily identifiable to the police, who would often turn a blind eye in exchange for a bribe. As Eddie Richardson explained to me, 'They can only operate by bunging[12] the police, otherwise they'd be nicked every time they went out. The police give them a sort of licence to operate and that means they are always close to the cops.' These relationships often lasted long after both the dipper and the police officer had moved up the ranks and often proved useful. The affable Kensit would personally deliver £25 per week to a senior CID officer at Bishopsgate police station in exchange for a 'heads up' if the Richardsons should come into the frame. In the straight world, it is called networking.

Kensit distanced himself from the Richardsons after their next business suffered a similar fire and his wife had a minor car accident, allegedly as a result of her brake cables being cut. However, Kensit was soon back working for the Richardsons in various capacities, until he was arrested in July 1966 on what was almost certainly a phoney charge of warehouse breaking.

In Lewes prison, the middle-aged Kensit was subjected to police pressure and, Eddie explained to me in a most matter-of-fact manner, 'He [Kensit] made a statement against Charlie, in return for which charges against him were dropped.' Kensit's statement to the police confirmed their description of him as a 'minor criminal' and 'a man completely under the domination of the Richardsons':

'I want to say that any association I have had with Charlie Richardson was because I have been scared and terrorised and worried because of my wife's safety. I have seen how violent he can be and I have heard

---

12 Bribing

about many other cases. My wife has been worried out of her life for me and herself and the baby. She has gone in fear ever since the brake-cutting incident.'

In 1966, with Charlie in South Africa, there was a dispute concerning the running of the door at Mr Smith's Club in Catford, in which one man was killed and five others, including Eddie Richardson and Frank Fraser, were wounded. Both men were later arrested, Fraser for murder.

The Richardson firm had dished out violence to a number of their team of long fraudsters who had either objected to Charlie Richardson's penchant for stealing stock and cash before the swindle had time to properly mature, or had indeed helped themselves from one of his long firms. When an associate of Charlie found himself on death row in a South African prison convicted of murder, in exchange for leniency, he gave key information to the British police on the Richardson operation. The resulting highly sensational 'torture trial' in 1967 featured shocking allegations of pliers being used to remove teeth and fingernails, along with a generator being wired up to the genitals of the hapless fraudsters. The judge came down heavily on the Richardson firm, with Eddie getting ten years and another five for the Mr Smith's incident, and Charlie receiving an astonishing twenty-five years. Frank Fraser was acquitted of the Catford murder but received five years for affray and ten years for his deviant 'dental practice'. The presiding judge was Sir Frederick Lawton, the son of Governor Lawton, the man who Fraser had attempted to hang on Wandsworth Common in 1951. Back in the prison system, Fraser carried on where he had left off and was one of the ringleaders of the Parkhurst prison riot in 1969, when he was beaten by prison officers and subsequently spent six weeks in the prison hospital.

In 1990, Eddie Richardson was sentenced to 35 years after being convicted of his involvement in a £40m cocaine deal. Eddie learnt to paint in prison and his work featured in a number of exhibitions. He was released from prison in 2001 at the age of 65, collaborated in writing a book, and continued with his legitimate business career, as well as developing a side line as an after dinner speaker intent on deglamourising 1960s gangsterism. He had become increasingly estranged from his brother, seemingly as a result of a dispute over one of their legitimate enterprises, and they were never reconciled.

In 1980, Charlie Richardson escaped from an open prison, remaining free for just under a year before giving himself up. He was eventually released in 1984. Shrewd, manipulative and addicted to business, he went against the old gangster stereotype in many ways. He was ahead of the game in his moneymaking ambitions that went way beyond the celebrity obsessed concerns of some of his peers. Nobody could swear quite like Charlie Richardson, and he reserved his most heartfelt oaths for the ex-business associates and members of the Establishment who, he insisted to his death aged 78 in 2012, had conspired to deprive him of his liberty for 18 years.

Charlie remained bitter, not only about his sentence but about his portrayal in the press. In his autobiography, he summarised his trial: 'Nobody was dead, maimed or even bloody scarred. I had slapped five hooligans around and had defrauded large companies.' While the sentencing in the so-called 'torture' cases was probably due to a combination of the UK's growing fear of American style 'organised crime' and Charlie Richardson's phone-tapping escapades on behalf of the South African secret service, I have found that the truth is difficult to unpack and official files relating to the Richardsons have been sunk deep into the long grass of British officialdom.

The Richardsons were by far the most potent, competent and business-like criminal entrepreneurs of the 1960s. They did not play at being gangsters, they were the real deal: shrewd, manipulative and, when required, quick to dish out violence to fellow denizens of the underworld. However, while violence was integral to their success, their shrewdness in nurturing relationships – in particular with corrupt police officers – was undoubtedly as important as the threat of a knock on the door from Frank and Eddie. Their ability to constantly mutate and replicate many of the workings of legitimate business was also a big part of their success.

Having spent a total of 42 years in prison without a single day's remission for good behaviour, Frank Fraser was finally released in 1985. In 1991, he survived being shot in the head at close range outside a nightclub in Clerkenwell. His new-found celebrity status among the 'lads' mags' popular at the time suited Frank Fraser and he became a regular guest on TV programmes and documentaries, as well as acting as a gangster in a feature film. He also conducted guided tours of 'gangland London' and toured the country with a one-man show.

He remained a first-class intimidator. After interviewing Frank for a radio documentary, the producer Matt Thompson and I were preparing to leave Frank's home when he politely checked the amount that he would be receiving for his fee. Matt replied that it was £75. Frank smiled, quietly said that this was wrong and that the fee that he had negotiated was £100. Matt became just a little rattled and repeated, but this time in a slightly terse manner, 'It was definitely £75.' And then I witnessed at first hand a master at work.

Frank retained his smile and sat down on the settee very close to Matt who was busy packing his equipment. Frank placed his right arm along the back of the settee behind Matt's head, paused until Matt looked up into those cold black eyes and then said, in a soft but clear tone, 'Now, that's all right boy, and I aint going to argue, but I just want you to know that it was £100,' before withdrawing his arm and standing up. The pace of Matt's packing increased and we hurriedly shook hands with our host, thanked him and flew out of the door into the street, whereupon a pale-faced Matt turned to me and said, 'I have just remembered, it was £100.'

I glanced up to see Frank looking down on us from the window of his flat. He was smiling.

Even in his old age, Frank Fraser never proclaimed to be reformed and in his dotage he was involved in a number of feuds with villains from across the generations. There was little in Frank Fraser's life that was not criminal and three of his four sons followed in their dad's footsteps. He was an unrepentant violent criminal who rigidly abided by a samurai-like code of the underworld, where respectable working people are mugs (he had a particular antipathy to clerks) and you were loyal to your friends and colleagues in crime. The greatest sin was to co-operate with the police – 'You couldn't do a worser crime.' At the age of 89 and suffering from Alzheimer's, Frank received an anti-social behaviour order after a row with a fellow resident at his care home. He died in 2014 aged 90.

Chapter 6

NOSTALGIA, CELEBRITY AND MURDER: THE KRAYS

'We were fucking untouchable.'

RON KRAY

Mere civilians living outside of the alluringly iffy frontier of the underworld were generally dismissed by professional villains as mug punters. If you found yourself in their company, you would either be ignored as a total irrelevance or treated with an exaggerated courtesy that bordered on condescension. Either way, you seldom had to buy a drink and in their company you were in the safest place in London.

One afternoon in the mid seventies, I was in a pub in Shoreditch owned by a notorious crime family when somebody poured several bottles of bleach over the floor of the gents toilet. The fumes were overwhelming and a number of punters, including myself, came coughing and spluttering out of the toilet into the bar. An extremely angry barman checked out the gents before interrogating several of his customers, making clear the fate that awaited the phantom bleacher. As he towered over me, a man built like a medium-sized refrigerator, albeit a refrigerator dressed in tasteful, medium-weight worsted, stepped in and explained to the barman, 'Well, he never did it, he's doing O levels at fucking night school.' The barman apologised and the remainder of the afternoon went swimmingly. The bleach stunt was an act of aggression by a competitor or old enemy and such an obvious civilian as myself was to be excluded from any conflict.

EARLY INFLUENCES: HOXTON AND HOLLYWOOD

The pub I was in was, of course, 'owned' by the UK's most famous criminals of the 1960s, the Krays, who have remained for over half a century indivisible from the concept of organised crime and the benchmark for British gangsters. Indeed, whenever some new psychotic mob of jack the lads come to the attention of the mass media they are inevitably compared to Reg and Ron. And yet, the curious legacy of these murderous twins was an empire that failed to extend much beyond their own backyard. Indeed, the hand-stitched, photogenic career of the Krays was based upon style rather than economic power. And the Krays had style, subtly mixing Savile Row and the Hackney Road with the violent panache of 1930s Hollywood gangsters such as Edward G Robinson, James Cagney, Humphrey Bogart and particularly George Raft, whose style and sartorial swagger they slavishly mimicked.

During the 1960s, the twins had a very good relationship with the editor of a local newspaper. I remember the front page often featured a picture of 'Sporting Twins Reginald and Ronald Kray' handing over a turkey/birthday cake/ bouquet of flowers/cheque to a pub full of grateful pensioners, while on the back page of the same edition the self-same 'sporting twins' were pictured presenting a trophy to a skinny kid in a singlet at a local boys' club boxing night. Boys' clubs, local charities and the elderly all benefited from the Krays' sense of publicity. They were tough, successful and highly visible local gangsters who were usually accompanied by an entourage of thugs, mugs and hangers on. A friend of mine, Phil, was once standing at the bar of a pub in Stratford trying to look 18 when a large man gave him a five pound note and told him to buy a round of drinks and join a group of besuited men sitting in an alcove seat. Phil told the man to fuck off, which he did, but when the barman explained that the fiver belonged to the waiting Ronnie Kray, my friend ran home and was sat in front of the TV with his parents in time for *Match of the Day*.

Of Romany/Jewish heritage, Reg and Ron Kray grew up in the East End in an environment that had changed little since Dickens' day. They were brought up in a family of fiercely independent men and powerful, resourceful women. Their father, Charles, made a good living 'on the knocker', buying second-hand clothes from affluent suburban households and selling to traders in the East End, and their mother, Violet, and her sisters May and Rose, became important influences on the twins and their older brother Charlie. While Charles declined to join the hostilities at the start of the Second World War and went 'on the trot', Violet and her sons were evacuated to rural Suffolk, before invasion scares drove the family back to bomb-scarred Bethnal Green.

Neighbourhood hard men such as Jimmy Spinks, Dodger Mullins and the brothers' grandfathers, Cannonball Lee and Jimmy Kray, had a huge influence on the twins, who followed their talented older brother Charlie into the boxing ring. But by the time they became professional boxers at the age of 17, Reg and Ron Kray had already appeared at the Old Bailey to face serious assault charges that were subsequently dropped. Their boxing careers ended after Ron assaulted a police officer and the PC's colleagues left Ron bloodied in a police station cell. Soon after, Reg located Ron's victim on the street and punched him in the face. A local priest intervened at their trial and the twins were given probation.

Ron had suffered a series of severe childhood illnesses that had rendered him slower and less outgoing than Reg, and he developed a fantasy world that revolved around notions of charismatic leadership. For instance, while still a teenager, Ron copied one of his heroes, Al Capone, by paying a local Italian barber to come to his house each morning to shave him.

The twins' compulsory military careers ended in the guardhouse after just 15 months, most of which was spent AWOL. They were employed by Jack Spot on the door of a Covent Garden club before he set them up in the racetrack game at a minor point-to-point course in Essex. A shooting at the Central Club in Clerkenwell, where the allocation of bookies pitches was overseen by Albert Dimes, was soon followed by a breakthrough into the big-time racecourses. But the twins were never really racing people and by the age of 20 they had taken over a billiard hall, a base from where Ron could play out many of his fantasies as the twins gathered a group of both young and old villains around them.

Clubs were their forte, though it brought them into direct conflict with the Watney Street Mob, a loose-knit group largely made up of interconnected families of dockers from the wrong side of Commercial Road. Ronnie was sentenced to three years' imprisonment for GBH when a revenge attack on the gang for beating up one of Ronnie's associates ended with an innocent young man being kicked in the head and slashed with a bayonet.

Two years, later Ron was certified insane but escaped from the secure hospital after his identical twin swapped places with him during a visit. A spell on the outside resulted in Ron's behaviour becoming increasingly bizarre and he gave himself up before being eventually released in 1959 to find the firm thriving under the increasingly business-like Reg.

The brothers' Double R club in Bow was a particular success, but when Reg was imprisoned in 1959 for extortion, Ron ran the club down and eventually the police opposed the renewal of the club's licence. The Kentucky club was opened in 1962 as a replacement for the Double R and attracted West End celebrities who ventured up the Mile End Road for a slice of newly fashionable East End lowlife. However, this proved to be another short-lived venture, and the police closed the club down in 1964.

The twins provided 'security' for some of Billy Hill's illegal gambling clubs, which should have set them up nicely for the legalisation of gambling in 1961. But they were always more comfortable at the simpler, bloodier end of the protection business and continued to collect weekly 'pensions' from clubs, pubs, spielers[13] and a wide range of legal and illegal businesses in North and East London, while also enthusiastically dipping their beaks into any successful theft or scam that came to their attention.

---

13 Illegal gambling clubs

THIRSTY WORK: TEDDY'S STORY

For instance, Teddy, who we met on the corner in The City Arms, pondering his next small-scale scam, had a cousin who set up an illegal drinking club in the basement of a Turkish-owned clothing factory and Teddy applied himself to stocking the bar. Theft was the most obvious strategy and the family were always on the look-out for stolen whiskey in particular. However, Teddy's major success was in his collaboration with a school friend whose father had worked all his life for a gin manufacturer. One of the long standing scams at the distillery involved the theft of labels that were then attached to bottles containing a potent home-brew that, when combined with a mixer, could pass for gin. This scam had been running for years in collaboration with a handful of local pubs and was designed to exploit the indiscriminate boozing that took place over Christmas in particular. However, Teddy could smell a good earner so he decided to expand. He printed thousands of labels and obtained facsimile bottles and cartons before setting up a business selling 'stolen' gin to pubs and clubs all over London.

Unfortunately, Teddy sold his moonshine, without first explaining its true origins, to the Krays, who at this time had a stake in a number of local spielers. This was regarded as a gross insult to a firm who were not to be treated as mug punters. Teddy took a terrible beating and the stoic manner in which he accepted his punishment established him as a 'face' in all the right places. But he kept a low profile and he was never considered as part of the cast of characters who were to appear in the subsequent books that created Krayology.

LORDS, LONG FRAUD AND LIBIDO

Like the Richardsons, the Krays did dabble in long-firm fraud but violence and clubland remained their primary interests and, whether it was imposing order, protecting their investments or dealing with eternally recurring feuds from their adolescence, the twins had formidable reputations to protect. While Reg was serving time for extortion, Ron had put the arm on notorious housing racketeer Peter Rachman, which resulted in the Krays taking possession of Esmeralda's Barn, a fashionable West End gaming establishment with a gay nightclub in the basement. Homosexuality was still illegal and the club became a vital venue for Ron to network, extort and act as a procurer on behalf of high-profile gay men, including members of both the Lords and the House of Commons.

In 1964, Ron's relationship with Lord Robert Boothby, the Eton-educated former MP for East Aberdeenshire and a former private secretary to Winston Churchill, was the focus of a story in the *Sunday Mirror*. The Krays had been approached by the son of the Labour peer Manny Shinwell to invest in a building project in Nigeria and when the development ground to a halt, Ron approached Boothby, a fellow member of the gay underworld, for funds. The story appeared in the newspaper, omitting names but leaving the reader in no doubt as to who was involved. It went on to discuss 'the private weekend activities of the peer and a number of prominent public men during visits to Brighton', and much more. However, in the wake of the Profumo scandal just the previous year, these revelations were not regarded as to be in the interest of either of the main political parties and after lawyers intervened, the *Mirror* backed down and Boothby received £40,000 in an out-of-court settlement (£700,000 in 2021). The political classes distanced themselves from the possibility of another scandal and the police were directed to back off from the Krays and abandon their ongoing operations. Meanwhile, in Nigeria, the Kray team had badly mishandled a backhander to a local contractor, the project went sour and they lost their investment.

But the twins were now bulletproof and free to revel in the social and commercial opportunities on offer. When Reg was married in 1965, David Bailey was the official wedding photographer. They had become fashionable hosts in a glamorous, smoky, boozy East End wonderland, where criminals, film stars and the aristocracy briefly mixed.

MURDERS

Esmeralda's Barn, like most businesses tainted by the Krays' inevitable mismanagement, collapsed in 1964 but there was always another source of easy money ripe for plunder. Via the Colony Club, where the Krays' boyhood idol George Raft now worked as a meeter and greeter, American organised crime was investing in London's newly legalised gambling industry and, along with other prominent London criminals, the twins were getting some crumbs from their table, even managing to strike up a relationship with the Philadelphia mob.

However, as the sixties progressed, the twins became more impudent in their confrontations with authority. Frank 'Mad Axeman' Mitchell, a man of great strength and low intellect who the Twins fancied having around as a pet and not-very-secret weapon, was sprung from Dartmoor prison and secreted in an East End flat. However, Mitchell became a problem for the Krays; his physical strength, short temper, and unreliability made him difficult to control, and the Krays had him murdered.

In March 1966, when the core of the Richardson firm had been arrested in the aftermath of the Mr Smith's shooting, George Cornell visited a patient at the London Hospital in Whitechapel. Cornell was an alumni of Stepney's Watney Street Mob who had married, settled south of the Thames and worked with the Richardson brothers in a number of enterprises. After visiting his friend, he was having a drink in the nearby Blind Beggar when Ronnie Kray, prompted by a misinterpretation of a threat to Fred Foreman's pub, shot Cornell dead as he sat on a stool in the saloon bar. The killing was carried out in front of witnesses and details of the murder rapidly entered East End folklore. However, while local schoolchildren openly discussed this latest Kray atrocity as if it was the result of a football match, no witnesses could be found to identify the assailant to the police.

Ron's mental condition continued to deteriorate and Reg, who was increasingly abusing pills and alcohol, became unstable in the wake of the suicide of his wife in the summer of 1967, resulting in a series of shootings and knifings. Ron urged his twin to commit a murder of his own and Jack 'the Hat' McVitie was nominated. McVitie, who Frank Fraser described as a 'lovely man', was a fringe member of the Kray firm with a penchant for pills and violence. After botching a murderous errand for the Krays, McVitie threatened to shoot the twins and was generally violent and disruptive. He was lured to a flat where Reg butchered him with a knife in front of several associates.

The Krays were arrested as the result of evidence provided by an agent provocateur working for the United States Secret

Service and when they were off the streets, witnesses to the killings of both Cornell and McVitie were found. George Raft and his colleagues abandoned London and Reg and Ron's 'empire' shrunk to a couple of pubs in Bethnal Green. There were two trials at the Old Bailey: the first for the murders of McVitie and Cornell was presided over by Justice Melford Stevenson and the second trial, regarding the death of Frank Mitchell, almost inevitably by Justice Lawton.

The trials became show trials for the sixties; the twins were the most obvious manifestation of what working-class boys might achieve beyond the factory gates and outside of the safe controllable worlds of sport and show-business. Most members of the firm so cherished by Ron Kray appeared not in the dock but in the witness box in exchange for leniency, with a few exceptions such as the Lambrianou brothers and Charlie Kray. Although acquitted for the killing of Frank 'Mad Axeman' Mitchell, the twins were sentenced to life imprisonment with a non-parole period of 30 years for the murders of Cornell and McVitie. But it was all irrelevant to Ron, who called the prosecuting counsel 'a fat slob' before he disappeared into the prison system.

Ron's marriage in 1989, subsequent divorce five years later and the sometimes bizarre antics of those who campaigned for the twins' release kept Ron in the public eye. But this was a soap opera limbo that was a parody of the years when he was part of the most notorious criminal alliance in the land. He was certified a paranoid schizophrenic in 1979 and served out his sentence heavily medicated in Broadmoor hospital. Ron Kray died in 1995 of a massive heart attack.

Reg Kray served over 30 years, which he spent writing autobiographies and books of poetry and keeping fit. In 1997, he married 38-year-old Roberta Jones in a brief ceremony in Maidstone prison and in 1998 expressed at a probation assessment some remorse for killing McVitie. In August the same year, he was diagnosed with bladder cancer and the Home Secretary ordered his release on compassionate parole just weeks before his death in October 2000.

Charlie Kray, who received a ten-year sentence for helping in the disposal of Jack McVitie's body, had been the 'meeter and greeter' on a thousand and one smoky nights when criminals, film stars and the aristocracy mingled in a swinging London pantomime. Charlie divorced his wife Dolly after she had conducted a long-term affair with a known villain and dedicated himself to campaigning for his brothers' release, while simultaneously exploiting the Kray name to the brothers' best advantage. Charlie was in constant financial trouble and when, after many years of speculation, the Kray brothers sold the film rights to their life story, it was not for the £2m that Reg had envisioned, but for £255,000. Charlie was the chief negotiator and was in dire need of cash due to the overwhelming debts and failed business deals that had marked his post-prison career. The twins refused to speak to Charlie for almost a year.

Charlie frittered away his proceeds from the Kray nostalgia industry, which apart from the film, included T-shirts, books, videos, autographed photographs, special edition prints, media interviews, Kray waistcoats, belt buckles and other dubious items. When his son Gary died in 1996, Charlie did not have the funds for the funeral expenses and Reg, who by that time had been incarcerated for 28 years, paid the bill. That same year, Charlie was arrested following a bizarre police sting operation.

The details of the case are worthy of a script written for Barbara Windsor, one of Charlie Kray's paramours of the 1960s. It involved Charlie borrowing £500 from an undercover police officer, a night out with the Spice Girls in an Essex hotel and an undercover police officer having a 'quickie' with a club hostess. At the trial, Charlie's two main character witnesses were an actor whose best known role was playing a dodgy CID officer and Frank Fraser, who, like many friends and observers of this quiet, polite, 71-year-old man, had trouble associating him with the drug trade. Nonetheless, in June 1997, Charlie was sentenced to 12 years' imprisonment for supplying two kilograms of cocaine and promising to supply cocaine to the value of £39m. Although he had never seen the drugs, what was probably just another scam cashing in on the family name had dire consequences and Charlie died in prison in April 2000 aged 73.

The Dickensian East End, of which the Kray family and their ilk were among the last remnants, has gone for ever, demolished or made irrelevant by gentrification, rehousing and economic change. A merchant bank has been built on the site of the Bluecoat Boy pub where, in 1975, after serving time for disposing of Jack McVitie's body, tanned, suited and booted, Charlie had held court looking like Robert Mitchum. The Krays were hapless criminal businessmen with a flair for violence and public relations. Had they been born 50 years later, they would have been prime candidates for *Celebrity Big Brother*, *I'm a Celebrity... Get Me Out of Here* or *Strictly*. Perhaps they would have rivalled Ant and Dec as Saturday night family favourites.

The peak period of the Kray twins' career coincided with some of the UK's key legislation changes of the 20th century, in particular the Betting and Gaming Act 1960 that legalised gambling, the Murder (Abolition of Death Penalty) Act 1965 and the repeal of the Sexual Offences Act in 1967, which decriminalised homosexuality. Gambling had given their careers a massive boost and opened up the West End; they could no longer be executed by the State for their crimes and, by the time they were imprisoned, the sexual preferences which, when prohibited, had helped shape their personal and professional lives no longer applied.

The potent mixture of money, violence, sex, madness and rolling nostalgia ensures that they will never be forgotten. As their biographer John Pearson explains, their story is, 'part black farce, part cockney tragedy, part sick saga in the overheated culture of celebrity'. The Krays barely made a mark outside of the old East End. As criminal businessmen, they were disasters who were only comfortable making their money the old-fashioned way, from extortion and intimidation in the style of Jimmy Spinks, Dodger Mullins and other much admired hardmen of their youth. Yet they attracted the attention of show-business celebrities and had contacts in the House of Commons and the House of Lords. Despite their very limited achievements, it is the Krays, in their mimicry of a Hollywood mafia, who contrived Britain's most enduring imagery of organised crime.

During their long incarceration, the Kray twins morphed into icons of a brief 'golden age' of the post-war criminal era. They are regarded by some deluded and sentimental punters as symbols of safer, more predictable days, when white working-class boys in sharp suits ruled their manor by hard but fair means. Certainly, as this quote from Ron Kray makes clear, the twins knew their audience: 'When Reggie and me looked after things in the East End there was never any of this mugging of old ladies or child killing. If anybody had started pulling strokes like that they would soon have been stopped.' The notion of Reg and Ron as community policemen is interesting, but the reality is that the Krays were glamorous, mother-loving street fighters who contributed to local charities, and whose unambiguous embrace of the gangster ethic at the expense of commercial rationality now seems as dated as National Service and black and white TV.

Chapter 7

GANGBUSTING WITH BERT: POLICING THE POST-KRAY CITY

'They were the hope of a frightened city as it struggled feebly in a web of bombs and bullets, alcohol and assassination.'

ELIOT NESS, THE UNTOUCHABLES

Post-war full employment and crowded shops had not pacified the British population and crime doubled in the 1960s. Telephone ownership allowed more crimes to be reported and property insurance became common, which further encouraged the reporting of crime, while the relative affluence of the population meant that people had more possessions to steal. Drug and motor vehicle offences were now impacting on the crime statistics; armed robbery became more prevalent as the cash economy boomed and professional criminals became ever more innovative in their quest for money and the avoidance of working for a living.

However, the police as an organisation was also evolving. Until the 1960s, serious crime was seldom regarded as a national, let alone international, issue. Periodically, in response to a particularly intense outbreak of professional skulduggery, it was recognised as a local problem in certain cities and the British police would respond by creating special squads to counter specific forms of criminality. For instance, the Metropolitan Police's Flying Squad had been formed in 1919 to work across divisional boundaries to counter burglars, robbers and pickpockets, often by forging close relationships with active criminals. But generally, the UK's individual police forces operated in isolation; force boundaries were sacrosanct and there was fierce resistance to centralised state policing.

However, the increased mobility of criminals created a need for a degree of flexibility within the police organisation and in 1964 Regional Crime Squads were formed with a capability to operate across police boundaries, but with a regional rather than national agenda. As indicated by the clientele of The City Arms, relations between the police and the communities they policed were complex, and local officers would often turn blind eyes to the activities of routine embedded criminal activity. Sometimes the motivation for so doing was cash but was more often inspired by a desire to make their working lives a little easier and ensure a quiet life.

By the late 1960s, while the big marquee names of London's underworld were buried deep in the prison system, or busy slopping out and planning their biographies, out on the streets, any neighbourhood crime firm that showed ambition was quickly crushed by a police force that feared attempts to fill the 'vacuums' left by the Krays and the Richardsons. The Kray and Richardson cases had mesmerised the British public and exposed the extent to which local police had been corrupted by gangsters. Investigative reporters and a police force increasingly attuned to the benefits of good public relations ensured that the public were much more aware of the activities of serious criminals than they had been in the past. Serious villains were being portrayed as examples of the nation's decay and special squads of detectives were more than willing to play whack-a-mole with any groups of likely lads poking their heads above the parapet. With the perceived success of the Regional Crime Squads now firmly established, incorruptible sheriffs from out of town were fashionable, for this was the era of the specialised squad.

THE OLD GREY FOX

In 1971, ex-Special Boat Service member Chief Superintendent Bert Wickstead, a local boy made cop, took over Scotland Yard's Serious Crime Squad, which to Wickstead's delight was given the nickname 'the Untouchables', after a highly popular 1960s TV series based very loosely on the exploits of Eliot Ness, the self-publicising American prohibition-era Treasury agent and his elite squad of gangbusters.

What burglar Peter Scott was later to christen 'Wicksteria' had arrived. Wickstead was a master of the witness box who arrived with a reputation that was both formidable and pock-marked with allegations of being creative with the verbal evidence of men that he deemed to be 'well at it'. The audio taping of interviews did not become part of police practice until the late 1980s, and with the enthusiastic support of the commissioner, Sir Robert Mark, Wickstead – or Bullwhip Bert as he was known to some of his subordinates – played the game according to the unwritten rules of the day exceedingly well.

The Metropolitan Police and its political masters were especially keen for Wickstead to keep an eye on the supposed vacuum created by the demise of the Kray firm and proceeded to apply a tactic that has proved enduringly popular in police circles: he exaggerated the threat. By the time they were arrested, the Krays' so-called 'empire' was almost non-existent. Prior to their final arrests, the twins' increasing unpredictability had drawn so much unwanted attention to nooks and crannies of the underworld that, as their former associate Fred Foreman noted, 'They were a danger to everybody – they were out of control.' In short, the Krays were bad for business and, according to Foreman, it is most likely that they would have been 'ironed out' by their peers if law enforcement had not intervened. In other words, there was no vacuum to fill.

Nonetheless, on taking on his new job, Wickstead asserted that the distinctly low-key Dixon brothers, along with successful publican and Kray schoolmate Phil Jacobs, were about to step into the shoes of the twins. While George and Alan Dixon were associates of the Krays, they were hardly gangsters, just local hard cases and debt collectors who dabbled with long firms and 'minded' a number of pubs and clubs in East London, including those owned by the diminutive Jacobs, who the Krays had attempted to extort shortly before they were arrested. Wickstead and his team converted a little light protection into heavy duty extortion and, in 1972, his newly formed squad of 'Untouchables' gained successful prosecutions against six men, including George Dixon and Phil 'Little Caesar' Jacobs, who got 12 years each, and Alan Dixon, who received a nine-year sentence. As the reader will no doubt have noted, during this period both the mass media and their friends in the police liked to use nicknames from the Chicago gangster era and Wickstead's sobriquets 'The Old Grey Fox' and 'Gangbuster' came into being.

SCRAP AND METAL

Canning Town's Tibbs family was designated as 'a highly organised gang' by Wickstead, despite no evidence other than their involvement in a four-year violent feud with the Nicholls family who, according to Wickstead, were 'a loose collection of criminal friends'. The Tibbs was a prominent family of scrap metal dealers, a trade which, during the 1960s and 1970s, required heavy hands and amicable relations with local police officers. But they were also highly visible and accessible locals who were primarily known via Jimmy Tibbs, who, in the late 1960s, was a local celebrity due to his outstanding career as a professional boxer. With a wide range of friends and associates who were part of the general population rather than of some exotic underworld, if the Tibbs were 'at it' then they were not alone in the East End of the 1960s and 70s where crime was normal. But they were not gangsters.

The Tibbs tit-for-tat feud with the Nicholls clan was an entirely personal affair between two tough East End families and their associates that appears to have commenced in 1968, when one of the Tibbs elders, George, who was in his sixties, had an argument in a Poplar pub with Albert Nicholls, a mini-cab firm owner in his twenties. The disagreement turned into a fight and George received a beating, which led three days later to a visit to Albert's mini-cab office from Jimmy, Johnny and young George Tibbs. A shotgun was discharged, Nicholls was seriously wounded and at the subsequent Old Bailey trial, the Tibbs trio received suspended sentences and a fine, the leniency of which is remarkable.

Two years later, Robert Tibbs survived having his throat cut outside a pub in Canning Town and the feud between the Tibbs and the Nicholls quickly escalated into a cycle of revenge and retribution. Stabbings and shootings, often featuring friends and associates of both families, became commonplace – one such attack that involved knives and an axe resulted in the victim receiving 180 stitches. In 1971, business premises owned by the Tibbs were bombed and Jimmy Tibbs and his four-year-old son were lucky to go unhurt when a nitro-glycerine bomb connected to the ignition of his van blew up. This very public act of violence ensured that the conflict could no longer be ignored by the authorities and it was then that Wickstead switched his attention to the Tibbs. They were the more coherent unit compared to the loose-knit Nicholls and the assorted villains who had antagonised the Canning Town firm, and it was the Tibbs that Wickstead chose to present as gangsters. At the time, Bert Wickstead was living in East Ham with his family just around the corner from prominent members of the Tibbs family. When he claimed to have received death threats, the family were forced to relocate to Essex where they lived for a time under an armed guard.

Wickstead had previously been a detective in East Ham and Leyton, and so avoided cooperation with the local police who he considered to be corrupt. Instead, he chose to carefully nurture relationships among enemies of the Tibbs. The family were headed by James Tibbs senior, a man Wickstead ludicrously branded 'the Godfather of the East End'. This fabrication of an organised criminal threat assured that seven members of the Tibbs family and their associates received sentences of up to 15 years from Mr Justice Lawton for various offences including perverting the course of justice, attempted murder, wounding and possession of a firearm.[14] Nobody

---

14 Jimmy Tibbs emerged from his ten-year sentence to become one of the most successful boxing trainers in the world.

was ever convicted of the bombing of Jimmy Tibbs' van or of cutting Robert Tibbs' throat.

SOHO

In 1973, Commander Bert Wickstead and his squad were then unleashed on Soho, where 'the Syndicate' and a number of 'Vice Czars', who were mainly of Maltese origin, were running a lucrative prostitution racket. Although Nipper Read, the police officer who arrested the Kray twins had an alternative and somewhat more nuanced description of the 'syndicate', as a 'co-operative, running clubs and near beer and clip joints'.[15]

Especially after the 1960 Street Offences Act took prostitution off of the streets and into premises, the real money made by these 'emperors of vice' and 'vice kings' was from investments made in the West End property market For example, sex impresario and pornographer Paul Raymond, who died in 2008, appeared annually in the *Sunday Times* Rich List and his property empire, which in 2007 owned 60 of Soho's 87 acres, was thought to be worth some £650m. Although highly visible, foreigners involved in the vice trade were in the minority; in fact, the most enduring criminal firm during the 1970s was the powerful alliance forged between pornographers and corrupt police that culminated in the arrest and conviction of, among others, pornographer James Humphreys, two ex-Commanders and an ex-Detective Chief Superintendent, all who had contributed to making the sexual exploitation of women in the West End such a prosperous business.

---

15   Near beer and clip joints are establishments where customers are enticed by the promise of sex into paying large sums of money for watered-down alcoholic drinks.

TAKING TURNS

Much of Wickstead's reputation was founded upon his success in investigating murder. After he left the Serious Crime Squad, he took on the torso murders investigation of 1976–77, culminating in the longest trial in British criminal history, which resulted in two known villains, Reg Dudley and Bob Maynard, being jailed for life for the gory murders of Billy Moseley and Micky Cornwall. Dudley was paroled in 1997 and Maynard was released on bail in 2000; both maintained their innocence claiming that Wickstead had 'verballed'[16] their confessions. The case against the two men also relied upon evidence from a man who was facing a long sentence for armed robbery, who later admitted that he had lied. In 2002, Dudley and Maynard were eventually cleared at the Court of Appeal. As veteran *Guardian* writer Duncan Campbell reported in Wickstead's 2001 obituary, the Old Grey Fox had predicted at the time of the conviction that 'do-gooders' would claim it as a miscarriage of justice.

CID officers of the era were often practitioners of 'turn taking', where members of the criminal fraternity and their associates could be connected to crimes that they may or may not have committed. As these villains were regarded as having got away with committing multiple crimes without being punished, the logic was that in response to pressure on detectives to get a result, the villain must play the game and take his turn to be prosecuted, regardless of his innocence. For CID officers, the bottom line was always the clear-up rate, which they strove to keep as high as possible in order to justify their existence and keep managers off of their backs.

---

16 Attributing false and incriminating remarks to suspects as part of a police interrogation.

However, turn taking was part of a game that the detective not only played but also umpired. Arthur Saunders, who was jailed for his role in the 1970 Barclays Bank robbery that was investigated by Wickstead, had his conviction overturned when supergrass Bertie Smalls, who had been on the robbery, established that Saunders had not been part of the £237,736 raid, which made Saunders' alleged confession a little more than suspect.

After the Richardson/Kray era, any London-based working-class family involved in crime was assumed by the hierarchy of the Metropolitan Police to pose an especially dangerous threat to law and order and therefore had to be dealt with by any means necessary. The cases constructed by the 'Untouchables' and their ilk featured a lot of verbal testimony and many of the accused switched sides to give Queen's evidence against the main players. But there is a large element of turn taking suggested by the choice to prosecute the Tibbses while ignoring the violence of their opponents. It was also easier to brand the Tibbses with the highly emotive stigma of organised crime. Wickstead claimed that on convicting the Tibbs family, 'some measure of tranquillity had been restored to the streets of the East End'. Which was news to the citizens of East London because, once things calmed down, low-key neighbourhood firms continued to come and go as they always had. However, because they were not associated with the Hollywood/Ealing comedy vibe of the Krays or with the business acumen of the Richardsons, they did not attract the overtime budgets so essential to fighting the war against crime.

Bert Wickstead had claimed, with absolutely no evidence, that the Krays were afraid of the Tibbses, and in doing so displayed a shrewd understanding of how the portrayal of police work impacts upon the public's understanding of crime and criminals. By turning a violent, alcohol-fuelled family feud into an example of organised crime, the reality of the random, chaotic nature of crime is distorted into a convenient stereotype familiar to any Hollywood film buff, or fan of *The Untouchables*. Hype and exaggeration is a crucial police tactic for, as armed robber Terry Smith explained some years later, 'If the police do not portray and publicise their quarry as Premier League villains, it will not consolidate or enhance their own careers and prestige within the police force.'

Chapter 8

HEAVY HANDS AND VIOLENT WORK

'One day, he'll be an old man with ten pence in his pocket whacking people with a fucking zimmer frame.'

GRAHAM ON JIMMY

While gangsters have always been part of life in the city, they had in the past tended to be based in local neighbourhoods, initially as groups of youths defending their manor from invading mobs, before extending their influence by attacking bordering domains. Indeed, working-class London was traditionally made up of a patchwork of distinct local cultures and nearby territories were regarded with suspicion and outright hostility. For instance, the New Cross Boys fought with their rivals from the Elephant; a loose-knit group of violent men from Hoxton engaged with the Italians in neighbouring Clerkenwell, while the inhabitants of Watney Street, adjacent to the river Thames in Stepney, became traditional enemies of anybody from Bethnal Green. Canning Town fought with Stratford and Mile End fought with everybody.

THE BUSINESS

As a one-time urban terror who grew up in the 1960s before going on to run a successful building company explained:

> 'As a young man, I was out every night. And every one of those nights was spent expecting to fight. I think back and there were stabbings. I got stabbed in the back, and I had [to go to] hospital when I had my jaw broke by a chisel. I had a little sheath knife for a while, screwdrivers, anything really. We would go over Hackney, Stepney and have full-on rucks. Then they would come over to us and do the same thing. I fucking loved it. You was taking on an area, it was exciting. But people were starting to get really hurt, and when a boy, just a boy, got murdered at Stratford, it pulled me up a bit. It weren't funny no more. Then you started watching people getting put down [sent to prison], stabbed up. One of the boys I was at school with lost an eye. I just eased off bit by bit. I was married at 19, but some of those boys went on and on.'

Not all of these boys and young men who fought their local rivals became 'kings of the underworld' or 'crime lords', but some did go on to grind out a living as violent predators. These men were never destined to become icons of the underworld, with their own entourage of ghost writers, agents and groupies. There was no glamour in their world and the violence that they were willing to dish out had nothing to do with skill, or the nobility of combat. They were unable to compromise or negotiate. They were merely extremely violent men who found that their willingness to destroy any opposition was a marketable resource.

JIMMY

Jimmy had come through as a violent youth before making money in a local firm which provided a platform for his subsequent violent career, a career that is as unremarkable as it is unheralded. As the mafia scholar Diego Gambetta explains: 'He who beats hardest not only does away with the beaten competitors, but advertises himself as an adequate protector.' And Jimmy beat hard.

In the 1950s, Jimmy's father was the first of his family to settle down into regular employment, working as a railwayman, bringing up a family in a quiet street a short bus ride from the docks. His ancestors had bought and sold scrap metal, old gold, jewellery, horses and, more recently, cars and lorries. They were street fighters and drinkers. Jimmy recalled:

> 'He was the first one to settle, like a real, what you might call a proper job, working for another person, not just like family. We were the only ones with a house. The others were always moving about, so they come to our house a lot. I never thought of it at the time but the place was always full of kids and the old man did shift work. Some of my uncles and that, they was working away, and when the kids were old enough to go to school, they got prefabs down from us, so we ended up all in the same school.'

While at primary school in the 1950s, a routine playground scuffle became more serious, and Jimmy's opponent spent several days in hospital. Local kids started to take notice.

'I got cousins all local. All fighters they were. Soon as I got big enough to play out I was out rucking, they was rough people, and you had to be rough too. I mean, we was always fighting with anybody. School, street, it's like a way of life really. And you could never cry, never cry. You just go mental, hurt people. Sometimes I was frightened though, like if somebody was really hurt. Once we was playing in the old school, we all got out the playground, over the fence, over the big metal gate. This kid goes under it, it was on a slope and we all did it. Your head could just squeeze under it, and one little kid was just getting under, and as his head is just sort of wedged under the metal, my cousin, the oldest one, Ricky, he ran at him and kicked him in the side of the head. He was only a little kid, eight or nine, and we thought he was dead. We run anywhere and when we looked round he was just there, not moving with his head stuck under the metal. We all did things like that, and you just did it, no questions. This kid, the little kid, they took him to hospital. His dad come in the playground few days later – we was playing football and he goes up to Ricky to give him a slap. Ricky just lashes out with a pump, bike pump. First time I ever see a boy fight a man. He was about 17. No, less, 14, 15.'

By the time Jimmy moved on to secondary school at the age of 11, he had forged a formidable reputation which was enhanced by the brutal potential of his large extended family. 'We would all back each other up. But that was the way it was then, everybody was in big families. So if two kids started a little row, they all got into one. Big brothers, sisters, mums and dads, old people.' This point was elaborated on by Kray associate Tony Lambrianou: 'If you didn't have a family of brothers with you, you were nothing. Brothers were your strength, All the major villains of our generation were brothers.'

For Jimmy, school was just another arena.

> 'We run the place. We all had knives, it was the thing; boy got stabbed in my last year. One who did it was like with us, me and my cousins. He was put away and I remember thinking, "Fuck that, that could have been me." The thought of it, prison like, or borstal, it was the one thing like that made me wonder, what's it about? We just kept on. Started earning.'

Once a group of youths have acquired a violent reputation, there is always the possibility of making money. Jimmy started working for a scaffolding firm run by one of his uncles.

> 'Good money, good money. Out and about a lot. My family, cousins and that, they was all on the firm. It was good and we had a good time all of us. We earned well and night-time we was all out. We was faces, you know, known faces. If you took us on, it was all of us and you had to go for a real result with us. We took places over. Pubs and that, the bouncers – nothing. We knew all of them so they never bothered. If we had a row we dealt with it, then that was it, over.'

Before he was out of his teens, Jimmy, his cousins and their associates were increasingly regarded as calming influences by the landlords of 'trouble pubs' and were welcomed in as benign influences wherever violence blighted business.

> 'Word got about that we could like do the business. Thing is, I would get right up front if there was a ruck. I would be right up there. You had to, it was what you had to do. We'd fight anybody, and with us, what you got it was like hospital, serious. People knew with us it was all off. We was murders. We started getting tooled up when we went out. I was still on the scaffolding and so was the others, either that or the building. Once we all put our belts on under our jackets, like scaffolding belts with all the tools round them. We waited for a little ruck to start and we was off, all the tools come out and we was into them. We used anything, then. But as we were all together, all in a little mob, then nobody could touch us.'

Soon they were able to graduate beyond free drinks and earn hard cash in exchange for a high visibility presence at pubs and clubs in and around the neighbourhood. Smartly dressed in expensive casual wear with neatly styled short hair and a sharp, attentive, intense group presence, Jimmy and his team could be seen in the background of numerous nightspots around East London, ready to react if trouble erupted. But violence by now was rare and, thanks to their reputation, their presence was normally sufficient to impose control. However, on the occasions when violence was used, the result was usually serious enough that the involvement of the police was inevitable.

Jimmy was arrested after two men were stabbed and badly beaten at a disco.

'Anybody wants a row we are there for them, they know who we are and where we are. We did them, all the way down in the lift and out the front, but one went down the side stairs and me and Alan goes down and gets him by the fire door. I never even had a screwdriver what they reckon they was done with, just a piece of plumber's metal wrapped round me hand. But I got tugged [arrested] in the Indian [restaurant] about an hour later. Even when they dropped it [the case] my card was marked and I started to get pulled regular. It got so the old man had enough of it and slung me out. He was always coming home from work in the mornings and the Old Bill be on the doorstep with the fucking milk, waiting to give me a pull.'

In the early 1970s, at the age of 21, and after numerous encounters with the police, Jimmy received his first taste of prison, two years in a shared cell, and a long way from the pubs and clubs that were his bread and butter. By the time that he was released from prison, members of his firm had started to settle into long-term relationships and several had started families.

JIMMY AT WORK

After prison, Jimmy went back to working as a scaffolder and become involved with a woman who owned several small businesses in a small commuter town outside of London. They met when Jimmy worked on the renovation of a large country property adjacent to a pub where he stayed during the week before returning home on Friday afternoon. Soon Jimmy had moved into her comfortable home and seldom returned to London. His mother died of cancer and three months later, Jimmy and his girlfriend married quietly at her local registry office. Jimmy's father was the only member of his family present. There was no stag night and no trace of a traditional London working-class wedding.

> 'There was a lot of work down there as it happened, so I put myself about and it was all right. Doing building and that, plenty of work. I mean, if anything come up, I still had to know about it. Like with any snides[17] or bits of gear, but I never went to work, I never got involved. I mean, she had her business and I never wanted to naus it up.'

Jimmy's girlfriend owned an apartment on a Mediterranean tourist island. The couple were frequent visitors and Jimmy invested in a small bar, going into partnership with a builder from the Midlands who had retired to the sun some years earlier. Jimmy's friends and family took full advantage of free accommodation and the bar became the focal point of their stay.

Back in England, Jimmy received a telephone call from the builder's wife to say that her husband had been arrested. Jimmy's friends and former colleagues had been using the bar to launder counterfeit £10 notes, changing thousands of pounds into local currency. Jimmy never returned to his island in the sun and a rift developed with his wife: 'She slung me out, to be honest, and it weren't working out, so

---

17   Counterfeit notes.

I come home. I let it go, she sold up. It was in her name, so fuck it.'

Jimmy returned to London and began working for one of his cousins who had started a mini-cab firm. He was soon involved in a business dispute with a competing cab company. 'There was a load of stuff going on round then with the cabs, like if you was going on another firm's plot and that. We had a motor burnt out and we kept a sawn-off under the counter. Then that was that really, we just went to work.'

The cab firm dispute resulted in shootings, a number of beatings and a four-year sentence for Jimmy. The day his father died, Jimmy had spent the day vomiting. He was in the first three months of his sentence and his body had yet to adapt to the rigours of prison cuisine.

'I come off the hospital wing and the screw says that I'm wanted in the principal's office. I just tells him that I aint going nowhere. I couldn't fucking move, felt so fucking rank. So he says, "All right, your father's dead." That was that. He weren't having a go, nothing like that. He just thought that was the right thing to do, like telling me last night's football.'

A hard-working family man, Jimmy's father was the antithesis of the uncompromising villain. He died alone after falling down the stairs at home and it was several days before Jimmy's eldest sister discovered the body.

'Never took it in at first like, I just lie there retching. Then the geezer I'm banged up with comes in with a fucking great plate of some shit they was serving up.

Geezers out of Watford or Cheshunt or somewhere, starts whacking this stuff down his neck with a spoon, and all the time he's talking to me. Then I clocks on he's on about his old man, and he never really knew him and all that old bollocks. So I says to this geezer, "No offence, Brian, but if you don't walk out that fucking door I will kill you." Now the geezer is no fucking mug, but he looks at me and just goes, no questions. I put in for special leave but I never got out for the funeral.'

Prison was not an experience that Jimmy valued and he despised the sentimental reminiscences of the 'old lags'.

'All this you read about being inside, I read all them books, you know, us against them, taking on the system – its bollocks. You get the old boys, they all reckon they knew the Krays, all the real fucking stars. They talk about it like it's a fucking boys' club, like *Porridge* on the telly. Hard men, funny men, all taking on the system. It aint like that. If we was all the same, like all in for violence, then I suppose that *McVicar* [film] it might be true. But not now, most of 'em are just losers, kids, car thieves, fucking car thieves and smellies. Old drunks come in to clean up. You get a few old weekend gangsters talking about how back when the twins were about nobody grassed and that, but it's like when your mum goes on about the good old days. All I know is that when things go wrong inside, there aint no fucker gonna help.'

On his release from prison, Jimmy briefly joined a robbery team focusing on relatively soft targets but he was badly injured in a stabbing at a drinking club, the result of an argument between one of Jimmy's cousins and a man suspected of having an affair with his wife.

It was many months before Jimmy was able to work again. During his convalescence, Jimmy met a new girlfriend and they set up home in a suburb adjacent to the old neighbourhood. Soon after Jimmy had commenced his come-back, he was arrested at his new home, only to be released with an assurance that 'your turn has come' and now he found himself as one of the usual suspects rounded up after every armed robbery committed in London and the Home Counties. The pressure proved too much and his girlfriend moved out.

Eventually, Jimmy was convicted for stabbing a man – a builder with whom he had struck up a potentially lucrative arrangement involving the theft and recycling of building materials. A contact working for a local authority would deliberately order goods that were superfluous to requirements and channel the surplus into a business operated by Jimmy and the builder. This business was able to undercut all local competition and it quickly established itself, particularly with developers wishing to renovate properties. The business employed the builder's brother, a roofer who took his Dobermann to work with him, leaving the dog in his van while he climbed ladders with piles of roofing tiles stacked on his head. He was known as a particularly volatile man with a reputation for violence.

There were numerous disputes involving the roofer and resolution was usually reached by the builder handing over large wads of cash. The roofer was working on a house in the suburbs when Jimmy, as arranged with the builder, arrived to tell the man that, due to the rates that the roofer was charging, his services would no longer be required. The argument was brief and the inevitable fight somewhat truncated. The roofer went down and as Jimmy continued his assault, he found himself being attacked by his business partner, the builder. As Jimmy turned his attentions to his attacker, the roofer ran to his van and released the Dobermann, which instead of attacking Jimmy as commanded, proceeded to bound down the street before disappearing into a nearby park. As the roofer set off in pursuit of his dog, Jimmy stabbed the builder in the chest and buttocks.

STEAMING

For years, the ritual of a session in the local Turkish baths after work was a fine prelude to a Friday night rehydrating in the pub. This was where the weekend started. Men would flock to the baths wearing their work gear and change into clean clothes after purging themselves of the working week. However, there was a class of Turkish bath clientele who did not have to work on Fridays or, in some cases, on any day. These were the duckers and divers and outright villains, the leisured retirees, the self-employed, gamblers and ex-boxers. But there were also those who were preparing to work on Friday night, such as cab drivers and bouncers. I had used the baths for many years, it was a place of stories, fables and legends, of bullshit and dodgy deals, promises and lies, and both before and after I started studying crime formally at university, it was a place where I could watch, listen and learn about the attractions of life beyond the nine-to-five.

A Friday afternoon in the Turkish baths was the one part of Jimmy's routine that was non-negotiable. He would arrive just after noon and steadily work his way through the four rooms that are graduated by heat, from the soothing balm of the 'dry-room' to the eyelash-singeing, lung-searing intensity of 'number four'.

In any such bath house, routines are ritualistic and heavily coded. Bodies are scoured, scraped, soaped and lightly flagellated. Young men stretch, old athletes perform press-ups and newcomers fret over the correct response to offers of 'an all-over soaping'. Small co-operatives of cleansers work silently, alternatively foaming and sluicing, before despatching their charges to the needle-sharp power showers.

At the centre of this steamy temple of hygiene stood the Beast. Short, squat and with his long grey hair tied back in a pony-tail, the Beast wore a minuscule towel and his long plaited beard lay over the heavy gold chain around his neck. His industrial-weight Wellington boots encased legs vividly mapped with varicose veins. The Beast ran the still centre of the baths occupied by a stone altar. Upon this altar, anyone with a few quid could sacrifice themselves to the relentless attentions of the Beast's massage. So Jimmy paid to be pummelled pink by a man who, some said, received the cat-o'-nine tails while in prison, while others maintained he had learnt his craft while languishing in a North Korean prisoner of war camp. The dates never quite measured up but what was certain was that the Beast had the power in his vast steely mitts to send a relaxed Jimmy, now wrapped in towels heavily festooned with the council's logo, into the rest room to consume two poached eggs on toast before a quick game of brag and a nap.

The rest room at a place like this functioned most crucially as a marketplace where goods, services and ideas were exchanged in an atmosphere of bonhomie and relative trust. Like all gentlemen's clubs, the leisure options were strictly prescribed, although members were licensed to bullshit at will. The Turkish baths was a place of elaborate performance, where individuals went naked into a world enhanced by steam, and tales from the pub and the backs of lorries were skilfully arranged to enhance reputations that could suffer, were they exposed to the icy chill of the street. Like The City Arms, there was a strict hierarchy and there was no shortage of willing masseurs hoping to ingratiate themselves to celebrities such as the villain who returned to the old neighbourhood every Friday afternoon. In the rest room he was always offered extra towels and a member of the kitchen staff constantly refilled his tea cup, while a queue of men waited to play rummy with the ex-gangster. Two men in their twenties followed the gangster everywhere, mimicking the bodyguards they'd seen on TV.

By late afternoon, the leisured elite who languished here all afternoon were leaving before the wage slaves arrive. In the changing room, Jimmy dried himself and put on his street clothes as a naked man, some six inches taller and thirty pounds heavier, aggressively searched for a bottle of shampoo. Kicking lockers and slamming doors, eventually he focused upon Jimmy, who was carefully combing his hair. The atmosphere created by the man standing about ten feet behind Jimmy had drained the Friday evening changing room of its usual bonhomie.

'Where's my fucking shampoo?' These words were spoken quietly into the back of Jimmy's skull, causing customers in various states of undress to pay immediate attention to their shoes or the insides of their holdalls. 'You got it?' The man stepped closer and pointed to a fat young man dressed in a towel and a pair of flip-flops. 'You saw him, you said. Yeah?' Flip-flops nervously grunted his agreement. Jimmy continued to arrange his hair and quietly uttered, 'I've not got it.' One step closer and Sammy the towel collector stopped to watch. 'You fucking got it, give me yours.'

This was no playground stand-off. Jimmy suddenly stepped forward and drove the man, whose nakedness suddenly seemed pathetic, into the lockers. He would have slumped to the floor but Jimmy's blows held him up. When he finally went down, Jimmy stamped on his shoulder and the side of his face. I didn't see the blow that split Jimmy's lip, he merely wiped it with a towel as he picked up his holdall and walked out.

Real violence has little to do with skill or bravery. These are not warriors or gladiators. Willingness to obliterate an opponent is what counts. No restraint, no mercy, no points for style or mock aggression. A pulled punch is no punch at all. It's all about maximum damage and humiliation. Jimmy was committed to violence; it was the foundation stone of his identity. He was unable to compromise because that would have made him somebody else, somebody lesser, more vulnerable. Jimmy defined himself as the very opposite of the bulk of the population whose daily strategies feature compromise and the avoidance of conflict.

Chapter 9

THIEVES ARE US: THE PROFESSIONALS

'On the box they say, "I got in with a bad crowd and they just led me on, your Honour." That just don't stand up, cos I was in with a good crowd, good meaning good earners, always got plenty of money. So when I get the chance I don't go in the factory knocking my pipe out for a two bob job, I'm going ducking and diving with the people who know what the game is.'

ROBIN

East London's post-war 'golden age' of the 1950s and 1960s, as documented in chapter one, was extremely short-lived. The area's decline can be traced back in part to the demise of the timber and furniture industries between 1961 and 1971, which resulted in the loss of over 26,000 jobs, and the disappearance of 40,000 jobs in the East End's clothing and footwear industries. But it was the slow death of the London Docks that brought about the most significant change to the area.

Throughout the 1960s, containerisation and new handling

methods reduced the demand for manual labour in the docks and the modernisation upriver at Tilbury, where the Thames could accommodate the gigantic new container ships, with plenty of cheap land alongside for the storage of containers, marked the end of the East End's most important industry. By 1971, the Port of London's workforce had shrunk to 6,000 and London's five Dockland boroughs lost 150,000 jobs between 1966 and 1976, mainly in dock-related activity. This represented 20 per cent of all jobs in the area and the London Docker and the communities that nurtured him either disappeared or were literally sold down the river.

The good times of the post-war period had been a brief blip of relative affluence in a long history of poverty, insecurity and unemployment, and, as traditional jobs and trades declined, East Enders, just like their fathers and grandfathers before them, ducked and dived, merging legal and illegal strategies as part of a chaotic, dynamic, yet well-established way of life.

As many of the dock-related warehouses and distribution centres either closed down in the 1970s and 80s, and the few that remained were reinforced by an expanded security industry and technology such as CCTV, there was a sharp decline in criminal opportunities. The cheap imports from the Far East coming in on the containers that had driven the docks out to Essex were undercutting the hookey gear that used to be joyously knocked out to bargain hungry punters in pubs, clubs and workplaces. From the late 1980s onwards it was no longer amateur hour: if the thief was to avoid being a mug the prize had to be worthwhile and the odd carton or parcel turning up in the pub became a rarity, as thieving and the trade in stolen goods became the preserve of more strategic, committed villains, for whom skulduggery was not about a bit of cheap leisurewear, fire-damaged woks or pina colada glasses. For these men, thieving was a way of life. They were professionals.

TELEVISION HUSTLE

The TVs were being stored in what used to be a thriving scrapyard and with the thieves' agreement, the yard's owners had sold some of the loot to the tune of £8,000, which was due to be handed over to the thieves along with the remainder of the TVs. Bryan and Ollie were the thieves – middle-aged all-round villains with a smattering of low-level convictions to their names and a penchant for discounted sportswear. The yard was pristine and, apart from a small pile of car doors and a few lumps of ancient machinery, there was no sign of a scrap metal business. Three family cars and an immaculate 4×4 pick-up with a ladder in the back were parked adjacent to what looked like a very old dog kennel. Most scrapyards have dogs but in this yard there were none.

Bryan and Ollie stubbed out their cigarettes before entering the Portakabin that served as an office; ten minutes later, they emerged and walked grim-faced to the rented van, followed by three more men who left the office and made their way towards the other vehicles parked in the yard. Bryan started to get into the van but hesitated, turned, and walked purposefully back towards the 4×4 where the three men were lighting cigarettes. Bryan engaged one of them in a quiet but clearly intense conversation, while the other two men, including Tony, an established thief who had worked with Ollie several years earlier, eased away from the conversation that had rapidly became louder. Bryan's antagonist said, 'No money now, knock it all out and divvy up on Wednesday.' An exasperated Bryan upped the ante by getting into the man's face and sarcastically repeating, 'No money now, knock it all out and divvy up on Wednesday?' This prompted Tony and his colleague to focus on Ollie who, despite having reduced the distance between the van and the 4×4, was now standing very still, showing no intention of intervening.

The argument escalated. Faces nearly touching, Bryan and his opponent grabbed the sleeves of each other's jackets and, as their knees and ankles became entwined, tottered across the yard. At this point, Ollie, palms outwards at head height, walked slowly towards the combatants while maintaining eye contact with Tony. The third man, who had been standing in the shadows, put down a metal tool box and stepped slowly towards Tony while remaining fixated on Ollie. The argument between the two men degenerated into variations of 'fuck', 'money' and 'cunt'.

Ollie placed his hands lightly on Bryan's shoulders, while demanding with some authority, 'Leave it, let it go', before gently peeling Bryan's clenched fingers from the bomber jacket of his opponent, who reciprocated only when he was free of Bryan's grasp. The spell had been broken and violence had been averted. Bryan and Ollie got into their van and reversed past the car doors, old machinery and the empty dog kennel.

JONJO

The TVs were down to Jonjo, and he was a different kind of thief. A man of long silences and edgy stares. I was never on close terms with him, although I knew he had made his reputation years earlier as a nasty bastard, one of many local men with a penchant for recreational violence. A one-time associate of Jonjo explained:

'That little mob were always tooled up with blades and hammers. If it went off somewhere they were the first to start chopping away at people's heads. Blood everywhere, screaming and that. And Jonjo was at the centre of it. He was a horrible bastard. But by the time we were about 21 or so it got a bit much. A lot of people was hurt and it was all the time. We just faded away and settled down, but him and that other little mob got into thieving.'

I met Jonjo in an old haunt, a pub that no longer had a clientele, where the fixtures and fittings have been stripped out and the only beer on offer was bottled. It felt like an abandoned waiting room in a haunted hospital. This lunchtime we were the only customers and, while we went through what passed for niceties, I bought the drinks from the barman who looked at me as though I was a burglar – although with a pint of lager coming out of two £4 bottles I knew which one of us was the thief.

When I asked how was business, Jonjo replied, 'Nobody wants to pay any more. You send a driver out to pick up a trailer, you sort out a slaughter and line buyers up, and when they come to pick up the gear they want to pay in fucking instalments. Other times, you put some gear away cos it's warm and when you go to pick it up its gone. "Been sold for a good price, not got the money now. See you in a few days." It happens too much now.'

Jonjo had organised the theft of the TVs but the buyers he'd lined up had let him down, which meant that the goods were being stored in several different locations. For someone like Jonjo, this was highly unsatisfactory. He had been used to buyers taking entire loads of prime goods such as TVs, but by dividing up the load, he made himself vulnerable to predators he considered some way below him on the food chain: 'It wasn't those cunts' gear to sell. It was mine.'

On this occasion, the situation was resolved when Tony and his scrapyard pals had paid up promptly and the price was right. However, I got the impression from Jonjo that the spectre of a reputation-destroying rip-off had not been entirely exorcised. Jonjo was not a top-class fence but he knew his way around a lorry park. Furthermore, his connections in the transport industry went back over 20 years. At one point, he had worked as part of a team stealing and exporting cars and heavy plant machinery. He was also well acquainted with the Fat Boys.

FAT BOYS

When Fat Laurie announced, 'Going for a shit, coming?' I felt strangely compelled to put down my coffee cup and follow him. The lavatory in the Fat Boys' car lot was a public health hazard and Laurie had learnt to synchronise his bowel movements with the nearby pub's opening times. At 11am precisely, six days a week, he left the car dealership and gingerly crossed the main road to enjoy a shit and a scotch in the tranquil environs of The Dog. In the bar, against a toxic backdrop of pine disinfectant and the phantoms of last night's beer and cigarettes, Fat Laurie gave me his philosophy of life.

'I aint a villain, never have been. The motors is straight. I do deals with anybody gonna put money in me pocket but everybody does that. I look at it this way: it's Friday afternoon, all week I aint sold a fucking bean. I got the VAT and the tax on me back for money I haven't got. I got a little sort I'm supposed to see later on and the wife's in me ear. In my pocket I got nothing; I'm lending sandwich money off that old cunt who washes the motors. Then in comes some punter, not a mug, ordinary geezer like yourself, maybe out for a bit of a bargain. But when you come in I make up my mind that whatever money is in your pocket I have to have it, cos I am desperate.

'An hour later I've done a cash deal for money and everything's sweet. It don't matter if Monday morning you come back screaming that there's no fucking engine, whatever. I give you a cheque, cos fuck it, customer's always right and that. I just start all over again and I've had a loan of your money over the weekend.'

The three Fat Boys had owned the car lot for over a decade, running the business from an old shop adjacent to the site of a demolished building that had once housed workshops where craftsmen lived with their families in the rooms above. The faded outlines of stairways, fireplaces and mantelpieces, signs of a long-dead domestic order, were ingrained into brick buttressed by weathered wooden props that neatly dissected the rows of high mileage ex-sales reps' cars.

Laurie and his brother Stan had been in the motor trade for most of their lives and at one stage operated three car lots that specialised in trading redundant fleet vehicles. However,

Laurie served two years in prison as the result of being convicted for his minor role in a major fraud. On his release, he found that his wife had left him and that the Fat Boys were down to one car lot. Laurie took up golf and married a woman who ran a successful hairdressing salon. He regularly smoked dope in the office and there was frequent confusion when without informing Stan, one of his roster of girlfriends was allowed to borrow a car from the lot. Looking like a bucolic golf pro in his primary colours, immaculately coiffed hair and gold-buckled casual shoes, Laurie would have looked at home in any Euro-trash resort, although his aura of relaxed well-being owed more to Moroccan Black than to an upturn in the FTSE.

Stan, on the other hand, didn't play golf and, in marked contrast to his younger brother, had adopted a formal style that complemented his sense of business decorum, favouring a sports jacket, shirt and tie, and addressing customers as sir or madam. Stan also had a prostate problem that made him less squeamish regarding the car lot's unsanitary toilet facilities. No matter what the weather, if Laurie lit up a joint, Stan opened the door and all of the windows, and then stood out on the car lot checking the stock until the smoke cleared. Fat Stan spent a lot of time at auctions buying stock and disposing of vehicles taken in part exchange. In contrast to his brother's more *laissez-faire* attitude, Stan took the business very seriously; Laurie confided to me that on the day of their mother's funeral, Stan was back at the office by mid-afternoon to catch any trade that might drop in from the passing rush hour.

When I dropped in to see the Fat Boys it was clear that business had been slack for some time and, as Laurie practised his swing, Stan worked hard on the telephone: 'You won't get cheaper. If you make me an offer – and I'm gonna say this to you just so you know – if you make me an offer it's got to be close. You're fucking killing me. No, I can't do it, our mark up on that won't pay the weekly phone bill. You're taking the piss, you know that? What are you, the fucking revenue?'

The Fat Boys liked to eat. They arrived for work with food and very soon afterwards would venture to the cafe next door, an establishment that had once provided substantial breakfasts and lunches for local workers but had declined into a sparse snack bar owned by an ex-chemical worker who had invested his redundancy money into a long lease, a Formica refit, a frying pan and a microwave oven. Laurie and Stan brought their food back to the office where they had their own bottle of ketchup and ate on the hoof. Pie and chips, bacon sandwiches, sausage and chips and fried egg rolls were staple items on the Fat Boys' menu. Lunch sent the Fat Boys a little further afield in their search for sustenance. To the pie and mash shop for double pie and mash every Friday, while the local fish and chip shop was a particular favourite. Stan did not like the batter that encased the fish and so would remove it and give it to Laurie, who regarded it as a delicacy. All of this was topped up with frequent visits to the microwave in the cafe next door for afternoon snacks before their colossal lager intake commenced at around 5:30.

Peter, the third Fat Boy, though unrelated to the other two, seldom came into the office. He operated a repair workshop at the back of the car lot just the other side of a narrow service road that was always jammed with cars awaiting his attention. Competing with a backdrop of grinders, drills and sanders, an unrelenting soundtrack of country music emanated from a portable CD player. Peter transformed the vehicles that Stan bought from auction into a saleable condition. Even bigger than his partners, Peter was permanently covered in oil and grease and his T-shirts hardly looked any different whether fresh or dirty; everything was faded to grime. His army surplus trousers were perfectly complemented by an ancient pair of boots, which, after years of hard wear, revealed a glint of steel from the toe cap.

Relationships between Fat Peter and the two big eaters were often fraught. When the backstreet became busy, Peter put cars on the main road and the noise generated by the kerbside bodywork irritated Stan in particular. One day when Peter came into the office, he found Stan complaining to the young man who occasionally helped Peter, who Laurie had christened YTS (Youth Training Scheme).

> Stan: I know it's a drill, you cunt, it's not a fucking hoover. How do I do business?
> Peter: It's a sander.
> Stan: A what?
> Peter: A sander.
> Stan: Oh, that's all right then. How do I do business?
> Peter: It is business, this is what it is. He's earning, the last thing you moved was your arsehole over the pub.

Peter's contacts in the car trade were extensive and he was well established as a dealer of black-market car parts. He owned a smallholding where he kept chickens and a couple of horses, and was proud of his rural existence, shooting rabbits at weekends and building go-karts for his teenage son. But his rural lifestyle offered more than mere relief from ducking and diving in the urban wasteland – the space and anonymity of the countryside also created opportunities in the form of several outbuildings full of car parts, and who knows what else.

SLAUGHTER

Any time I attempted to move a conversation beyond the second-hand car business or black-market car parts, Peter would smile and gently but firmly change the subject. But when Mickey walked into the pub one evening after work, it quickly became obvious that the senior partner had arrived. Thieves need a discreet depot for the dissection and distribution of their loot – a slaughter – and Mickey's warehouse was ideally situated: close to London, several motorways and south coast ports. Thieves could pay a straight fee or more for storage or labour. On occasions, Mickey or the Fat Boys would find buyers for goods coming into the slaughter or they would invest in part of the load themselves.

Mickey's office was on an industrial estate at the top of a row of delivery bays rented by different firms. Apart from a calendar from a stationery supply company on the wall, there was none of the usual trappings that you might expect to find in a modern office. Mickey was keen to commence our interview, so keen that when I took the tape recorder out of my coat pocket, he delved into the desk drawer and brought out a fistful of various size batteries, 'in case you lose the power'.

As a teenager, Mickey had been a recreational car thief with a penchant for Minis. 'Up West for a night out, get pissed and nick a motor to get home. Minis were the easiest – just whack out the little quarter light and pull this little wire they had instead of a handle and that was it.'

His enthusiasm rapidly turned to an expertise when he acquired a bunch of keys.

'I bought them from a geezer in the pub. Yeah, I know! It's what you say to the Old Bill but it's true. I knew this geezer, a wannabe you might call him, always shooting his cuffs and talking big. Then one day he comes in with a fucking great ring of keys, waving them all over the place. Reckons he can get in almost any motor. We all piss ourselves. So he takes us outside and does nearly every motor in the car park. So I gets him pissed and buys 'em off him for 75 sovs.'[18]

Overnight, Mickey became a professional car thief, sometimes renting the keys out but often stealing cars to order.

'But the joke was people thought the keys was magic, and a lot of motors I couldn't get into so I had to find other ways. But I had to be so quick and although I say it myself, it's a question of bottle. Having a nice BMW and it's sitting all plump and ripe, and I know that I have got a punter with a large pile of notes waiting, then I must be able to go and take it. Don't matter about skill. Honest, anybody can do it. The Old Bill, even them, if you forget your keys they will turn up and do it for you. Difference is the pressure; the buzz

---

18 Pounds.

is on you to do it under pressure. The thing was, I got a good name as a thief before I was really good. People think it's harder than it is to do a motor, at least they used to before kids started doing motors for radios. Some thieves would have radios but for me I was doing it to order and class motors too, so I never really fucked about with anything in the car.'

After serving a sentence for car theft, Micky was forced to reassess his career.

'The market all changed. Well, yeah, but you change yourself as you get older. I mean, the two stretch I did, it shook me. I had to think about the future. I met this geezer inside who was part of a firm of ringers and I did some work with them. The thing with ringing[19] is that there is not the money in pulling[20] the motor. But the ringing, doing the chassis number and re-registering it from the number on a write off, there is so much to be made there. That's why now it's just boys taking the car and handing it over to a ringer, and if he got a buyer, then within a day he's laid out a couple of hundred sovs top and pulled anything, nice few grand.'

After falling out with the ringers over money, Mickey set up his own car workshop with another thief who was part of a group selling high-end vehicles to continental Europe. The new business was almost over before it began when Mickey's

---

19 Stealing cars and changing their identities by replacing their identification numbers with a set from another – usually written-off – vehicle.

20 Stealing.

new partner was captured by the police as he was about to drive a recently stolen car onto a cross-Channel ferry. After serving his 18-month sentence, he and Mickey renegotiated with the German importers to accommodate the expanding demand in the Middle East for high-quality European cars. The stolen vehicles were now to be put in shipping containers accompanied by documentation for cheap, undesirable cars and modifications were made in Germany before being transported to the Middle East.

Mickey explained:

> 'We would buy old shitheaps at auction, half a dozen at a time, store 'em away, stash 'em till we needed 'em. Usually old Japanese motors – buy 'em for £150–£200.'

A high-end vehicle would then be shipped out in a container using an old Datsun's documents.

> 'Just to be safe, we would have the Datsun crushed at the same time. So any come-backs it's, "Sorry, it was a Datsun when it left us." But it was costing us a lot of money and we felt, well, on offer, really, cos any come-backs led to us.'

The next step was to establish a series of limited companies that would 'own' the vehicles bought from auction and Jonjo, now operating as a shipping agent, exported the goods.

Mickey told me:

> 'We knew what the Germans want, we just ship 'em out. For a special price, I would drive out or let

somebody drive a motor over but that is going to be very expensive. After having it, it gets laid down for a while, ringed, you know, engine and chassis number changed, sometimes sprayed but not often. Then, after a while, we will drive it out, drop it off, get a train to, say, Frankfurt, away from the depot, and fly back from there. We did that, what, only four times in nine years. It costs loads but for the right motor, they will pay the money.'

Mickey went on to describe how when cheaper competition emerged his firm expanded into a scheme devised by their German partners to exploit the market for heavy plant and road-making equipment.

'Sometimes, again for the right price, we get all the documentation arranged beforehand and the lorry takes it straight to the docks. Heavy plant vehicles are good; it's working at night in out-of-the-way places with plenty of time to work. The only problems we come across was when we sold some stuff to a firm of tarmackers and about two years later the gear turns up at an auction in Kent. They couldn't trace it to us but the site manager [who was working with the thieves], he was nicked. Since then, I won't deal in this country, I just move the stuff quick. Say a 'dozer, it's up on a flat bed [lorry], down to wherever docks and away. I will arrange it all, the paper whatever. I don't often touch motors any more. I am just a businessman who stole a few motors when he was a kid.'

The export business dissolved when a number of the key players were arrested but Jonjo's role had established him as competent operator and gave him an opportunity to collaborate with a wide range of criminal businessmen. One of these businessmen was Kenny.

SUBURBAN KENNY

Kenny bought his bungalow and an adjacent chunk of land before housing estates wrecked any illusion of rural paradise. He had done well, sharing the suburban penchant for four-wheel drive vehicles, home improvements and koi carp. He wore designer sportswear, was on first-name terms with local restaurant proprietors and had firmly held views on both international politics and sex offenders. He was a businessman who dabbled in a number of legitimate enterprises but had become an established dealer in stolen goods at the tender age of 17.

As Charlie, Kenny's cousin and work associate, explained: 'He was always better at the selling than the rest of us. He could sell anything, always turn a profit and not upset people. They all liked Kenny and even now, people from when we was kids will go to him and if he can't do something then he will put them into somebody who can.' Kenny quickly forged a reputation as a shrewd wheeler-dealer, but one who was 'a real pleasure to do business with'.

Kenny married while still in his teens and was soon rehoused in a council house, the lock-up garage of which provided the neighbourhood's very own 24-hour slaughter. According to Charlie, 'Even as a kid he was stone cold reliable, sensible with prices and that, could always move stuff that others would hum and ha over.'

In his early twenties, Kenny bought a huge consignment of stolen tinned food, was arrested and his 18-month sentence gave him his last taste of prison for 15 years. When Kenny was released from prison in the mid-1970s, he set up a mobile cafe on wasteland adjacent to a major freight depot, providing tea, bacon sandwiches and the best prices for any spare case, parcel or crate. Kenny quickly moved on to purchasing part-loads, particularly of top-of-the-range clothes, reams of cloth and electronic goods. He'd then carefully liaise with loaders and clerical staff, who in turn would collaborate with lorry drivers. Consignments were checked against the relevant paperwork and confirmed as complete. In terms of security, these were slack times and usually nobody at the freight depot noticed when extra goods were placed on vehicles. Before computerised systems, multiple versions of delivery papers or manifests usually did the job, although on occasions staff at the point of arrival received a pay-off to ignore missing goods. Drivers would stop off for sustenance at Kenny's greasy spoon, making sure to park away from the glare of the terminal's floodlights, and the goods were then transferred to a waiting vehicle, which would then deliver them to prearranged customers or to a slaughter. By the time any abnormality in the load was discovered, the goods had been wholesaled, retailed and made indistinct from legitimate goods.

Kenny became a reliable outlet for a wide range of thieves, including Bill and Ben. In the early 1990s, these men were part of a team plundering all-night lorry parks, which was, in Bill's words, 'a piece of piss'. They included one team who would put false number plates on a borrowed lorry, enter the lorry park, check in with the security guard, park the empty lorry and the driver would leave. Meanwhile, the thieves, who had been playing cards in the back of the lorry, would exit and plunder vehicles at will, before returning to the back of their own vehicle with their loot and wait for the driver to return at dawn. Both the thieves and their plunder would be driven to a nearby goods yard, the number plates were switched back to the original, and the goods distributed via a network of outlets, including Kenny. However, without prior knowledge of the contents of the lorries, this could be a haphazard enterprise. Once, the team of thieves got out of their vehicle in the middle of the night to find the lorry park empty, except for a 40-foot container full of unmovable engine blocks. The team broke up after that.

Meanwhile, Kenny built up an extensive network of contacts, including drivers with 'spare' loads, companies with surplus goods following a fire and numerous thieves, burglars and jump-up men. Lorry parks without CCTV cameras, hidden corners of motorway service stations, warehouses, lock-up garages and slaughters were all vital to this vibrant and profitable trade.

'Anybody with a lock-up who wanted to earn could just give us the keys and forget about it,' Charlie explained. 'We had lock-ups all over. We got people to front up on warehouses and we put gear in them. There was rented vans coming and going. He [Kenny] was trusted and he had a good eye for a deal.'

But for Kenny there was a price to be paid. Pre-dawn meetings in lay-bys, negotiations over a full English breakfast, bits of business over lager and a pie at lunchtime and more lager in the evening. The hustle was 24/7. Then it all stopped.

FRY UP, BURN OUT

Long before middle age, Kenny's hair, along with his wife and child, were gone. His drinking was having a marked impact on his judgement and two close associates were convicted of GBH before he was ripped off by Jonjo, who by now had a reputation for violence and sharp practice. He had paid Jonjo for a consignment of goods without realising that the lorry's refrigeration unit had been turned off, rendering the load worthless. When cousin Charlie confronted Jonjo he was badly beaten, and soon after this Kenny was rushed to hospital with a perforated ulcer.

Kenny was no longer a competent villain and he was shunned by former accomplices and associates. In an effort to get back in the game, Kenny moved his mobile cafe to a lorry park and made himself available to any passing driver with the odd carton or pallet to sell. By his early thirties, he was especially partial to cheap bottles of whisky purchased from drivers returning from trips abroad, consuming them while serving tea and bacon sandwiches, before sleeping off the effects in his van.

After more than a decade as a professional fence, he was arrested for possession of 500 handbags and cardboard briefcases. Soon after his release from prison just over a year later, he married, sold the mobile cafe, became teetotal and invested in a consignment of contraband tobacco, which paved the way to suburbia. He looked up some of his old contacts in the haulage industry and reconnected with Charlie, who took responsibility for hiring trailers and seeking out legitimate consignments in Holland as a cover for the smuggling operation. Meanwhile, Kenny kept his distance from the day-to-day running of this tobacco business and concentrated on a legitimate enterprise that he established close to his new home.

Eventually, the tobacco business suffered a series of setbacks. First, a business associate of his was exposed by a Sunday tabloid newspaper as a major smuggler and then, suspiciously soon afterwards, at least one consignment that he had financed was hijacked. Kenny drifted into a rather unremarkable life as a legitimate businessman, punctuated by trading in the odd part load of consumer durables, not to mention some subtle investments in drugs, pornography and counterfeit foreign currency. It is just business.

Kenny and his kind are not outsiders living in the underworld on the edge of society but residents of an overworld festooned with kitchen extensions, hot tubs, barbecues, nail bars and gyms. For Kenny, as for many other residents of this world, the passing of time has rendered the modern world a disappointing place lacking in structure, discipline and morality. At the annual award night of Kenny's son's football team, Charlie told Kenny that I taught courses on crime at a university and Kenny decided to give me his views on law and order:

'I wish you could tell me about it then. Nobody has any respect. But by the time kids get to school they just do what they like. The rapes and that, there's no stopping people from doing what they like. There's a clampdown coming and I'll tell you, and I mean this, I'll be there when the time comes. Something's got to be done. It's getting out of hand.'

Back in the worst pub in the world, Jonjo remained reluctant to put his hand in his pocket and the drinks were on me. Like most villains of Jonjo's ilk, he did not give too much away regarding his current activities but everything about the man told me that he was still 'at it'. He, along with Mickey, Kenny, Charlie and the Fat Boys, have made their money and they have all 'done well'. Money-making defines them. They deal in anything with a sell-on value but seldom feel any compunction to make uncalled for payments to the Inland Revenue. That is for mugs and straight goers. Professional criminals are more committed, knowledgeable and ruthless than the everyday amateur, and while they have always been part of life in the city, they are not daring outlaws cocking a snoot at conventional society, they are conventional society. It is all about the money, and the only Robin Hoods that I encountered were pubs.

Chapter 10

CRAFT AND CRACKERS: SPECIAL SKILLS

'You open a safe and you think this is the one, and you open another one and this has got to be the one. It's like the gold prospector, he keeps digging and digging until he finds, and you find that a lot of criminals are very persistent people. They keep at it, sometimes until the day they die and never realise, but some do, but they keep trying.'

DICK POOLEY

In 1951, the director of the National Maritime Museum appeared in an early BBC TV broadcast discussing a recent acquisition: a remarkable *chelengk*, with a plume of more than 300 diamonds, awarded to Nelson by the Sultan of Turkey after the Battle of the Nile in 1798. Shortly after the broadcast, a lightweight ladder was placed against the wall of the museum, a window was forced and the glass case containing the *chelengk* was smashed. Over 30 years later, George Chatham claimed responsibility and said the jewel had been broken up and the diamonds sold 'for a few thousand'.

Professional criminals come in many shapes and sizes;

they are not all violent and many are driven by hedonistic desires that include a wide variety of needs and vices. Funding drug or sexual needs, a penchant for expensive motor vehicles, or a desire to reimagine their lives as a perennial party that can take in all of the above and more is far more common than the drive to acquire the trappings of corporate respectability or conventional affluence. However, many committed criminals are dedicated gamblers and at the top of the old underworld's hierarchy were a few daring men of rare skills for whom risk – gambling with the possibility of great riches or personal disaster – sat at the core of their very identity. As the British economy blossomed in the years following the Second World War, professional burglars plundered exclusive shops and the homes of the rich and famous. George 'Taters' Chatham was the most prolific of these burglars.

TATERS

While most fictional accounts of professional burglars tend towards the atypical upper-class amateur cracksman Raffles or technical proficiency against a backdrop of breath-taking exotic glamour, such as the 1955 film *To Catch a Thief* or 1964's *Topkapi*, Taters Chatham's story is a little more down to earth, and very British. Born in Fulham in 1912, the son of George Chatham, a waiter, and his wife, Jenny, *née* Hewson, he showed an early talent for football, played for England Schoolboys and had trials with Queen's Park Rangers before crime staked its claim. His first conviction for theft was in 1931 and by the end of the decade, he was burgling some of the wealthiest homes in London, specialising in stealing furs, works of art and jewellery.

In 1948, Taters commenced his long-term relationship with the Victoria and Albert Museum by stealing two of the Duke of Wellington's swords. Encrusted with emeralds and diamonds, one commemorated his victories in India and the other was a gift from Tsar Alexander I. Although today the swords would be worth many millions, to Taters they represented little more than stake money and he called a bet at a gaming table by prising a stone from the hilt of one of the weapons.

Chatham was also prepared to branch out into armed robbery. He was a member of the successful team that pulled off 1952's £287,000 Eastcastle Street robbery of a post office van organised by the eminent thief and gangster Billy Hill. Chatham's £15,000 share, which is over £400,000 in today's money, was quickly lost at the rigged tables of Hill's gambling club, which prompted Taters to make an unsuccessful attack upon the gangster's bulging safe.

Like many thieves of his era, Chatham despised gangsters who he considered to be 'thieves' ponces', feeding upon the risks taken by others. Before his gambling habit drove him to foolhardy risk-taking, Chatham researched his targets via *Burke's Peerage, Country Life* and *The Tatler,* as well as cultivating insurance clerks and blue bloods with intimate knowledge of the treasures of Belgravia, Mayfair and Regent's Park. A skilled and fearless thief, Chatham developed an educated eye for plunder and his thefts, which his equally notorious colleague Peter Scott described as 'Just George with a bit of wire and a knowledge of how to bend glass doors,' were branded by the media as the work of an 'international art gang'.

Chatham was part of a rare breed of thief targeting the glamorous high society of 1950s Britain who flaunted their enormous wealth at parties, film premieres and exclusive events. Taters detested both the social elite and the criminal justice system in equal measures. As he explained to journalist Duncan Campbell, 'They were usually very, very rich people, millionaires. Some of them regarded it as a nice thing to talk about at dinner parties. I was a rebel against authority and I had no respect for the police. If I could outwit them in any way, I would.' Other victims of Chatham included the Maharaja of Jaipur, Lady Rothermere, Madame Prunier and Raymond 'Mr Teasy Weasy' Bessone, the society hairdresser. Having attempted to burgle Lady Diana's future stepmother, the Countess of Dartmouth, Taters fell four floors from her roof and spent six weeks in hospital before returning to his chosen profession still swathed in plaster and bandages. Exclusive shops, including Bourne & Hollingsworth and Harvey Nichols, as well as numerous furriers, jewellers and galleries, also fell victim to Chatham. A Matisse and a Renoir found their way into Taters' swag bag, respectively fetching a mere £7,500 and £5,000.

His 35-year association with thief and fellow degenerate gambler Peter Scott lasted well into the 1980s. The flamboyant Scott, a self-styled 'Gentleman Thief' who met Chatham in prison, was the only thief to rival Chatham for both risk taking and his high profile targets, including the Shah of Iran, Vivien Leigh, Zsa Zsa Gabor and Sophia Loren. Both solo and with Scott, Chatham continued to attack central London targets and was caught stealing furs in his sixties. In his 70th year, 34 years after the theft of the Wellington swords, Taters returned during a blizzard, via scaffolding, over the rooftops to the V&A. However, gambling and time eventually took their toll and at the age of 76, he received a six-month sentence for shoplifting a piece of bone china from Harvey Nichols. Decades earlier, he had penetrated the same shop via the roof and got away with several hundred thousand pounds' worth of furs.

In 1997, after a 60-year career as a thief that reaped 35 years' imprisonment and an estimated £100m in loot, George Chatham died aged 85. He had taken his chances, lost a lot of his liberty and spent millions at the bookies and at the gaming tables. Unlike most thieves, the big prize did not elude him: he regularly exchanged it for a pittance before obsessively gambling it away. Yet there is much to be learnt from Taters Chatham's life. About the irrelevance of the criminal justice system as a deterrent, the make-up of Britain's post-war criminal and non-criminal elites and, most importantly, the nature of the criminal marketplace that later was to oust craftsmen like him and replace them with venal, largely anonymous entrepreneurs.

BUSY MAC THE BURGLAR

Not all professional burglars were as reckless or notorious as Taters, for by investing in careful reconnaissance and nurturing outlets in legitimate markets, something approaching longevity in the business could be achieved. Mac worked closely with Sammy, who subcontracted for a firm of furniture fitters in the south of England. During the course of Sammy's work, he collected details of houses that he had worked on, including photographs of their contents, and passed them on to Mac. Mac, a man in his fifties, would sometimes set up other people to carry out the burglaries for him, passing on all the relevant information and giving strict instructions as to what should be stolen, while on other occasions, he would lead the team. Either way, Mac would pay the burglars a fixed price before moving the goods on very quickly. Mac targeted country houses, always relatively deserted, quite often with no one living in them. He was quite prepared to take windows and doors out completely in order to remove large items and at times emptied entire rooms.

Zac, who worked with Mac for a while in the early 1990s explained:

'He told us that what we had to do was take out about ten or twelve panes of glass. He said that we had all night. He said that if we loaded up carefully we could make about, maybe, £15,000 each. He told me to hire out a van using a nicked licence. All through this, I couldn't make out whether he was on it or not. He was talking about "we" but I wasn't quite sure and cos I didn't know him that well, I never asked. But on the night he was as good as gold. He was there, he did it. For an old man, I mean the way he moved, he was very good, very good. Took out the panes of glass and he just pointed at these lumps of furniture and we started moving them out. We did have all night, he was right, cos the place was empty, but we had to walk across fields. At first it was really bad news, cos walking across fields carrying big lumps of furniture, you know you don't know what you're fucking doing or what you're going to bump into. But after a while, you got used to it and we just cleared the place out, all the ground floor anyway. Never went upstairs far as I can remember, but he was as good as gold, no problem at all.'

Zac claimed that he was only paid £1,000 for his night's work. He knew he was probably ripped off but he had absolutely no way of proving it. The goods were taken to a lock up on an industrial estate and that was the last time that Zac worked with Mac. However, some of Mac's hired help became greedy and consequently several of his brigade of burglars were arrested for stealing whatever they could lay their hands on, as well as those items pre-identified by Mac. This made Mac vulnerable and he was always talking to solicitors and friendly policemen to find out who has been nicked and what for.

Mac was constantly looking for new collaborators. Ian was a jobbing burglar. He was regularly arrested by the police and served a number of convictions for crimes ranging from burglary through to petty vehicle crime.

> 'I was always being had over,[21] that is when I tried to get rid of my gear. I don't know too much about it, you just grab what you can from the bedroom and all you want to do is get out, you don't want to be handing it around, but they'd only give me pennies for it really, just nothing. I'd be satisfied with whatever I could get. I mean, it could be worth five grand – if I got a hundred quid, two hundred quid I'd be happy with that.'

Sammy the furniture fitter provided some information to Mac who selected Ian to assist him. Mac promised to teach Ian a more refined version of the burglary business, in particular the trade in stolen antiques. This, Ian said, was the procedure: the house would be empty apart from sometimes

---

21 Ripped off.

a housekeeper on the other side of the house. They parked the van approximately a quarter of a mile away and went in about midnight, taking out the panes of glass using cutters and a blow lamp before quickly walking around the room where the targeted loot was stored. They then came out of the house and waited near their van to see if the police had been alerted by an alarm. When the coast was clear they entered the house again. Mac reminded Ian not to touch anything other than the targeted items.

In the back of the hire van they had a lot of old blankets and bedding so that the goods could be transported carefully. When they left the property, they waited until just before dawn before changing into light-coloured overalls and joining the early morning commuter traffic. Just another van load of tradesmen commuting to work. On one burglary, Mac diverted from the usual procedure and also took some items of china, later explaining to Ian that he would not get a share of this but that he would receive a share of the proceeds from the rest of the loot, which was mostly furniture. The china was packaged up and sent the same day to a Scottish auction house.

Sammy gave an example of a job that he'd set up for Mac in a flat in central London where he had worked. On locating some items that he thought might be interesting to Mac, he passed him the details and the burglary was successful. However, while Sammy was paid for the information, he wasn't satisfied with the fee. Mac had claimed that only the china had been taken but Sammy discovered that all of the items that he had photographed, as well as some additional items of jewellery, had been stolen.

Mac exported antiques and, despite his shabby appearance,

according to Sammy, he lived in some style in a house full of legitimately purchased antiques. Mac also had an irregular side-line selling counterfeit currency and MOT certificates. His run-down antique/second-hand shops, which never had anyone working in them, were rarely open to trade. Mac would keep receipts for items that he had bought legitimately at auction. Very little detail is given on these receipts – for instance it might simply record the sale of some porcelain. This meant that, in the event he was arrested for stealing an ornate 18th-century vase, he had a convenient receipt for an item of porcelain stashed away. Another part of Mac's *modus operandi* was to place an item of stolen property in an auction under one name and buy it under another, becoming the *bona fide* owner for the price of the auction house fee.

Essential to Mac's network were the craftsmen that he employed on a casual basis to alter any stolen or potentially problematic jewellery. One man who worked on Mac's goods in the back bedroom workshop of his semi-detached house had a son-in-law who worked in the family furrier business and two nephews who ran a shipping agency. Mac was very close to this family.

While Taters' qualities lay in his identification of ripe targets and his skill and daring as a thief, Mac was a far more modern felon, with a skill set encompassing the recruiting and running of a team, including specialist consultants, the physical act of theft and knowledge and manipulation of legitimate markets. An admiring Ian explained: 'He's always busy, that's why he's always floating about the country. Little deals here, little deals there. He'll be at auctions, he'll be in dealing rooms, he'll be absolutely anywhere where he can get receipts, make money, keep money moving. He's always busy.'

CRACKERS

One evening during 1969, in the Edward the Seventh pub in Stratford, a muffled explosion was heard coming from the bank next door. Almost immediately, three smoke-blackened, plain-clothed policemen came coughing and spluttering into the crowded bar from the adjoining toilets. They were gripping the arms of a wiry middle-aged man wearing a smouldering golfing sweater and a huge grin, who politely tried to order a beer before being roughly hustled away by the police.

Like the cat burglar, the safecracker is an iconic craft criminal. While homes, shops and museums offered scant protection from Taters Chatham, safes represented a ripe target for another kind of knowledgeable criminal craftsman. Particularly during the post-war era, cinemas, theatres, departmental stores and other cash-based businesses kept their takings in safes overnight. And as in those far-off days most people were paid in cash, offices, factories and warehouses also stored large quantities of money, particularly on the night before payday.

I interviewed Dick Pooley in the early nineties at his elegant home in the suburbs of a northern city. He was a fit-looking stocky man in his sixties with an alertness and vitality that filled the room. His former profession was that of safecracker and he had been introduced to the craft by his elder brother. 'I timed myself once on a clock in this particular place. We took the back off in 20 minutes, and we got right in and there was nothing in it. So we cast around and found the money in a gas oven – they'd put it in the gas oven.'

Safes were vulnerable to 'picking', drilling, cutting or having their doors or backs levered off but these methods could be exceptionally time-consuming, a problem that was solved by the use of explosives. However, it was only after he was caught and imprisoned that Dick Pooley learnt to take his craft seriously.

'I was put in a cell in Wandsworth and I met a man who was probably one of the best safe-blowers in London. They called him the Silver Fox of Camden Town and his name was Alan Robinson. A big, big man and he was one of Billy Hill's boys. He took me to a place in New Cross and he loaded a safe up, so I watched him do it. We came out of the room to set the charge off and it didn't work, so we tried wiring it up to different electrical gadgets and it still wouldn't work. So Alan said to me, "Go and have a look and see why it's not working." So I walked up to the safe and I wriggled the detonator about, little knowing that it could have killed me stone dead.

'There was three of us. Alan must have been in his sixties, the other man was in his seventies – an old-age pensioner he was. I always remember him saying to me, "Dick, do you mind if I don't come up the stairs? If it comes on top [goes wrong] I won't be able to get away." I said, "You stay there," so he stayed and we went up and done the business, got the money and come down, helped the pensioner over the wall.'

Access to explosives was no problem during the 1950s and 1960s.

'We used to go to quarries and we used to use explosive to open up the magazines [explosives store]. You imagine enough explosive in there to blow a whole town up and we used to blow it open. I remember once in Maidstone blowing a big magazine there, and I had two blokes with me and they ran and kept running because when they found out I was going to blow the magazine open they thought I was crazy. I was like an apprentice. So we, my pal and I, decide to do our own safeblowing. We managed to get hold of some explosives and our first job was on a safe. I can't tell you where because we've never been nicked for it, but we opened the safe as easy as that.'

Practice and familiarity enabled Pooley to acquire an intimate knowledge of explosives and the way that he recited the rituals associated with his craft is testimony to the pride that he retained in his skill.

'[This kind of explosive is] very easy to handle, it's not dangerous, you can throw it on the fire. It's called Polar Ammon and it was like mincemeat, red with all little red globules in it, and it was powerful enough to knock a door off a safe. The detonators were of a size that just used to fit into the keyhole of the safe, so you would take the baffle plate off, load it up with enough explosive, put it all round in the lock. Then you press your detonator in, run the wires off if it had wires. Or if it had a fuse you just light the fuse and get out the way, and the explosion occurs and you run back in. The door's usually lying on the floor, it was so easy. We were the scourge of London because we did all and sundry. I think I counted up when I was in jail and we did over two hundred safes.'

Before he became known as the leader of the Great Train Robbers, Bruce Reynolds had a shot at the cracker's art and vividly explained the sensual enjoyment to be gleaned from a successful assault on a safe: 'I couldn't believe the buzz blowing a safe gave me. It was the ultimate power trip. Unless you've been there, you can't understand how a little block of jelly and a handful of detonators can make you feel almost omnipotent. I couldn't wait to try again.' However, safecracking, for all its attractions, was not for everyone. 'I discovered that it was far more technical than most people imagine. So many things can affect it – the atmosphere, the temperature, the positioning, and the vagaries of metal.'

Like Taters Chatham, Dick Pooley was a consummate professional with a fierce streak of independence. But while he could see no advantage in aligning himself to a criminal organisation, he was heavily reliant upon the cooperation of civilians with strategic knowledge – a clerk, cleaner or relative of someone whose workplace stored money in a safe – who were willing and able to pass this information onto the safecracker without taking any risks.

'The thief is only as good as the information that he can glean. But we used to get people into us, that's why we blew so many safes, people would sidle up to us from the criminal fraternity and say, "Just seen it in the safe," and we'd say to them, "How much?" "Well, I dunno, there's loads and loads of money going in, probably about a thick six inches or a foot and they were piling it in the safe." So we'd go and blow the safe open and probably find less than £100 or £200 and they were using our liberty really to get a few bob because if we got good information we'd give them a third. So people who knew this would take liberties really and do us up, so we used to do lots of safes and find nothing in them.'

Dick Pooley was proud of his craft and, unlike most of the professional criminals mentioned in this book, for him it was not all about the money – he gained a great deal of pleasure from his villainy.

'Actually, it used to get the old adrenalin running and the two of us we loved what we did, and even today I never regret anything that I've done. When you're in front of a safe putting explosives in, the sweat used to pour off you and there'd be a pool of water on the floor by the time you got the explosive in. It would run down your back, your legs, and drip on the floor, you were covered in sweat, and each time you blew that safe you would get nitro poisoning. You would get a terrible headache, and it was the daddy of all headaches. Apparently, if you work where there is explosive, you're only supposed to work with them for 20 minutes, you must come out cos you get poisoned, and I was poisoned every time. In the end, it seemed that when the explosion occurred then the head would come and I'd be sick and it seemed that the explosion set it off. So in the end I would load the safe, put my fingers in my ears and then my partner who was the lookout man would leave his post as lookout, come back in and he'd blow the safe so that I couldn't hear it. Every time I blew a safe I got nitro poisoning; it got through your fingers. I couldn't wear gloves cos I had to put the stuff in and if you had gloves on, like tight rubber gloves, then it would restrict the blood, and your hands had to be loose so as you could get the stuff in quick and pack it nicely. It used to do me up, the noise, and I can't stand noise now, noise really does me up. In fact, I'm going deaf – the doctor says, "Did you use to work among a lot of noise?" I said, "Yeah, I used to open safes with explosives!" But you know we done some nice and good things, and we lived well.'

The safecracker was a thief but, unlike most other thieves, he had to possess skill, intelligence and daring, and he was often glamourised in popular culture and acquired a certain iconic status among the fellow members of the underworld. However, for the criminal justice system, which regarded criminals as members of a dangerous but ignorant underclass, these qualities were regarded as a threat to the status quo. The safecracker of the 1950s and 60s contradicted this stereotype and was consequently given special attention by the police, who regarded these craftsmen as elite prey.

'[The Police] hated us. They beat us up and beat us up badly. We got into this place and I had a strange feeling . . . The safe was there, we had the explosives, we were ready to blow the safe. It was on a main road but next door there was a pub, but I always get feelings – even today I get feelings and they turn out right. I said to Joe, "Joe, it's not right, there's something wrong here." So all of a sudden, we heard noises and we got out the back, out the window, and went towards the gate. I landed up getting over the gate; Joe couldn't get over the gate. He was pulled back and sticks walloped him over the head, smashed his head, got him down – I'm away.

'But they got into a car and they see where I'd hid in the front garden about half a mile away, and they come in and put the sticks on me. These two people [police officers] from Scotland Yard were the two people who nicked the train robbers, and in evidence they said that they had been waiting in doorways across from the pub for Hindsy [Alfred Hinds the notorious prison escaper], and they were given information that he was going to be drinking in the pub, but they heard us in the place next door. But we believe that we'd been set up and they were coming to nick us, which they did, and the Hindsy bit was a load of nonsense and indeed Hindsy never showed up at that pub.'

Judges too were keen on the demise of safecracking.

'I went out with another bloke who was a bit of a lunatic and we landed up over in Lincoln blowing a safe, and it just so happened that when we blew it a policeman walked by. So we had to leave the safe and the contents, all the money, and we got chased in our car. The judge, a cunning man, Michael Argyle, terrible man and I think a very dishonest man really, one of the most evil judges. The barristers hated him. He used to come down to our cell to check on the bolts to see we hadn't been sawing the bolts and bars to get out. I thought to myself, are we going to get a good crack of the whip with him? And then he said, "Never, never in the history of" this little place, and you know the wind blows and rocks, and the wind was really pounding the place, rocking it about like, you know, "never has there been a more important case", and he went on, and on, and on.

'When we were casing the job, I went into a library and looked at a poetry book, and I come across a poem which I like to this day, it was by Christina G. Rossetti, so I wrote it down. "Remember Christina G. Rossetti". Well, when they found the car, this piece of paper was in it so the police spent weeks scouring London for a Miss Rossetti, but the judge pointed out to them during the summing-up that although the police were looking for this woman, they weren't to know that she'd been dead for 90 years.

'And at the end, before he sentenced me, he said, "I think there is no doubt in this court's mind that this man Pooley is one of the top safe-blowers in this country and as such, the public needs to be protected. But before I sentence him, I think Pooley would appreciate this," and he got a poetry book out and he read, "Remember me when I am gone away, gone far away . . ." I can't remember it all but this was a poem that she wrote about death and he read it all out in the court to me. My pal said to me, "Dick, we're going to get away with this." I said, "Dave, this is the most cunning man I've ever been in front of, he's going to ten us up."[22] He said, "No, he's reading you a poem."

---

22   A ten-year sentence.

When he'd finished then he came out and said, "You are known to the police to be one of the top safe-blowers in this country and as such the public needs to be protected. I sentence you to ten years in prison. TAKE HIM BELOW." And when he sentenced the other bloke to ten years he fell down the stairs! So we both got ten years for nothing really. So I decided to do me bird, come out and turn it all in and to finish it.'

Dick Pooley has no doubts about why safecracking is now no more than a nostalgic blip in the annals of professional crime.

'Well, I think because of me they got better safes and I knocked over 200 safes and they were so easy to knock over. They used to cement them down so you'd blow the door off. But if they weren't cemented down, 20 minutes you could have the back off. So Milner, who I could open their safes quite easy, joined up with Chatworth, and they now have a safe which is virtually blow-proof. In fact, when you blew it, it set off on springs a secondary mechanism so the bolts were shot home again. You'd made a lot of noise so you couldn't blow it again, you had to get out of there.'

The shift towards a security-conscious, more risk-averse society had a huge impact on criminal craftsmen, and cash targets such as department stores, cinemas and theatres started to use banks and safety deposits, effectively removing some of the safecrackers' prime targets. In addition, the era of criminality in which Dick Pooley and his species had briefly thrived had many similarities to what was going on in the straight, non-criminal world. Here, apprentices also studied under acknowledged masters of their craft and an individual was judged according to his occupational skills. In the underworld, highly skilled 'time served' apprentices were similarly afforded respect. But times were changing, and in both the over and underworld painstakingly acquired skill sets were fast becoming redundant.

Alternatives to the safecrackers' art – such as argon guns, high-powered electric torches that could carve through metal, thermic lances or oxyacetylene cutters – were tried and although these methodologies made some impact, before this new technology could be applied to a safe, the thief first had to get into the building. As arch-villain Fred Foreman explained, these innovations required vast amounts of heavy cumbersome equipment: 'about six suitcases and several oxyacetylene gas bottles weighing two hundredweight each'. Together, these changes accelerated the passing of craft crime and hastened the emergence of a cruder, less cerebral form of skulduggery.

As Dick Pooley explained, 'See, people graduated during my time from safes to banks, or to "jugs" as they'd call them. It was quicker to go and get it out with a shotgun and they used to take all the money. That was the easy way. Doing it in the safe, you had to take a bit of time, lot of effort, lot of noise.'

Dick Pooley served a total of 20 years in prison, during which time he was one of the founders of the Preservation for the Rights of Prisoners (PROP), which in 1972 organised a 24-hour general strike involving 10,000 inmates in 33 prisons. On his release, Dick Pooley continued the work on prison reform that he had begun while he was incarcerated and ran a home for ex-offenders. He died in 2010 aged 82.

Craft criminals often acquired their skills by serving an apprenticeship at the bench of an acknowledged master or developed key skills as part of a quasi-commercial network where a precise understanding of the market for specialised stolen goods was crucial. These skilled operators, like the notion of a criminal code, faded like an old tattoo, leaving the plunder of barely imaginable riches to more violent project criminals working in specialist teams.

Chapter 11

OTHER PEOPLE'S MONEY: ARMED ROBBERY

'The nervous tension I used to feel before a job didn't stay with me all the time, only till I got started. Once I start I feel completely calm, 100 per cent, everything comes brilliant to me. I might be fogged up a minute or two before, but the minute it's on it's like the sun coming out from behind a cloud.'

BERTIE SMALLS

Villains like to get their money without working for it and, for most of them, blowing a safe was too much like hard work. They were just not equipped technically or temperamentally for such painstaking endeavours, and as violent action was such an integral part of their lives from an early age, it made perfect sense to just get tooled up and take the money by force. Unlike the safecracker, the robber was not reliant upon an intricate craft but on traditional qualities of toughness, physicality and endurance. This new criminal elite that started to emerge in the 1960s were project criminals, intent on going after the money. But as the robberies became routine features of British life, so the robber became the most valued prey of the police, giving rise to a new sort of criminal, one prized by the police and reviled by his fellow villains: the supergrass.

The Great Train Robbery in 1963 was a project crime *par excellence* that immediately gained worldwide notoriety – partly because of the sum involved: £2.6m (which is over £46m in 2021) but also because it became a benchmark for a new kind of criminal activity. Most aspects of the robbery were carefully planned; there were no firearms involved and the amount of violence used was relatively low, yet the robbers were given sentences on a par with those awarded to murderers. Although its aftermath appeared to be cursed, the robbery nonetheless became symbolic of a kind of underworld brotherhood beloved of the mass media and despised by the Establishment. This was a fraternity of flash working-class men with no interest in working for a living and the Establishment decided that, like their gangster colleagues, they needed to be put back in their box.

ENTER THE BLAGGER

Before villains turned their attention fully to banks, wage snatches were a popular and startlingly simple way of accessing other people's money. When workers were still usually paid in cash on a weekly basis, a cosh was the only bit of kit a predator needed when targeting a wages clerk leaving a bank carrying a briefcase or holdall full of cash. However, when villains became interested in the larger prize that a bank job could deliver, the security industry reacted with technological advances and the robbers responded accordingly. Glass screens were constructed on bank counters and so sledgehammers were added to the robbers' armoury. The glass was hardened and so instead the money was attacked 'over the pavement' as it was being delivered or removed by security guards. The resulting pitched battles between robbers armed with crowbars, pickaxe handles and ammonia sprays, and guards wielding batons and wearing crash helmets with visors burnt up valuable time and in 1961, after one of his colleagues was shot and allegedly killed by a bank clerk guarding cash in the back of a security van, robber Fred Foreman expressed the view of many members of this violent elite: 'Next time we'll be armed as well.'

'It saves time,' Bobby Cummines explained when he was asked why he used a gun. By the 1970s, the sawn-off shotgun had supplanted blunt instruments as the standard weapon for intimidating guards, bank staff and customers. With guns, the blaggers could avoid battles with security guards, considerably speeding up the robbery process: a blast from a sawn-off into a bank's ceiling motivated bank staff and ensured that a large quantity of cash could be liberated in less than two minutes. In response, the banks continued to improve their security, which resulted in robbers placing a greater emphasis on attacking security vans in transit. To which the van manufacturers reacted by inventing airlocks and interlocking doors for their vehicles. When the robbers learnt of this they brought chainsaws. This technological arms race was accompanied by a ramping up of violence. By mid-1972, armed robberies in London occurred once every five days, and as the decade progressed, Bobby Cummines was responsible for his share.

Half a century ago, working-class London was still essentially a cluster of self-contained villages boasting their own distinct occupations, football teams and skulduggery, and so for straight-goers like myself to hear about villains from another manor was most unusual. However, I couldn't help but notice that Bobby Cummines' name was increasingly being mentioned in somewhat hushed tones in pub conversations across London.

From an honest hard-working family in Islington, Bobby left school at the age of 16 to start work in a shipping office but his life took a turn for the worst with his first serious encounter with the police: 'I was in a park with my mates and the police were called and began bullying these younger kids. They were aggressive and shouldn't have been talking to these kids without an adult present. I stood up to them.' The police left and returned soon after. 'They pointed to a cut-throat razor that was on the ground and claimed it was mine. It was a fit-up. My dad was a straight-goer and thought the police were like *Dixon of Dock Green*. He said the police would never plant evidence and that I should plead guilty; I'd get a fine and it'll be forgotten about in a few years.'

He did as he was told and his dad paid the ten shilling fine. However, Bobby's employers found out about the case and sacked him. 'I was gutted, I thought, if you want me to be bad I'll show you how bad I can be.' Within a year, he was in the Old Bailey charged with possession of a shotgun and armed robbery.

At five foot six inches tall, Bobby learnt early on that he had to be more violent than the opposition and his weapon of choice was a sawn-off shotgun. 'When people ask why I used guns I always tell them I was sick of getting my nice suits messed up.' However, he stood trial for murder when a robbery went wrong and a man that he had tied up choked to death. He was found not guilty of murder but served five years of a seven-and-a-half-year sentence for manslaughter. 'Over the years that unnecessary death has haunted me.'

On his release, Bobby became deadly serious about the crime business. 'I made sure that there was never any photos of us floating about, and I didn't drink, I always had bitter lemon. I needed to stay sharp.' He lived in an environment where violence was an ever-present possibility and Bobby was on the receiving end as well as dishing it out. In a drive-by incident, he was shot in the leg while walking down the street and on another occasion he received a stab wound to the stomach that required 26 stitches. In the end, he was grassed up by the man who supplied his weapons, arrested by armed police and sentenced to 18 years. 'In the end it was almost a relief,' he explained. 'I've done some horrendous things – extreme violence – I never deny that I deserved every day I got in prison because it was lunacy. If I had carried on I would either have been shot dead by the police or innocent members of the public would have been shot.'

IMPENDING DEATH

By the time that I encountered Mick, he had retired from crime and was able to reflect on the armed robbers' task, which included making their victims believe that they were facing impending death.

'It's like an act; you've got to convince the people that you mean what you say and you're there to do a job. You haven't got Dickie Attenborough standing at the end behind a camera saying, "Sorry, duckie, can we do that again," if you crap out. You've got one chance, one take to do it, so you've got to convince those people that you mean what you say and make them understand that their life is much more important than somebody else's money. Usually, there's nothing like firing off a gun to convince them. I know people would use salt and bird seed sometimes – they'd stuff that into the cartridge. It would create a blast effect: they'd fire it into a ceiling, it would bring down a bit of the plaster, everyone would scream, and before you knew it everyone's on the floor face down doing what you want them to do.'

However, while most armed robbers preferred to go to work wielding an uncompromisingly lethal weapon, loading a shotgun cartridge with rock salt is not quite as benevolent as old pros like Mick would have us believe. While salt will inflict less permanent damage than lead pellets, from close range, penetration into human flesh is possible and the pain of salt slowly dissolving in a wound will be excruciating.

The sense of professionalism that this generation of armed robbers had in their work is clearly expressed by Robin, another man who agreed to talk to me about his bank robbery days.

'I just used to get a sawn-off given to me by one of the others and go to work. In the door and either hold the floor so it was nice and calm or over the top for the money. I never even noticed the others in there, I just did the job and got out. I was a steady worker and it did feel good to be respected like that. You can't panic and people respect you if you just do a good job and don't let anybody down. That goes for the people you rob too. They want to feel that you are in control of everything so that they don't feel that they have got to have a pop. They just want to lie there till it's over and the quicker the better. The better you are at the job the better they like it.'

Robin had been a reasonably successful thief before teaming up with two men with reputations for violence and proceeding to rob a number of building societies. Initially, the working arrangements were almost casual, with a cavalier regard for detail and little planning or preparation. As Robin explained, 'We would sort it out about a week beforehand and just take the prize.'

Eventually, Robin's luck ran out and after weapons were found in the garden shed of a relative, he was sentenced to 14 years. On his release, the money had evaporated, an attempted reconciliation with his family did not work out and soon he was offered employment at his old trade. 'This time we were more careful about things and we made money. This time we knew what we were doing a lot more and we took it serious.'

GOOD TIMES AND THE RISE OF THE SUPERGRASS

The robbers of the 1960s and 70s were working-class men who had experienced wartime childhoods and the shortages that continued well into the 1950s. The rewards on offer for a successful bank job or raid on a security van opened the door to a whole different world. In his autobiography, key member of the Great Train Robbery team Bruce Reynolds recalled nights out at London's most fashionable high-end restaurants: 'We would be celebrating at the Astor or the Embassy and we would spy another group of crims supping magnums of champagne. Bottles would be exchanged as we toasted each other's success amid much rivalry. It was exciting. This was the recognition I had always craved.'

As Fred Foreman remembered: 'You could go from one club to the other and see the same faces. We could easily tell which pavement firm[23] had a touch on a particular day by the way they were celebrating in the afternoon. They'd be walking around with bottles of vodka or scotch. Money just flowed.'

By the 1970s, while armed robberies had become a routine feature of city life, the robbers themselves were anything but mundane: they were part of an exclusive professional community that seldom overlapped with the world of straight goers. Membership was limited, though the rules were quite flexible – however, there was one line that could not be crossed.

Robbers were prime targets for the police. Although as one professional robber told writer Laurie Taylor, 'For a policeman to catch a bank robber is like a fisherman catching a 20lb trout,' during this era, convictions for armed robbery were rare and the loot was seldom recovered. The ideal robber was a 'good worker' who could be relied upon to act resourcefully in tight situations, avoid capture, remain stoic and never implicate either himself or others. As for grassing, Frank Fraser summed it up thus: 'All self-respecting villains in the underworld find such people contemptible. You couldn't do a worser crime.'

However, most strategic-thinking villains of the day valued relationships with police officers: the Krays and the Richardsons

---

23 Team of armed robbers.

did in the 1960s, as did Billy Hill in the 1950s and the Sabini family in the 1930s. Fred Foreman's long career at the forefront of British crime was partly due to the successful relationship that he was able to nurture with senior police officers, and Soho pornographer James Humphreys' friendship with Head of the Flying Squad Ken Drury in the 1970s was testament to the value of having Old Bill 'on the firm'. But these were business relationships and while they may have been mutually beneficial, as we saw in the saloon bar of The City Arms, the currency traded was often information rather than money: a favour for a favour. CID officers were entrepreneurs of knowledge, which by necessity was often acquired by associating with villains, rendering the line between corruption and competent detective work indistinct. But one man was about to step out of this grey area, destroying the idea of a functioning underworld and contributing considerably to the demise of armed robbery as a profession.

Born in 1935, North London's Bertie Smalls was the eldest of five children. At the age of 15, he was arrested for breaking into a railway restaurant car and served his sentence in an approved school. From then on, he dedicated his life to crime and soon became part of a team of robbers who plundered over a dozen banks in London and the south-east. By the mid-1960s, Smalls was at the forefront of the switch from coshes and pickaxe handles to firearms and a key figure among the high-spending, hard-partying underworld. Although he was regularly questioned by the police, Smalls' alibi always stood up and his only adult convictions were comparatively minor: living off immoral earnings and a fine for possession of a loaded gun – the latter indicating the relatively lax attitude to firearms in the 1960s.

Smalls' house in Selsdon, South London, was raided by the police and, although he was absent at the time, he did later telephone the local CID office to make an appointment, but he failed to turn up. Smalls then became part of a seven-handed team who, in 1970, in just 90 seconds inside the Wembley branch of Barclays Bank, stole £237,000, over £3m today, before decamping to Torremolinos with their families. Meanwhile, an informant back in London had named two of the Wembley robbers and Bruce Brown, a golfing partner of Cecil Saxby, head of Wembley CID, was arrested. This success inspired the formation of a specialist robbery squad that combined officers from previous competing units, such as the Regional Crime Squad and the Flying Squad.

Despite visiting Spain, the 25-strong team had no further success but Smalls' name was being increasingly linked with a portfolio of robberies across London, and in November 1972, his house was again raided and the family's au pair gave the police an address in Northamptonshire. Bertie was arrested and immediately offered to 'do a deal', which the police refused. Within a month he offered to give up 'every robber in London' in exchange for immunity but again the police showed no interest. At the committal hearings in March 1973, Smalls was served with papers indicating some very strong evidence against him in relation to the Wembley robbery and another at Palmers Green, as well as a Hatton Garden robbery that netted £296,000, over £4m today, in cash and jewels. Faced with the probability of a 20-year sentence, Smalls again offered to 'do the royals': offer Queen's evidence in exchange for immunity. This time the proposal was put before the director of public prosecutions, a deal was struck and the term 'supergrass' entered the public lexicon.

Smalls confessed to 15 robberies and named 32 bank robbers and a number of associates. The Wembley robbers alone were sentenced to a total of 106 years and, over the next 14 months, a further 21 men received sentences totalling 308 years. Smalls also secured the release from prison of Jimmy Saunders, who had been falsely imprisoned for his part in the 1970 raid on Barclays Bank in Ilford that had netted £237,000. When Smalls finished giving his testimony at the Old Bailey in February 1974, his ex-colleagues gave a rendition of 'Whispering Grass' from the dock, before launching into 'We'll Meet Again', their fingers copying the shape of a gun, an episode that was replicated in the 1984 British crime film *The Hit*, starring Terence Stamp, John Hurt and Tim Roth.

Chief Superintendent Cecil Saxby, Bruce Brown's golfing partner, was accused of stealing £25,000 from Brown's safety deposit box, although the subsequent police investigation cleared Saxby who then retired from the force. Another police inquiry highlighted a common practice of the day. Detective Constable Joan Angell, a member of the Flying Squad, alleged that an informant of hers, 'Mary Fraser', had named Bruce Brown and Bryan Turner as two of the Wembley robbers, who were then arrested. Angell claimed a reward for 'Fraser' but the paperwork for this claim disappeared and the police inquiry found that the reward had been paid to a 'William Wise'. The officers who had claimed the money on behalf of Wise were Saxby and Detective Chief Inspector Vic Wilding, who were both eventually cleared by a police investigation. Angell resigned in disgust, although in 1976 'Mary Fraser' received a £1,000 reward, over £6,500 today, and Vic Wilding left the Met to become a security officer for Barclays Bank. By 1973, two officers a week were voluntarily leaving the Met as a result of a general anti-corruption purge led by Commissioner Robert Mark and the number of bank robberies in London fell from 65 in 1972 to 26 in 1973.

Smalls' case was the only time that a self-confessed criminal was allowed to escape all punishment in return for turning Queen's evidence. The now Lord Chief Justice Frederick Lawton subsequently decreed that the arrangement between Smalls and the Director of Public Prosecutions was an 'unholy deal' and required that all future supergrasses should serve a prison sentence, albeit one that was significantly reduced.

Until Smalls broke rank, the code of the underworld, at least theoretically, had dominated professional criminal life, and while he was beaten up at least once, nobody attempted to claim the £1m bounty, worth over £6m today, that members of the underworld were alleged to have been willing to pay for his murder. Smalls spent the rest of his days with an assumed name living under police protection but he was able to return to his old drinking haunts long before he died of natural causes in 2008.

Smalls had set a trend and other supergrasses quickly followed his example. In 1976, armed robber Maurice O'Mahoney was able to dub himself 'King Squealer' after passing on more than 150 names to the police in return for a five-year sentence, which had become 'the grass's tariff'. O'Mahoney served his time in Chiswick police station with a free supply of alcohol, conjugal visits with his girlfriend and fishing and golf trips with his guards. On his release, like Smalls, he spent the rest of his days with an assumed name living under police protection.

The genie was out of the bottle and the old underworld was in decline. The emergence of the supergrass had undoubtedly damaged the armed robber community, even though after an initial decrease in robberies during the immediate post-Smalls era, armed robbery continued to rise. However, now there was an even higher premium placed upon trust and the formerly loose-knit robbery teams evolved into tightly bonded units, often with family or neighbourhood connections. But as the risks increased so did the rewards. In 1980, a team of robbers stole 321 ingots of silver valued at £3.4m, over £13m today, that was being transferred by road to Tilbury Docks and the fallout from the supergrass-inspired investigation sparked allegations of police corruption.

Robbers also turned their attention to the depots where bullion and cash were stored. In 1983, the Security Express depot in East London was robbed of nearly £7m in cash. John Knight had planned the crime, which involved one guard being threatened with lighter fluid and a box of matches in order to ensure compliance. However, a man responsible for minding some of the money turned informant and the robbers, along with others charged with handling the loot, were convicted.

Six months later, £26m pounds of gold bullion, worth over £80m today, was stolen from the Brink's-Mat depot at Heathrow, a robbery that featured petrol being poured over security guards as a means of gaining compliance. Within 12 hours of the robbery, the world's gold markets had reacted and the value of the haul increased by a million pounds. The insider who had provided keys and information turned informer, arrests were made and the violent aftermath of the robbery continued for many years, with at least five men associated with the robbery being murdered.

DECLINE: DUNROBBIN

In the decade preceding the Brink's-Mat raid, armed robberies had risen from 380 to 1,772 per annum, an increase of 340 per cent, and the police ramped up their response. In July 1987, police shot dead two men during an attempted robbery of a wages van at an abattoir in South London and in November the same year a robber was shot dead by police in a wages snatch at a south-east London supermarket while a television crew filmed a documentary on the Flying Squad. In April 1989, two men were killed by police during a raid on a North London post office and in 1990 a robber was shot dead by police during an attempted raid on a security van in Surrey. In a shootout near the post office in Brockham, near Dorking, in August 1992, police injured both the robbery gang and members of the public; the officer in charge explained that, 'sometimes it was necessary to fight fire with fire'. Professional robbers had reason to believe that the police were operating a shoot-to-kill policy and in the words of robber Terry Smith, 'The risks involved were very real and were not worth it.'

Advances in security technology, including smoke and dye boxes, voice speaking intruder alert alarms, satellite vehicle-tracking devices, CCTV and DNA all had an impact on the viability of professional robbery. The days of professional villains openly toasting each other after a good day 'at the office' in London's smartest restaurants were over. However, businesses unable to afford new security measures went unprotected, even if they offered low returns. Convenience stores, garages, supermarkets, restaurants and off licences remained fair game for amateurs who were often connected to a violent drug subculture rather than to a specialist professional elite. Meanwhile, even professional armed robbers get older.

Robin reflected on his last venture: 'When I was nicked the last time, they did the full bit with the early raid and the door gets put in. By now I was known, and it was a matter of time anyway, but I can honestly hold my hand up and say I was stitched up totally. They marked an *A–Z* that was in my motor on the page where there was a blag. Then they rowed in a shooter that they found and lumped it all in one.'

Mike explained:

'You see people you know get nicked and in the end you start to think about maybe there's a better way of getting your money than sticking your neck out. Sooner or later, it starts to get to you. First of all, you do need to be fit, you can't go into something like that if you're not in good nick because if things go wrong you've got to scarper. I mean, these days, 30 fags a day, I wouldn't get 50 yards down the road if I tried to do something and there was an off. And I think also the younger you are, the less fear you have. You know some people might call that stupid – call it what you like but you're more brazen when you're young and the older you get the more cautious you get.'

In prison, Bobby Cummines enhanced an already formidable reputation. At one time, he held the governor of a maximum security prison as a hostage: 'Well, they said that but he was on his rounds and I knew that they was taking prisoners down the wing and giving out beatings. So I pulled him about it and he screamed that he was being taken hostage.' The incident added considerably to his notoriety.

Eventually, with the support of his probation officer and

a sympathetic prison governor, Bobby enrolled on an Open University course and started to think about the future. However, on leaving prison Bobby at first struggled to make a living, finding potential employers reluctant to take on an ex-con. 'To live an honest life, I had to be dishonest about my past.' He persevered, taking a £100-a-week job stacking shelves and volunteering with the Kent Probation Service, dealing with hostage negotiations and suicide management. Bobby gained a degree in housing and eventually became CEO of Unlock, the National Association of Reformed Offenders. 'Few people seemed to know what they was talking about when it came to the needs of somebody coming out of prison. How to get a job, insurance, a bank account. Employers were saying that they couldn't employ ex-offenders as staff were paid through the BACS system, and former offenders didn't have bank accounts.' Gradually the banks, and insurance industry – sectors not renowned for their social awareness – came on board, and the lives of some of the UK's most excluded were materially changed for the better.

Bobby has proved to be a more successful campaigner, fund raiser and government advisor than he was a criminal and does not flinch from the realities of his past life: 'I've been stabbed, I've been shot and obviously I've shot other people. It was a violent, vicious life.' When Coutts Bank awarded £10,000 to Unlock, 'One of the directors said that he was pleased to see me in his bank without a crash helmet and a gun.'

FANTASY AND INNOVATION

Both safecracking craftsmen and tooled-up project criminals were part of a distinctive criminal fraternity or underworld where specialised knowledge clearly marked the boundaries between the professional and the amateur. However, armed robbery now holds little appeal to career-minded individuals, except as a way of putting together a chunk of cash to invest in entrepreneurial activities. But while professional armed robbery, which according to one ex-blagger was 'just like going to work, but easier', has all but disappeared, 'big hits' remain attractive to a small minority of project criminals.

For instance, in 2000, a group of experienced thieves attempted to steal diamonds from the Millennium Dome using a JCB digger and a speedboat. The potential prize was worth over £350m (£520m today) and the police used unprecedented resources to follow the planning stages, as well as filming the entire progress of the actual robbery before triggering an ambush involving 200 police officers. Although they were not armed, and nobody was injured, the two principal robbers were given 18-year sentences each. As with the 1963 Great Train Robbery, the raid on the Dome shows that spectacular robberies result in spectacular sentences, regardless of the lack of violence.

In 2006, an attack on a cash-storage facility in Kent yielded the UK's biggest ever cash haul of £53m and while a number of men have been convicted, approximately £30m is still missing. Like an earlier cash robbery at a bank in Northern Ireland in 2004, the Kent robbery involved a 'tiger kidnap', where the family of an employee was taken hostage and threatened in order to force the employee to assist the robbers. Yet apart from these occasional spectacular attempts at obtaining fantasy riches, robbery has become largely deskilled and relegated from the Premier League of villainy.

However, armed robbery did not entirely disappear from

the portfolios of what armed robber and author Noel Smith has called 'unorganized lives of drifting destruction' and some blaggers continued to seek out softer targets requiring little or no preplanning, such as travel agencies or security vans picking up bags of cash from supermarkets, cinemas or bingo halls. But while these bandits retained their predecessors' devotion to life as a party, the game had changed.

As improved security technology, the emergence of the supergrass and the likelihood of being killed by a police marksman was making armed robbery significantly less appealing, rewards from entrepreneurial pursuits grew – in particular drugs – and came with markedly fewer risks. The old underworld had functioned as an employment and information exchange but it was breaking down, and the unwritten criminal code that provided a notional ethical framework for a community of professional criminals could not cope with the new free-for-all market driven by drugs. What emerged from the remnants of the underworld was a new criminal entrepreneurship featuring a weird mutant that was at times barely distinct from legitimate business.

A SUBTLE LIBERTY: VAT GOLD FRAUD

In 1979, Margaret Thatcher's new government removed the VAT on gold coins, such as the South African Krugerrand and the Canadian Maple Leaf, in order to give private individuals freedom to trade in gold. However, VAT on gold scrap – gold not in the form customarily traded, such as jewellery – was maintained and the rate raised from 8 per cent to 15 per cent. The difference made VAT fraud an attractive proposition, presenting an opportunity soon seized by a wide range of individuals and armed robbers were at the front of the queue.

It worked like this: fraudsters would buy large quantities of gold coins (VAT free), melt them down and cast them into gold bullion. The bullion was then sold through secondary dealers. One of the secondary dealers in this chain, although registered for VAT, would be in on the swindle and abscond with the VAT he collected from his customer. The purchaser of the bullion could reclaim the VAT he had paid as input tax and thus the only and substantial loser was the Exchequer.

One of investigative journalist Paul Lashmar's contacts, Sammy, described the fraud in a 1992 interview:

'You go and buy from one of the big bullion houses like Johnson Mathey, say £100,000 worth of Kruger Rands, paying a small premium. The coins were then melted down and sold back to another bullion house for slightly under the price of gold. So the team might get £98,000 plus 15 per cent VAT; that's £114,800. After expenses, their profit was £11,000 (although they still owe the VAT £15,000). The next day, the team would buy £114,000 worth of Kruger Rands. And so it would go on. It might be three or six months before the VAT were breathing down your neck – by which time the proceeds would be in the millions and the team would either have disappeared or started again under a different set of names.'

Lashmar quotes 'Terrence', a former armed robber: 'Suddenly the blaggers realised that instead of going across the pavement, tooled up and risking being shot by the Old Bill, or grassed up by one of your own and getting 15 years, here was a way to make millions. Even if you got caught, the maximum they could give you in the early days was three years. If you'd salted a few million away, even that was all right.' By 1993, it was estimated that VAT gold fraud had cost the taxpayer £500m.

By 1982, VAT gold fraud was booming, prompting Customs to run a number of investigations, including one that culminated in the arrest of two former Great Train Robbers, Charlie Wilson and Roy James, along with the armed robber Danny Redmond, and a dozen other men. They were accused of stealing VAT worth £2.4m – just short of the amount stolen from the Great Train Robbery. After two trials where the jury could not reach a decision, the case was abandoned.

Customs started to crack down and a legitimate company was required for VAT registration. The fraudsters adapted. In 1992 Paul Lashmar interviewed Albert:

'So I sent a conman down to a small jewellery shop out in the sticks. The conman rolled up and told the owner he was from the VAT and demanded to see his books. On the sly, he photocopied the bloke's VAT certificate and I sold copies of it all around the Garden.[24] Some months later, the Customs tried to work out why some little bloke who had been turning over two bob a year was suddenly dealing £8m worth of gold.'

In 1982, the government re-imposed VAT on gold coins and the fraudsters quickly adapted again by smuggling coins from

---

24   London's Hatton Garden, the city's jewellery quarter.

anywhere that had no, or very little, VAT. In a 1986 interview, armed robber turned author John McVicar reported that some of his former associates were now shuttling between London and places such as Jersey, Guernsey, Liechtenstein and Switzerland, where gold coins could be bought without too many questions being asked: 'At peak, they [the fraudsters] would be coming in by private jet three times a week and they would bring as much as £2m a time. They made so much money they did not know what to do with it.'

Of the original first wave of 12 major Customs VAT gold fraud operations (1981–82), seven involved individuals with a record for armed robbery and it was believed that other VAT gangs involving armed robbers had avoided arrest.

MICKEY GREEN

Armed robbers Mickey Green, James Jeffrey and Ronnie Dark, who had all been imprisoned as a result of Bertie Smalls' evidence, left prison in the late 1970s and, under the tutelage of a notorious Hatton Garden jeweller, quickly adapted to VAT fraud. In just a few months, the trio made £6m by buying gold coins, melting them into ingots and selling the gold back to the bullion house, collecting VAT. When they clamped down on this particular team of ex-armed robbers in 1981, Customs claimed that the proceeds of the fraud had disappeared, along with the jeweller, Green and Jeffrey, to Spain.

While most of the professional robbers of the 1960s–1980s era were more concerned with long holidays in the sun than in investing in their futures, blaggers were now coming to terms with the drug trade. Many became commodity brokers, investing heavily in a relatively low-risk business that quickly came to dominate criminal life. Mickey Green, the head of the Wembley mob, put his VAT profits to good use and by 1994 he was described in a Scotland Yard report as 'probably the most prolific British drug trafficker in the world'. The UK had no extradition agreement with Spain until 1985 and Green used the country as a base to shift huge quantities of cannabis from Morocco to mainland Europe. In 1987, he was arrested for attempting to import two tons of hashish. When he was bailed he abandoned his drug-running fleet of power boats and yachts and fled to North Africa. He was traced to a flat in Paris where gold bullion and cocaine was found but Green had already fled. He was later sentenced to 17 years in his absence. He was also sentenced to 20 years in absentia in Holland.

Green proceeded to move huge shipments of drugs around the world and in 1994 he had one tonne of cocaine worth £200m seized in Merseyside. The FBI arrested Green as he lounged by the pool at Rod Stewart's Bel Air mansion that the ex-robber had rented under an alias. Following ten months in a San Francisco prison, he was put on a flight to France but absconded when the plane made a stopover at Shannon airport. In 1994, Green, who had dual British and Irish nationality, bought a home outside Dublin but his involvement in a fatal car crash brought his background to the fore and he swiftly left Ireland when the IRA showed an interest. The Irish government seized assets including two Dublin homes and Green returned to Spain.

In 2000, Mickey Green yet again became the victim of a supergrass when he was arrested in a Barcelona hotel after being named by the notorious drug dealer and money launderer Michael Michael. Michael claimed that Green had visited London twice in 1997 using a false passport and also maintained that he was responsible for killing two London-based villains. This time Mickey Green spent time in a Madrid prison before being released for lack of evidence. He then settled in Estepona on the Costa Del Sol.

There are many rumours as to how he stayed out of prison for so many years but the definitive story of Mickey Green remains untold. Whatever the truth, his ability to stay at liberty was not unconnected to his ability to hire expensive lawyers. At the time of his death in 2020, aged 77, he was wanted by the police in France, Ireland, Holland and Morocco.

One of the great British crime myths is 'in the old days villains didn't deal drugs', which in terms of romantic fantasy sits alongside 'all this mugging/burglary/rape etc. wouldn't have happened when the twins were about'. Most of the main players, including many of the iconic gangsters of the 1960s, made money from drugs. It may have not been their main source of income, but they were at it. Because that is what villains do, they make money. But while a few of the old conservative villains professed to be 'against drugs', often while simultaneously having a stake in a suburban pill factory, by the late 1980s the demand for recreational drugs was shifting the trade from the periphery of illegal capitalism to its very centre.

The best place to get an education in the possibilities of the drug trade was in prison, and while captured robbers were sharing cells with the new drug entrepreneurs, fellow blaggers enjoying the warmth of the suspension of the extradition treaty between Spain and the UK were sipping cocktails while watching speedboats full of cannabis travelling across the straits of Gibraltar.

PART TWO

Chapter 12

MAKE YOUR MONEYMAKER: DRUGS AND VIOLENCE

'There is no doubt that the type of man who once turned to piracy still exists, but is compelled to find other channels for his talents.'

THE HISTORY OF PIRACY

OPPORTUNITY KNOCKS

The appetite for recreational drugs had been growing throughout the 1970s and for anyone seeking to earn – and, to be frank, who wasn't? – the drug trade filled a lot of gaps. Joining forces with armed robbers, well-established family firms and 'other' villains were ordinary punters at the edge of the stolen goods trade – duckers and divers, thieves, lorry drivers, bouncers and football hooligans. These groups came together to make easy money doing what came naturally: buying and selling. Chaotic, dysfunctional broods of work-shy drunks who had previously been shunned by their neighbours became 'crime families' merely on the strength of their ability to pick up a parcel of dope or a few wraps of powder and move it on at a profit. Big dogs, big cars and gold-toothed consumerism took over streets that once housed the families of working men and women but now were home to CCTV cameras, steel-enforced front doors and barred and belled-up windows. Those shunning involvement in the drug trade were abandoned to diazepam and daytime television.

Some villains were quick learners and became very ambitious. For instance, Liverpool's Curtis Warren emerged as a violent teenage street robber at the height of the 1980s recession before quickly moving through the ranks to operate a global enterprise that spanned five continents. Warren was arrested in Holland in 1997 and by the time he was convicted, the *Sunday Times* listed him as the 461st wealthiest individual in the UK, with an estimated fortune of £40m. According to writer Tony Barnes, Warren's known assets included properties in Wales, Turkey, Spain and Gambia, 200 houses in Liverpool, a brothel and a football club. Clearly things had changed. Now it was all about mega-profit rather than merely dominating the pubs and street corners of a run-down neighbourhood or claiming enough bags of cash from a security van to pay for three months in Marbella.

New rules came to the fore, as robbing drug dealers became common. In the 1990s, one group created fear and chaos by alternating between either promptly paying cash on the nose for a parcel of drugs or stealing the dealer's entire stock. Dan, a dealer, described the dilemma in doing business with them:

'It happened over and over, nobody knew if they was paying or not. When they had the money it was on the table and thanks very much. But then another time they would just not pay. And from what I heard, shooters or heavy stuff weren't always needed. Just "Fuck off, it aint happening" and they'd walk out with the gear. That was when it seemed like everybody was getting tooled up with something and there was talk of shootings, kids with guns out riding their bikes at night.'

Ex-armed robbers with reputations forged 'across the pavement', and often smarting from the effects of many years 'behind the door', introduced a little old-school professionalism to this new market. Unrestrained by the somewhat flimsy rules of the old underworld, these bandits set about threatening, robbing and swindling the messy chaotic mob who constituted this new criminal community.

In the 1980s and 1990s, the ex-robbers were joined by teams of successful lorry thieves, who upped the stakes by hijacking the loads of cigarette and cannabis smugglers – from the hijackers' perspective, why not let somebody else take the risks associated with importation before taking the prize? However, anybody planning to hijack a lorryload of contraband had to be very certain that the load had not been at least part financed by somebody connected to one of the more violent firms, for when this happened there was only one outcome.

Trust was gone. Once you could rely on people you had been brought up with, worked with, drank with. It was an old-school way of life that was central to working-class culture. But the old communities were either gone or in the process of being dismantled and their straight-going members were trying to adjust to and make sense of a life of minimum wage jobs, new locks on the door, satellite TV and cheap booze from the corner shop. Meanwhile, more than ever, violence was being used to control the illegal markets that were the only local growth industry. The old trust networks of the underworld were no longer relevant, therefore if you wanted cooperation the threat of violence was crucial.

PUNCHING ABOVE WEIGHT

If someone refuses to pay for a parcel of cocaine, or a van full of cannabis, going to the police is not an option. There is no ombudsman to go to with your complaint. There is only one way to get revenge. A dealer explained:

> 'It's the threat of violence that keeps people in line because I mean, that guy he could say, "I've took your 25,000, I'm off, I'm not coming back." But what happens if I find him in two years' time? I'll murder him, or I'll want my mate to murder him, somebody will murder him and he knows that. So it's not worth his while to fuck off with 25,000.'

So either you wipe your mouth and walk away a much wiser, albeit bankrupted entrepreneur or you go and get your money with a gun and give yourself a chance to stay in the game. Commercial instincts with a violent default mode are essential to acquire and maintain a slice of the market. However, violence is not just a management technique, it is also very personal, and no matter how sophisticated and market-orientated illegal trading is, individuals must respond to a perceived slight to self, or to family, with the same level of ferocity and commitment as they would to a threat to their profit. In this chaotic marketplace violent reputation provides a guarantee of order, it is an obligation, a necessity, even if on occasions this proves to be bad for business.

For instance, a cannabis importation business, whose members also had interests in amphetamine manufacture, car ringing and a portfolio of property that included two pubs, crumbled when an ex-business partner was released from prison. Fifteen years previously, this man had publicly insulted the wife of one of the firm's founder members. On his release from prison the man was beaten and stabbed, and the legal and extra-legal fallout of this violence – firebombs, police raids, property boarded up and the imprisonment of a number of young men on the fringe of the firm – marked the disintegration of this profitable cluster of skulduggery. Within 18 months, the firm had imploded in a haze of smoke and paranoia, and while members either faded into obscurity or re-invented themselves within new clusters of opportunity, few would ever return to the same levels of strength and prosperity. Business had become confused with ego, and business suffered.

Violence and intimidation runs through drug markets like a thread. It is a way of ensuring contract compliance, in particular making sure that creditors do not default on debt. Geoff, who was serving a seven-year sentence for intent to supply, explained, 'It's part and parcel, isn't it? It goes with the business. If you can't pay for your drugs, what else can they use? I stood to lose too much by letting people walk over me, so I would deal with this guy severely: he was getting taught a lesson, he was getting took for a drive.' This dealer's arrest prevented this from happening but, 'At the end of the day, the guy's still there and as far as I am concerned he's still got to be dealt with in time.'

Debt also puts family at risk. The father of a man owing

a drug debt was killed when the creditor poured petrol over him and set him alight. A man serving 20 years for drug importation explained: 'I was paranoid, especially when I been arrested. I was scared cos my cousin he knows my house; the other person, he knows my family in Cyprus. They know I got two kids. I love my kids to death, my whole family can be in danger. Them people, I know what they can be.'

On a more mundane level, a boy, a naïve user-dealer with fantasies of becoming a drug kingpin, had had his legs broken and the next step was death or 'the vegetable patch'. His father had little choice. He gave over his life savings to two men in a car park in order to save his son's life.

When police operations are disrupting business this can often lead to attempts to buy leniency or safety through informing, and violence is an inevitable result. For instance, in the build up to a trial featuring an eight-handed conspiracy to import, one of the accused, who was suspected of being an informer, disappeared after the main protagonist had put pressure on him to be 'staunch' and not claim to be a mere courier. He was murdered while on bail.

However, some of the violence associated with drug markets appears to be more recreational than instrumental. For instance, an associate of a middle-market group of dealers owed a mere £400 to senior members of the group. He was met in a pub and, despite offering to pay the debt, was taken to the countryside where he had both of his hands broken. He was then taken out, kept captive and severely beaten. Eventually he was found rolled up in a carpet at the back of a fish shop, naked and badly beaten.

Many of the prisoners I interviewed mentioned how kid-napping was a useful tool in the drug dealer's kit, particularly as a way of enforcing the payment of debt. This could go one or two ways: either the debtor would be kidnapped and held until his family members got the money together, or members of his family would be kidnapped until payment was made. In one case, family members in Colombia were held hostage until someone based in the UK secured the necessary funds for release. In another, a financial dispute between an importer and a wholesaler resulted in the importer being kidnapped and held hundreds of miles from home until the debt was settled by his family. In yet another instance, the main player in a drug network had a debtor kidnapped. It had not been a particularly serious debt but the main man felt that he could use it to his advantage since the person involved was known as a waster, someone vulnerable with few if any loyal friends, and so there was little likelihood of any retaliation. The man was beaten and photographs were taken of him in degrading circumstances, before being shown around to local people. The message was clear: 'This is what happens if you mess around with us.'

Kidnapping and torture can also be used as a way of extracting funds from villains who are unable to turn to the police for assistance. One group of dealers inflicted life-changing injuries on a man who regularly transferred millions of pounds of his cash abroad. Over several days, a sledgehammer was just one of the implements used upon him before he revealed the whereabouts of his drug money. At the other end of the scale, in the early part of this century there was a spate of expensive 4×4 vehicles being 'kidnapped'. The carnappers would then send photographs to the owners of their pride and joy next to cans of petrol or paint stripper. Payment was usually made.

One of the drawbacks of placing violent, occasionally psychotic individuals in a business environment is that blood and guts not only attracts the attention of the police but also it deters potential partners and investors. As a highly successful criminal entrepreneur explained to me when discussing a murderous business associate, 'He became a fucking liability. You are trying to get a deal out of a man and he is on him cutting and plunging away. He never knew any limits, not what you want out of a money-maker.' What you need from a money-maker is sufficient viciousness to satisfy both personal greed and self-respect, but enough self-restraint to know when to take a step back.

In the 1990s, as the methods of the drug trade spilled over into other market sectors, the space between personal and business became blurred and violence was normalised, with even those not directly involved in the drug trade borrowing from it to enhance their commercial and individual reputations. The ever-present threat of violence polluted personal business as well as commercial troubles.

THE NAIL BANGER

A builder by trade, Stewart played down his expertise and training by claiming to be somebody who makes a living merely by 'banging nails in walls'. On leaving school, he worked briefly in a factory before taking up an apprenticeship with a local building firm. Here Stewart blossomed, and in his spare time he turned his hobby repairing cars into a part-time commercial venture. His mechanical skills made him popular among a loose-knit network of friends and business acquaintances, who, when Stewart completed his apprenticeship, provided lucrative building work in the form of repairs, renovations and house extensions. Via this network of largely self-employed men, Stewart worked with corrupt council officials who granted permission to build on land whose use had been limited to industry or agriculture.

Stewart was doing well and over the next two decades, he invested his spare cash in cars and property. But he was also married three times, and the subsequent chaos of his personal life resulted in him over-extending himself in the property market. When a business partner was declared bankrupt owing Stewart over a quarter of a million pounds, he turned to the corrupt cohort of public officials who had provided such a boost to his career as a property developer, only to find that they had retired, or become risk averse and unreliable with age. One incompetent clerk had spent his kickback before it was discovered that planning permission should not have been granted for a two-storey house built by Stewart and had to be demolished. While the clerk took an early retirement deal, Stewart unsuccessfully fought the demolition in the courts, and he was now running out of money. He turned to booze and while he could be nasty when he had a drink, he was no fighter. Ducking, diving and 'banging nails in walls' was his game, and he came off second best in a suburban ruck with a relative of one of his ex-wives. He crashed cars and punched walls, becoming a regular visitor to the accident and emergency department of his local hospital as he shed both friends and business associates. He needed help, he needed respect, but while he was no hard man, he knew a man who was.

A huge man with a face as blank as a paving stone, for decades Al had made his money from his willingness to hurt people. A famously degenerate gambler, Al had a cocaine habit that supplemented the rigid intensity that had marked his career as a bouncer. He was the go-to man for anyone picking up a bag of moody money, needing squatters evicted, a debt urgently repaid or an ominously mute back-up at a business meeting. Al became Stewart's saviour and the making of the second phase of his career. Although both Al and his new employer needed money, Stewart also desperately required an injection of personal and professional respect, and so Al accompanied Stewart whenever a dispute was likely, which was often. Cars were torched, a subcontractor and some of his staff who unwisely intervened were beaten up and a number of municipal administrators were reminded of their obligations. Al was also by Stewart's side at encounters with his ex-wives and their families and, on at least one occasion, when he arrived at their place of work in order to aggressively 'renegotiate' property arrangements. Al's presence was usually sufficient to ensure the non-intervention of concerned workmates or family members. For the first time in his life, the unprepossessing Stewart assumed a swagger of invulnerability.

With Al's brooding assistance, Stewart's life became relatively ordered. His domestic life was positively tranquil, he acquired a new business partner with whom he invested in a building project in Spain, he took golf holidays and cruises, and bought a small house in a quiet Mediterranean village. By the early years of the 21st century, he was the epitome of the tough, resourceful, successful working-class businessman and, although only in his early fifties, spoke to friends about one day cashing in and spending his retirement years floating from island to island in the Caribbean.

The swindle put an end to his dreams. The Spanish building

project was exposed as a scrap of undeveloped barren land pock-marked with discarded breeze blocks. The business partner disappeared, Stewart became a pisshead again, another wife left him and a group of his drinking friends were convicted of conspiring to import drugs from Holland. Stewart's life proceeded like a bad country and western song and his portfolio of debt was not improved by a dip in the property market or by a weekend cocaine treat that had morphed into a daily routine. Close friends reported that he became morose, obsessed by slights and perceived wrongs that had festered in his increasingly unstable imagination.

Back in his twenties, when Stewart was buying and selling cars and drinking away much of the profits with friends, he had become embroiled in a row with a younger man whose inability to cope with alcohol had made him something of a joke among the amateur car dealers. As neither Stewart nor his opponent had a reputation for fighting, they were ignored by the rest of the group until, completely out of character, the younger man threatened Stewart with a pint glass. To the equal amazement of the assembled drinkers, Stewart beat up the other man sufficiently badly to warrant a trip to hospital. But a few days later, before his stitches had been removed, Stewart's adversary flaunted a handgun and claimed to anyone who would listen that he was going to shoot Stewart in revenge. However, nobody took the young man seriously: he was a mere eccentric attempting to big himself up after a public humiliation. The incident was soon forgotten and Stewart was told neither of the gun, nor of the threat to his life.

Many years later, his old friends reminded Stewart about the threat at an evening of boozy reminiscences and he laughed it off as just another episode of their chaotic youth. However, he filed this information away in his memory and the toxic cocktail of an ego made brittle by failure and cocaine brought this long-redundant threat to the fore. The young man with a gun was found living a blameless family life and Al was despatched to break his arm.

Although Stewart's failing health made him heavily reliant upon the 'off the books' eastern European labour that he employed on a series of rapid turnaround renovation projects, he was back in the game. A row of shops proved a particularly prudent investment due to their generous storage facilities with discreet rear access, and he was able to offer a site for slaughtering lorry loads of stolen goods and parcels of contraband. Al was always available to ensure that Stewart was paid. By 2009, the shops were sold and he was once again a wealthy man whose hard graft, ruthless energy, obsessive predatory instincts and astute understanding of the role of violence had paid off. While it is unlikely that he has repaired his fragile ego, Stewart now appears to be on a relatively even keel, with a foot in both legal and illegal camps, but should his commercial or personal life become disturbed, Al is just a phone call away.

ALL INCLUSIVE

The vibrant alternative economy based in backstreet pubs and smoky spielers had gone the same way as the docks and factories. When the old territories had broken down, the ranks of villains trying to make sense of fresh opportunities were joined by a wide range of new players intent on not working for a living. The result is not an overarching Mafia but clusters of thugs, mugs, Tom, Dick and Ali, connected by nothing more than mutual desire to make money – a community of practice.

The drug trade was low on skill: it was easy money and welcomed both new entrepreneurs and the grizzled old guard fresh out of Parkhurst, stinking of boiled cabbage and intent on making up for lost time. The doors to this party were wide open and there were no barriers to membership, as villains became businessmen and businessmen became villains. There was also no need to be part of a big-brand family firm or to have a staunch reputation on the back of a ten stretch, although having a paranoid nutter prone to the odd drug-fuelled atrocity on the firm could be useful. Villains no longer shared a common cause or exchanged celebratory bottles of champagne at West End night clubs: the exclusive underworld of thieves, robbers and gangsters was finished, and the violence and rip-offs of the drug trade set the standard for the new skulduggery.

Chapter 13

BACK IN THE CITY: STAYING SHARP IN DIFFICULT CIRCUMSTANCES

'If you are asked why you favour a particular public-house, it would seem natural to put the beer first, but the thing that most appeals to me about the *Moon Under Water* is what people call its "atmosphere".'

GEORGE ORWELL

By the 1990s, the old props of community based on jobs and a sense of neighbourhood had splintered. As the drug trade became normalised, ordinary civilians without the resources to escape to the green-tinged suburbs were forced to distance themselves from the drug market by cowering behind barred windows as street level dealers, often of school age, engaged in drug-related as well as recreational violence. The local order had been seriously disturbed; the atmosphere was predatory and suspicion and insecurity became the norm. Pubs, once centres of community from Christmas clubs and football and darts teams to sub-retail outlets for mountains of hookey gear, were no longer what they were. There was a severe lack of beer money about and many of the newcomers to the area brought with them cultures that did not include alcohol consumption. As property prices escalated, many East End neighbourhoods were assaulted by gentrifiers. Old boozers were demolished or turned into flats; those with preservation orders on them, like Terry Jackson's Steamship, were converted into fast-food outlets, while others 'had a fire'. But for a while, The City Arms survived.

The City Arms was barely afloat on a reputation that had echoed down the decades. Occasionally, retired thieves made pilgrimages to reminisce about how in their day, money had been made in the traditional manner – the plunder of lorries, factories and goods depots – and the booty dispersed among a working-class population fully engaged with networks of loot. But there were precious few remnants of the old way of life and darker margins now shaded the boundaries.

The lunchtime trade in The City Arms had evaporated when the clerks sought out a more interesting sandwich and the CID found an alternative venue with a handy function room upstairs. Just around the corner, a crack house caught fire and while nobody knew much about the business, some elderly neighbours had complained about the dogs that barked and the car doors that slammed in the night. To most local youths, The City Arms was a joke, a ghost ship adrift on misshapen promises and inhabited by grotesque phantoms.

By the mid-1990s, the boozer was being run by a steady stream of disappointed men and women. Spending serious money on a pub like this was just flushing fresh dough down the Doulton, and the remnants of various Victorian light-fittings and early Tandoori wall coverings were all that remained of the 1980s, when the pub had served as a covered market for a thousand and one duckers and divers.

LAST ORDERS

It was one o'clock in the morning in The City Arms, two hours after the call for last orders. The glamorous couple who once ran the pub were long gone and, several licensees later, we were being served by a morose Welshman who clearly hated his clientele. There were fewer than 20 customers in the pub; on the muted TV was a thriller that broadsheet critics had claimed had a powerful feminist subtext, adding an additional light source to this bleak, bloodless boozer. However, at an alcove table, six men showed distinct signs of something resembling life, and were enthusiastically talking bollocks.

Bert the Builder: I tell you, it fucking sounds cold out there.

Nick: What?

Bert the Builder: You can fucking tell, it sounds fucking cold. Listen.

(quiet)

Bert the Builder: See.

Brian: Can't hear a fucking thing.

Bert the Builder: That's what I fucking mean; it sounds fucking cold. That's all I'm saying, you can hear it. Listen.

Nick: Fuck off.

Bert the Builder: Listen, when I was in Gambia it was so hot you could hear everything. Flies and fucking lions and that. The fucking noise you wouldn't believe it cos it's so hot.

Nick: Lions don't fucking live here, do they? You don't get a fucking animal zoo or nothing coming down the street.

Brian: This time of night the buses have stopped.

Peter: But you can get a cab.

Brian: But not a fucking camel.

Peter: Listen.

(Rhythmically chinks glass)

(Ensemble sings 'Santa Claus is Coming to Town')

This was an unremarkable, mid-week rendezvous for these men, most of whom made their money from crime but who were also committed to leisure. Apart from the pace and haphazard content of their conversation, they were marked out by their frequent visits to the toilet. Fat Bert had been dealing in cocaine ever since Peter became unreliable, demanding payments from people who he had failed to supply.

Fat Bert looked more like a glass collector than a central casting version of a drug dealer. He was dressed exclusively in polyester, his cheap trainers the same shade of grey as his skin, and there was more hair sprouting from his ears than on his head. Only after close examination is it possible to discern that the small crescent of acne-like scarring above his left eye was caused by a sharp instrument rather than a youthful diet of chips.

There were no more Christmas clubs for the elderly and the landlord was not an ex-cop or relative of a well-known face. He was not even local and did not see the point in sponsoring a football team or an annual Jolly Boys' outing to Margate. There is no money in the pub game any more, most people would rather booze at home, but Bert kept the punters drinking deep into the early hours by chopping Charlie on the cold smooth white porcelain of the toilet cistern, organising the powder into lines, and allowing his customers to enjoy it at will. Not dissimilar to the old days when the landlord used to put sausages and rollmops on the counter on a Sunday lunchtime.

On this particular night, Sammy was the cubicle's most frequent visitor. The youngest of the men at the alcove table, Sammy, was still benefiting from a successful burglary of a carpet warehouse, having succeeded in selling his entire stock within a week and earning the nickname Aladdin for making the carpets fly. Just a year previously, Sammy had not been a City Arms regular, but he was now snorting coke as part of an established urban elite, several of whom were old enough to be his father. He wore an expensive designer watch that did not turn his wrist green and everyone expected him to be a future money-maker.

On reaching the age of 30, Bert the Builder had claimed that the building industry was a 'young man's game' and retired. By that time, he had a long-standing arrangement with a local postman, buying anything from his mailbag and selling stolen credit cards to Fat Bert. Like half of the pub's clientele, he also distributed 'snide' designer clothing. He was always immaculately dressed for early summer, even in mid-winter, and on this particular night he was wearing gold buckled slip-on shoes and peach-coloured slacks with a red polo shirt under a pink cotton cardigan with white trim.

Bert the Builder was about to fly to the States with Brian to watch a world title fight. Brian, who always had 'plenty of money' and was also a regular visitor to Bald Bert's cubicle, wore dark denims, a tracksuit top and a black roll neck embossed with a golfing logo. His trainers were state of the art. A one-time amateur boxer, he had in the recent past sold amphetamines in conjunction with his elder brother and was the last to arrive at the pub after selling tickets for a mediocre derby match between two unsuccessful football teams. He worked with a group of men who had close connections to a major football club and could obtain tickets even for the most popular fixtures.

A regular customer of Brian's was Peter, who would never miss a cup final, or anything else if he could help it. He inherited the family market-trading business when barely out of school but the long hours, in particular the early morning starts, had a catastrophic impact on his social life and he soon passed over the day-to-day running of the business to one of his brothers. Not long after Peter married the daughter of a local publican, he became embroiled in a long-running feud with his in-laws after stolen goods were discovered by the police in a storeroom at the back of his father-in-law's pub. The subsequent police attention created chaos: his father-in-law lost his livelihood, followed by a conviction for Peter's brother-in-law when drugs were discovered in his car. Although Peter had only put the goods in the storeroom while they cooled off, the die was cast – it triggered a feud that ran for over two decades and periodically erupted into violence that drew on the resources of some of the neighbourhood's long-standing criminal families. The feud led to the shooting of one of Peter's cousins. He survived and the subsequent retaliation left two men with bad slash wounds.

Peter had lived abroad for a number of years working in a timeshare business but left his wife and children in a flat above a supermarket and returned to London, where he discovered cocaine. However, he was an unreliable dealer and never got to grips with the basic protocols of the trade, such as supplying the goods. Consequently, he was quickly usurped by Fat Bert as the neighbourhood white-powder provider. Peter was still showing the results of a bad beating that he'd taken several months ago following a succession of events involving a burnt-out car, a can of brake fluid and his now ex in-laws.

Peter was accompanied by two men in their early twenties who bought drinks for Fat Bert and co. They were there to pay their respects to Peter, whose brother had, until recently, been the cellmate of the pony-tailed of the duo. The previous Wednesday, both Pony-tail and his crop-haired mate were severely reprimanded for smoking dope in the bar as 'the guvnor don't like it'. Tonight's flashing of cash is their way of making amends for this indiscretion.

The last member of the group was Nick, a gambler who once stole a car from a car lot before selling it back to the same dealer the next day; he did it for a bet. He'd had a complete and regularly formed pair of ears before he sold some empty cigarette cartons to people who knew better and now one of his ears appeared to be made of plasticine. He had come fresh from the dog track and when he left the pub would head straight to a warehouse in West London that was storing large quantities of counterfeit goods. Christmas was coming and Nick had already taken his orders from local traders. The next afternoon, the horses will beckon him to the bookies. By this time the following day, Nick would likely be either cash rich or asking the custody sergeant for another blanket.

WAYNE'S WORLD

Wayne used to lurk in The City Arms. He liked cocaine but he loved the idea of the cocaine business. However, Wayne became a nuisance, failing to pay for his share of the coke and constantly attempting to arrange loans. Eventually, he was informally barred from the Wednesday group's alcove and hung around on the periphery for a few weeks, hoping to be invited back in, before eventually fading away. Peter was especially hostile. 'Soapy smelly cunt, a fucking junkie or what? Couldn't have a toot like anybody else. Well, no fucking money. Fuck him.'

Wayne talked constantly about smart clothes and glamorous women, of snorting coke and being invincible in a fight. His version of the future was totally wedded to cocaine, a dreamlike projection of a clean white world of crystal sharpness and unrelenting certainty. He enthused about his involvement in a 'little', 'big' or 'fucking blinding' deal, manipulating his world via his own use of the drug. All of which was at odds with the reality of the dishevelled figure in the saloon bar of The City Arms. His skin was semi-transparent and acne-scarred, his suit jacket appeared to contain someone else's shoulders, while the material of his shirt came from the same batch as Fat Bert's. On a warm day, Wayne would not smell too good.

Soon after he had stopped hanging around The City Arms, Wayne started telling anyone who would listen that he had bought a shotgun. This was followed by rumours that he had robbed an all-night garage. However, as it was now common knowledge that he was using crack this was all dismissed as 'junkie talk'. But Wayne's one-time flatmate was arrested for robbing shops and off licences and when the police responded to a neighbour's complaints of a noisy argument, Wayne was found with two rocks of crack in his pocket and a vintage air rifle under his bed.

On his release from prison he died of pneumonia after apparently living rough on the streets for a couple of months.

Wayne's story highlights the criminal fantasy that sits at the core of many modern identities. He did not set out to make money, but to be an outlaw, a maverick standing outside the everyday realities of a crap job and humdrum future. Cocaine gave him a focus that had little to do with the drug's pharmacology or its impact on his brain and everything to do with its image and association with sexy, glossy consumerism. But while Wayne's story is especially sad, criminal fantasies are not uncommon.

BENNY AND THE TROJAN CONTAINER

Now in late middle age, City Arms regular Benny, whose talent for making trailers, lorries and containers disappear had once been renowned, was coming to terms with the decline of his once-imposing physique by consuming vast quantities of the powdered protein drinks favoured by athletes and bodybuilders. However, lager, vodka and increasingly rare visits to the weights bench in his back bedroom had done little to enhance his general health. Benny appeared to be melting. His jowly buttocks, permanently encased in black tracksuit bottoms, hung either side of the barstool of the City, where he was now to be found most nights and much of the daytime. He had presided over the bar from this very spot for over a quarter of a century, while enjoying a life that had encompassed reckless outlaw, supplier of cheap goods, guardian of the decrepit old pub's moral order and now grand old man and resident sage.

Benny could not keep a fiver in his pocket, having made, spent, loaned and gambled a lot of money in an unruly cocktail of a career featuring low-level theft and a little violence. But then there was the debt. Owing money was as natural as sucking up a large pint of chemical lager. The trick here was never to rob an individual so badly that they would feel obliged to come after you and cause a row. You borrow a ladder and sell it. A set of tools 'got stolen'. Van repairs costing £250, £50 for an iPod for his granddaughter and, on one occasion, £800 to buy a British motorbike, which was promptly sold to a drinking partner for £1,000 before Benny borrowed it back for the weekend, returning it on the Monday morning, five years older and Japanese.

But age was catching up on Benny. He was no longer borrowing money to invest in a 'few parcels' of stolen or cheap goods but for household bills, rent and his precious stool in The City Arms. For many years, his ability and willingness to put himself 'on offer' – over a fence or through a window, to drive through the night and generally buy, sell, steal and scheme – had kept him and his family fed, housed and shod in the latest trainers, but now a £25 loan was all that was keeping Benny from a life behind drawn curtains with a bottle of supermarket vodka in the company of the ghouls and freaks of daytime television. The reasons for requiring a loan varied over the years but equipment such as tools, ladders that he could no longer climb, or vehicle parts were on rotation. Remarkably, most lenders swallowed it when they handed over £200 for Benny to purchase some essential item of kit, only to see him peel off a couple of £20 notes to buy a round of drinks. He had been getting away with this for years and most people regarded it as money well spent in exchange for his amiable company or, perhaps, in the hope that some of the fading glory associated with a man who could still do the business – albeit with a shuffling gait and lager sweat, jaundiced eyes and creaking joints – might rub off.

UPWARDLY MOBILE

Although the area around The City Arms had generally proved to be allergic to gentrification, a few bold members of the middle classes invested in the ex-council flats and small Victorian terraces, staying for a couple of years before moving out when the prospect of sending their children to a local school became beyond the pale. Some of these bourgeois pioneers even ventured into The City, where they were generally ignored, but Benny's olde worlde courtesy proved to be one of the few comforting features of their harsh new habitat and he made a point of striking up conversations with these nervous-looking strangers.

Delia was a privately educated woman who worked as a teacher in a local school and she dressed in a manner that marked her out from the local women who drank or worked in The City. As opposed to most of the male drinkers, local women who used the pub were smartly dressed but Delia was both 'scruffy' and 'posh', and the female bar staff were especially suspicious of anyone deliberately veiling their origins.

Delia's partner, Alec, had also been privately educated but his bohemian tendencies had included shoplifting, drinking and smoking cannabis, which resulted in expulsion from school. After a few years of volunteering for a little London lowlife by living in squats, he set up a small kitchen-fitting business in one of the more fashionable parts of the East End. By the time he started drinking in The City Arms he had picked up a slightly annoying mockney accent.

Both Alec and Delia enjoyed smoking dope but they had no ready local supply until Benny stepped in to oblige his new neighbours and occasional drinking partners, who, along with a group of their equally bourgeois friends, became his regular customers. Benny, who although at this stage was only earning drinking money, set about the enterprise with characteristic zeal and imagination. Eventually, he approached the middle-class couple with a plan to invest in a small consignment of dope that he had arranged via one of his old comrades in warehouse theft. After Alec and Delia shook hands with Benny, he invested their money and within just a few weeks the profit was split three ways. Benny, now clean-shaven and alert, exuded confidence. If he could have found a suit featuring trousers with an elasticated waist he would have been more Cary Grant and less Del Trotter.

Alec and Delia jumped at the chance to make a further investment in a part-load of dope that this time required them to find several thousand pounds. However, the news that Benny was once again earning had quickly spread and creditors were congregating around his stool in The City anticipating getting paid. These creditors included the pub's landlord who had loaned Benny money that had come straight back over the bar and Ernie, a milkman who had loaned Benny hundreds of pounds and now anticipated a pay-out. Then Benny went missing.

Rumour was rife in The City. From being holed up in his girlfriend's spare bedroom on the other side of the square to absconding to Spain, theories abounded on Benny's whereabouts. He returned a fortnight later to an embarrassed silence and Delia and Alec put their heads down, kept quiet and carried on drinking. Eventually, Benny hinted that payment was imminent but when nobody had been paid after three months of bluffing, Benny again went absent without leave, this time for three weeks.

When he returned to The City there was now an

uncharacteristic intensity. He claimed to have been in hospital with a serious intestinal complaint, which unfortunately differed significantly from the accounts given by members of his family, who had cited business abroad and varicose veins as reasons for his absence. At this point, some people clearly expected to get paid, while others were quietly speculating on how Benny would bring the impasse to a conclusion.

But where was this lorryload of drugs that Delia and Alec had forked out their savings for?

A JOINT ENTERPRISE

According to Benny, the drugs were in a 22-foot container in an Essex lorry park. There was no need to worry: 'We'll all make plenty of money.' Four weeks later, Benny announced that the container was under police surveillance and from now on he kept things enticingly vague. The container was probably in Tilbury but he could not be sure; he thought that the drugs were mixed with boxes of sweets or clothes or shoes but again, he could not be certain. He was, after all, a fellow victim and had no inside information. Delia and Alec were not the only investors in Benny's scheme and, while a few people naively persisted in waiting for the police to cease their operation and some walked away disappointed, most of Benny's creditors disengaged from the fantasy with some relief, feeling no compunction to confront Benny, which meant that he had succeeded in writing off all of his debts while simultaneously enhancing his status. For he was no longer a mere neighbourhood ducker and diver but an entrepreneur with serious connections in the world of drug importation; while this time fortune had not been kind, he was back in business. A sense of normality returned to The City Arms when Ernie was hit by Benny for another £25.

Delia and Alec counted themselves as unlucky: if the police had not been so efficient they would have received a substantial chunk of money. Although they became less frequent visitors to The City Arms, it emerged much later that they had recouped some of their losses by borrowing from some of their friends, who also swallowed their losses when the rumour of police involvement dropped into their stripped-pine lives. But Delia and Alec had enjoyed the buzz of transgression with little of the risk and there had been some great nights with Benny. The ladderless and bereft of tool maintained a stoic silence and the petty investors dreamt of what might have been if not for predatory cops lurking in Tilbury. By escalating the situation to the level of drug importation and involving undercover police and organised crime, Benny had called his investors' and creditors' bluff while presenting himself as someone with contacts in high places.

In the wonderful world of skulduggery, there are no official versions of events, no checking news broadcasts or newsfeeds and gossip and rumour fill the gaps in knowledge. The container under surveillance proved to be a very welcome rumour among a community of greedy, risk-averse individuals who embraced the story as a way of resolving the situation without any grief. Straight people do not like risk, that is why they are straight people.

Chapter 14

BOUNCERS: MINDING THE DOORS OF DECEPTION

'There's a big bouncer round now who's on all the doors . . . He's bigger than the police in our area, what he says goes.'

OFFENDER INTERVIEW, MALE, 16-YEAR SENTENCE IMPORTATION OF COCAINE

FRIDAY NIGHT AND SUNDAY MORNING

The old industrial way of life, with its mills, factories, mines and docks, had a strict rhythm and routine where the workforce grafted all week and went out at the weekends. But when the manufacturing base disappeared, so did the old way of life, and shops were relocated to out-of-town malls and city centres emptied out of any signs of life, especially after dark. This decline created an economic crisis which prompted British towns and cities to actively pursue forms of city-centre regeneration, and the night-time economy looked like the answer.

In the 1980s, Prime Minister Thatcher broke the brewers'

monopoly, ensured that tax breaks were offered to businesses and made it possible for redundant buildings to be converted into bars and clubs – all measures designed to boost the alcohol-based leisure industry. This policy was followed up in the late 1990s by Prime Minister Tony Blair, who had been mightily impressed with the fact that during his summer vacation, he could enjoy a late-night coffee and brandy sitting in a peaceful village square in Tuscany as smiling local families promenaded and elderly widows walked their dogs. The mistake was in trying to bring this idyllic scene to the cold, wet, pissed-up streets of the UK. Licensing laws were liberalised and the new seven nights a week night-time economy became a major generator of jobs in bars, fast-food outlets, taxi firms and much more.

But before Blair attempted to make his fantasy come to life, cheap Balearic holidays had already given British youth a taste of a different kind of hedonism and on their return home from two weeks in the sun they began to demand more from a good night out. While community pubs outside of city centres were closing down at an alarming rate, venues that mimicked the Balearic experience began to pop up in British city centres, which after dark became vibrant zones that were almost exclusively for the young. Like their Mediterranean equivalents, these new venues were generally much larger than the cosy Victorian pubs enjoyed by generations of British drinkers and the atmosphere of an Ibizan nightspot was recreated in empty shops, churches and schools.

However, alcohol remained the major drug of choice and the vast numbers of young people who flocked into the new night-time economies were drinking much more than their parents had. Violence increased, the police were overwhelmed and it was at this point that bouncers started to decorate our high-street boozers. For instance, by the early 2000s, Manchester city centre was attracting an average of 130,000 people on Friday and Saturday evenings – approximately 40 police officers were on duty along with an estimated 1,000 bouncers. Similar comparisons can be drawn in towns and cities throughout the UK. For example, Nottingham city centre, which regularly attracted 30,000 weekend night-time visitors, was 'policed' by over 400 bouncers but only 15 police officers at most.

The creation of the modern night-time economy was an enormous boost for criminal entrepreneurs; while villains had always craved a slice of nightlife, this was different. With entire towns and cities reliant on drink and drugs, muscle was now in high demand and those who supplied it saw doors to both legitimate and criminal opportunities kicked wide open.

Eric, a bodybuilder and businessman, explained how his close friend, a notoriously successful 'security consultant', drummed up trade.

'It worked like this. Jackie would walk in a pub, any pub, and speak to the owner saying words to the effect of, "This is a rough pub that looks like it needs doormen to keep out the wankers." If the owner refused this generous offer, then coincidentally, some of these "wankers" would fight in the pub that very night. The next day, Jackie would survey the damage, which was always high, and once again offer his services. The ratio of closed deals he got on the second visit was very high.'

Together with non-interference pacts with other bouncer firms, it became possible to create a monopoly of violence. Eric continued:

> 'Jackie played a pivotal role. If the "Smiths", "Jones" or "Browns" [organised crime families] or whoever wanted to do business, he had to approve it first. The Smiths were moving in on a number of doors that Jackie had no interest in on a first-hand basis. The club was held[25] by a sole entrepreneur who would not let the Smiths take control of the club, so they hired Jackie to teach him a lesson [which] consisted of Jackie beating him to within an inch of his life. The Smiths got the club and Jackie's service fee was 15 per cent, which reliable estimates put at around £20,000 a year. This is only one of the 30 or so clubs and pubs that Jackie had an interest in.'

However, as Ricky, who ran a security company, explained, these new opportunities also required diplomatic skills, and the ability to negotiate.

> 'There's certain areas and there's certain gangs, you cannot just put some person in there who's a doorman, you're going to have to get a member of a gang, who people recognise and they know who he belongs to. So what I would do in that area, I would put in the doormen from that gang in that area. That way they'll have a bit of respect and I can do my job.'

---

25 The door was run.

The young package-tour punters brought back something else from Ibiza, something that made the Balearic vibe possible: ecstasy. Then, as the quasi-religious fervour associated with the first wave of ecstasy use faded, Es became just one component of the cocktail of drugs that flowed through the night-time economy and the drug dealer became integral to the messy, chaotic mob looking to cash in on the seven-day weekend. Despite the hippie-like philosophy of many of its youthful punters, even the British illegal rave scene, which succeeded in making bundles of money while bypassing the high street entirely, required security. Whether it was played out in redundant factories or in fields off the M25, this new economy offered opportunities for door staff that involved collaboration with dealers. Then, when the government succeeded in putting the illegal events out of business, a legal, heavily diluted version of rave culture took over the high street, and the commercial competition became violent. Dealer Jason recalled:

'Then there was that shooting at the place in Surrey. Then it started to change, you could feel it was different. The people I was with, they just faded out of it and I was turning up and the new people, it was guns, baseball bats. Security, but if you weren't working with them they just rob you, I tell you. Understand me, a couple of times they tax me of everything I have right in the car park. There was some bad lickings at these places. I lost a lot of money and things started to go to the fucking wall for me.'

ON THE DOOR

Going back as far as the Sabinis and beyond, villains have always seen door control as a way of making both money and reputations, and increasingly through the expansion of the night-time economy criminal firms were linked with door supervision. This became more pronounced after acid house arrived in the late 1980s: in order to control the rapidly expanding trade in amphetamines and ecstasy, running the doors of pubs and clubs that targeted the youth market made a lot of economic sense. Although some bouncers sold drugs inside the venue, the norm was for door staff to 'license' dealers and provide security for them. In some venues, door staff wholesaled the drug to these dealers, while at others, the dealers were directly employed by the door staff team. If police pressure mounted, the firm would vigorously enforce a no-drug policy, after first licensing a dealer to operate from a local pub. Anyone entering the club had to consume the drug before entry, and if they required topping up, the firm would usually enjoy a discrete monopoly inside the venue thanks to unofficial security staff such as Taff, who explained, 'They want the stuff [drugs]; it's going in the place anyway, so all you can do is make it right for the kids who want to do it in peace.'

Unauthorised dealers risked having their stock confiscated and resold, and worse. Steve, an experienced bouncer, described the informal policing methods used in one venue.

'Anybody that sells drugs in their club will get the shit kicked out of them, they'll be lucky if they're half alive when they leave the place, they'll have everything taken off them – even their shoes. They'll have a serious beating, be dumped in some alley, and basically that's a warning, you don't come back. That happens all over the place. Them lads are bad bastards, you fuck about in some places you're going to be in big lumber, big, big lumber.'

However, as head doorman Frank North explained, unless your firm were willing to start a war, confiscating the drugs found on an 'unlicensed' dealer could be a big mistake:

'If you've got a runner in here and he's selling, I can guarantee he won't get beaten up by my doormen or have stuff taken off him by my doormen. I've had them turn up outside my clubs, five or six with shooters and everything. They've told us, "You've took the gear." "Aint took no gear, get the little shit in here now." So they bring him in. "Right, who's took the fucking gear, me?" "No, it weren't you." "Well, who was it?" I'll bring me doormen down, this was all who was working that night. "If I was you, I'd take this fucking cunt and throw him under a bus." A lot of people make mistakes by taking the drugs off them and then they get repercussions because [the dealers] want their money back; they've laid out say £5,000 and that's a £15,000 profit. You just don't know who you're dealing with.'

All over the country, incidents of extreme violence linked to security and the drug trade, and the intimidation of licensees and clubland entrepreneurs, became common. The demand for illegal drugs saw a stampede of players who had previously regarded the drug trade as a peripheral concern, and various combinations of robbers, serious gangsters, street gangs, football hooligans and others, fighting to get their noses in the trough, as law-abiding bouncers found themselves swept away by violent predators.

Darren explained the necessity for criminal alliances in such an environment: 'Let's face it, you've got to have people like that [with criminal connections]. Think about it: you're stood at the door and a group of blokes comes up and one pulls a pistol out, one pulls a machete out, one pulls a baseball bat out. You're put on the spot, the police aren't there, what are you gonna do? Say, "Sorry, mate, you've got trainers on, you're not comin' in"?'

Licensees and their staff were put under intense pressure. Journalist Matthew Collin writing about Manchester's night-life recalls: 'The staff were scared, the gangs would demand champagne and sandwiches; no one dared refuse. They'd want their people at the door, all their people in for free, to order drinks and not pay for them, and to openly sell drugs.' Manchester's street gangs regarded certain venues as extensions of their own territory and out-of-town security was dealt with especially harshly.

In order to work the doors successfully, it became increasingly important to be connected to local gangsters, although even when alliances were made, or accepted as inevitable, it didn't guarantee the business would be protected. As the owner of Manchester's iconic Hacienda, Tony Wilson, explained: 'In one 12-month period, the Hacienda spent £374,000 on "protection". Forget drug-dealing, that's what the gangs were *really* doing. Running protection rackets, taxing us – which would have been fine if they actually *had* protected us, instead of using our club as a shooting gallery!'

The inevitability of various levels of criminality in a legal venue that is reliant upon illegal drugs for its commercial viability is the reality for doorstaff, as Doorman Charlie explained:

'If you got a door which is very, very lucrative then it will be a drug-driven thing. People are either buyers or sellers, and you can't work such a door without being involved. You make your mind up whose market it is and you keep out the opposition. Money? If I am working five nights a week and putting myself on offer for whoever is placing their dealers inside, then it's hard to think of me not getting £750 a week. With subcontracting, which does work if you are shrewd, then many times that. A couple of us will have one of our own [dealers] inside and make out it's one of the official firm whose got the place. If I take too much of the trade then people are gonna get mightily pissed off, and I will be confronted with a degree of grief. First you get taken off the door as a bit of notice that you have been sussed by the head doorman, who is responsible for keeping everybody sweet, but if you are still in business for yourself, well, they are not going to slap somebody like me cos I might slap back. It is serious or it's nothing.'

Even in venues without a significant drug trade, where the bouncers were intent on providing a safe environment for drinking alcohol, the spectre of organised violence became a serious problem. Dougie worked as a bouncer for seven years. He stands six feet seven inches tall and weighs around nineteen stones. He explained the constantly evolving complexity in the venue where he worked, particularly in relation to the door staff's attempts to retain control:

'It's not really a drugs place, there's probably dealing going on, but just between friends and that, nothing organised, nothing major. You sometimes get problems from drug dealers, not with drugs, but just coming into the place thinking they can do this and that. Les once barred this kid, he's just a kid, tries to get in and he isn't dressed right, so all the shite starts coming out, so Les says, "Look, you're barred don't come back." The next day [Les] gets a call from the manager, wants him to come in. He turns up and this kid is sitting there with this bloke who's a bit known and it's like, "This is my fella, I want you to apologise." You know, the lad's just doing his job and now he's got to apologise to this little prick. Rightly enough, he says, "I want a couple of days," and the bloke says, "You've got 48 hours or there's going to be trouble." You can't just say you're sorry in a situation like that. I say, "If you apologise to that little fucker, I'll fill you in myself." So rightly enough he says, "No apology. He's barred." We get a few tasty faces in the place the next couple of nights and it's all for fuck all. Nothing happens. That's the kind of thing you have to deal with sometimes and people don't appreciate that side of things. I mean, he's done the right thing. Before you know it you're apologising to everyone and the club's not your own.'

In many cases, venues featuring a significant drug market were often regarded as less problematic than venues based around the consumption of alcohol. Although local criminal networks seeking to control the trade in drugs within the venue brought complicated politics and the threat of occasional violence, from the bouncers' point of view, at least the risk of customers punching each other's lights out was greatly reduced. As Charlie put it, 'All in all, I get paid a lot of money to keep things sweet and there is a lot less actual fighting [in drug-based dance venues] than in the usual old places with pissed punters wanting to whack you.'

The main problems tended to arise when a new group decided to make a challenge for the lucrative control of the door. Again, Charlie explained:

'Other firms' dealers we always treat well and just don't let them in. But you might get a firm work itself up between a little group of security who are running their own thing. Then the proper firm with the contract have to deal with it and you might get most of [security] sacked. But if they come back the next night and say, "We are the new door," then management just might have to swallow it and sack the remains of the old firm. Or at a push you might get two firms running the door, letting their own people [dealers] in and keeping the others out. Or the other thing is that the door breaks down and everybody has got their own dealer in and it's chaos, nobody can control it, so the gaff gets battles and the scream goes up and gets shut down. That's no good, it's dangerous, and nobody makes any money. That's why controlling the door is so important.'

In June 1990, Manchester's Thunderdome was forced to close after masked men brandishing shotguns knee-capped three of the club's door staff in full view of more than 300 people. After this incident, episodes of extreme violence, including murder, pock-marked Manchester's night-time economy over the next decade, as gangs moved from housing estates into the city centre and fought for control of the doors.

Alliances between legitimate businesses and criminal firms, while often necessary, could lead to commercial disaster and major security companies were forced out of lucrative regional marketplaces as a result of their unwillingness to subcontract to organised crime. For instance, when a nationally known nightspot re-opened after a spell of closure, the security company that had been contracted to control the door, in an attempt to avoid any friction, contacted the local criminal firms to inform them that they were taking over. The head of this company told me that this was vital and communications were put out to the effect that, 'You are welcome, but please play by the rules and control your henchmen and hangers-on.'

All seemed well and the pre-eminent local crime group was obliging. But problems soon developed. The head of the company explained that the city's other gangs were not as well structured, and control, therefore, 'not as tight'. After two weeks, a doorman attempted to search someone who was not normally searched at the entrance to the club. Fifteen minutes later, a car with blacked-out windows pulled up and a man wearing a balaclava and brandishing a hand gun at the doormen uttered, 'Do you know where you are? Don't fuck about here.' The company stopped working at the club and the venue was closed.

In some towns, this violent entrepreneurship spread to

restaurants, take-aways and clothes shops, as well as to venues beyond the bright lights of the city centre. Its influence was as extensive as an individual's or group's reputation, sometimes requiring periodic visits or demonstrations of power, but usually word of mouth sufficed. As this licensee of an out-of-town pub explained:

'I already knew Jimmy for a few years and he's a mate of mine. I knew he did the doors over at some of the pubs in town so I just asked him to call in. I picked a time when I knew some of the local lads would be in and he comes in and has a Coke. We talk for about five minutes and you can hear them go quiet then start talking about him. After a few minutes, he just walked over and said "all right" to them, and that he was working there now. They didn't say a fucking word. They knew who he was, obviously, everyone knows Jimmy, it's not like you can miss him. And that's it. He gave me his mobile number to phone if there's any bother and he comes in every now and then, just has a quick drink and leaves. With someone like Jimmy doing that, I don't need a bouncer on at all really. I'm still here all the time and I keep a pickaxe handle behind the bar.'

Local councils facing economic decline did manage to bring investment, jobs and vibrancy to run-down city centres. However, metropolitan dreamers such as Tony Blair did not quite achieve a continental-style 'cafe society'; indeed, Manchester DJ and writer Dave Haslam cited one local as saying, 'It's certainly very continental out there, but less like

Paris, more like the Somme.' Profitable order was imposed on this violent and chaotic frontline by firms of bouncers working to very different rules from traditional pub or music venues.

HOOLIGAN INSTINCTS: THE PEOPLE'S GAME

As the night-time economy evolved, the demand for security placed a high premium on muscle backed by local reputation, and when rave culture's early entrepreneurs required a way of policing these highly lucrative events – and protecting the sacks full of cash that they were collecting – they often looked to the old neighbourhoods. Many of the key players came from the generation who were flocking into the night-time economy as well as both the legal and illegal raves. Enterprise culture proved to be a seductive adventure for so many young people growing up during this era and, driven by a love of dance music and an even greater love of a pound note, football hooligans – playwright Al Hunter's '1980's Thatcher's eagles' – became central to rave culture and the night-time economy. The rise of this economy coincided with the peak of hooligan firms who formed tightly knit networks of trust that had been tested both home and away. What is more, they used ecstasy, understood the culture and were money hungry.

By the end of the 1980s, the peak years of hooliganism were over and the gentrification of British football, which had once been the property of the working classes, was underway. Most of the senior members of these now infamous groups of hooligans were in their mid- to late twenties and they were not dopes. According to event promoter Joe Wieczorek, 'The same geezers who would be standing across the road, throwing bricks and having silly fights over football, had realised there was no money in football.' However, the new security market, as another ex-hooligan Carlton Leach explained, was another matter. 'I'd already got a reputation as a hard case West Ham supporter and they knew I could handle myself. Fancy it? I took to it like a duck to water.'

More than mere muscle, these young men were sufficiently savvy to lock into the contemporary youth market, as academic Kenny Monrose explained: 'Most of these white working-class boys started moving around with blacks and the music/rave thing started. Blacks did illegal raves – blues, [parties], shebeens – for years cos they couldn't get legal premises to hire. Empty flats would be used, set your own bar up, five quid to get in, and make a bomb. These "illegal" dos had flyers printed and were advertised on black pirate radio.'

Soon entrepreneurial football firms were mimicking radio stations such as the Dread Broadcasting Corporation, generating publicity for their own illegal music events and directing ravers to events. Across the country, nascent entrepreneurs, including members of football firms, showed remarkable imagination and enterprise in driving this new business. Though for others, the drug trade, despite the risks involved, remained their focus.

RONNIE AND TERRY

Ronnie and Terry had been good friends since their schooldays on a run-down council estate in the Midlands. As supporters of their local football team they enjoyed fearsome local reputations, and via these football-based reputations they formed the hub of a small network importing ecstasy, amphetamine and occasionally cannabis from Holland, supplying a network of dealers in two nearby cities. The group had two regular Dutch suppliers: one who arranged for a lorry to be driven to a nominated town from where the drugs were collected and taken to their base, while in the second case, couriers would be sent to collect the drugs from Holland and bring them back to England. They maintained their hooligan connections and although violence was rare, it was always a distinct possibility if someone stepped out of line or failed to deliver on debts. Ronnie and Terry were still regularly involved in fights in pubs, unrelated to drugs, which helped to maintain their reputations originally gained through fighting rival football supporters.

DANCING IN THE DARK

During the nineties, as club owners and promoters cashed in on rave culture, almost every provincial town, all over the UK, boasted legal 'rave nights'. Viv and Taff's firm were just one of many hooligan-based firms recruited to provide an informal backup to the local bodybuilders and rugby players who normally ran the door.

In 1993, a dance/acid house club in a small provincial town had been running for several months using local security staff when the local newspaper reported that fights and drug-dealing were routine occurrences. In response, a firm was invited by those running the event to provide additional, albeit low-key security.

On one particular night, two members of that firm, Taff and Viv, had done their job, which meant slinging a young man, who had the temerity to try to re-enter the club with a portion of fish and chips, down the steps of what had once been a cinema to rest motionless among the residue of fast-food meals, cigarette stubs and various other messy remnants of just another Saturday night. When the police arrived, Taff and Viv retreated to a backroom inside the club. The police spoke to the two official bouncers, who had big suits, big necks but no memory of seeing the now fully conscious youth being thrown unceremoniously down the steps by their unofficial colleagues. The two PCs, one with a military campaign medal ribbon on his uniform jacket, were easily convinced that there had been a minor scuffle between local youths, routine stuff, and nothing to do with the club. 'Good as gold, must be the drugs that keep them quiet.'

Viv and Taff explained their role at the venue:

Viv: They don't even come on the pull most of them, so they don't have rows about who's going with who. So it's on the door that's where the work is. Make sure you don't get drunks, beer monsters going to naus it all up.

Taff: Then its 'Sorry, lads, just a kids' night.' You let the suits[26] do it first cos it's their number. 'Try down the road, half price tonight. There's a cab over there.'

Viv: We just sort of lurk a bit and gradually join in the talk. And it works cos we don't wear suits and as they keep coming and we join in they know it's getting more serious. If a bouncer goes down then they all want to get a kick in. If there's a bunch for a night out, say 20 or 40 and they're on a coach, if there's a ruck they all want to say they give the bouncer one.

---

26 Official bouncers.

Viv: He'd been inside got sorted, been dancing for hours, what's he want fish and fucking chips for?

Taff: Bottom line on this is 'you ain't coming back in with them [fish and chips]'. He got silly.

Viv: Wankers like him bad for business.

Drugs were OK, but fish and chips were beyond the pale.

ZAMMO

Imagination and the willingness to diversify were key features of a new wave of broken-nosed entrepreneurs and many of these ex-hooligans soon expanded from unofficial door duties to supplying the requisite drugs both in and around the venues. From there, they could then rapidly diversify into the profitable world of wholesale. Zammo's story puts the ecstasy era in perspective.

'I was in a club in Surrey, I had gone down there to see some girl I met on holiday, it never worked out, but I ended up in this club and there was something I didn't quite get, cos there was all these blokes dancing with each other. All night really giving it some, sweating away like I never seen before. I had heard about Es, not a lot but it was about. I never knew about drugs, I never knew anyone who did it. But after that night I started to see it more and more, different sort of a night out.'

Zammo had been watching his local football team since he was 11, and by the age of 14 was fighting for the team home and away.

> 'When I was 17 or 18, some of the hard core what I was on the edge of got the security gig for some DJ working a rave. Me and my pal Dave, we hooked on to this little mob, to be honest cos they were picking off people inside and robbing them, including the drugs – selling them on like to the others. Matter of time before we tried it [Es]. Changed me life, to be fair, never looked back. Music, everything.'

Zammo stopped robbing and worked with his hoolie pals providing Es to punters across the south-east of England. While more than capable of looking after himself, Zammo worked under the umbrella of his fellow hooligans and managed to avoid excessive violence, while simultaneously enjoying the remarkable way of life that sprung up around late eighties/early nineties rave culture.

> 'Best time of my life. I had money, bundles of it, I knew all the promoters and DJs, and there was a lot of sex, a lot of sex. We were still going to football and you did see faces from other teams in clubs and that. But it never went off over the football. It was money what did it. People were running doors on the strength of our name, getting the dough on the door, ripping off and hurting people. They were getting slung out by other firms who were then putting it about that they had slung us off the doors. So it started to go off, which was a shame, really.'

While a combination of gangsters and riot police eventually drained the romantic mysticism out of the ecstasy business, it had introduced Zammo to the wonderful world of the entrepreneur. So, in league with an event promoter, he invested in importing product from Holland. But after 'just a couple' of trips he lost a 'lot of money, don't even want to talk about it'. But Zammo had had a taste and, while sticking with an increasingly commercialised rave scene through the nineties, he also embarked on a 30-year adventure in entrepreneurship that encompassed a wide range of 'opportunities' from property development to the manufacture and distribution of high quality counterfeit menswear: 'I had the computer discs for everything from Lacoste to Prada. I sourced the materials and the buttons and had them made up by a friend who had access to his family business. Then, through contacts of my ex, I placed them all over, into legit shops in the high street, into duty free, some people were knocking them out on the internet, whatever.'

For some hooligans, access to the night-time economy opened up new opportunities and they remain commercially relevant to this day in fields remote from the unforgiving world of door security. They have made their mark on the music business, publishing, the film industry, the building and property industries, and a whole range of disparate enterprises. The bonds and connections that evolved around football hooliganism served as an introduction to legal and illegal security work, debt collection, extortion and niches at every level of the drug trade, as well as numerous scams and swindles. For Zammo, the snide shirt business became 'too much like hard work for the money' and he sold the computer programs before moving on to a legitimate home improvements franchise. The last I heard, Zammo was playing a lot of tennis.

The night-time economy – the marketplace in which dance drugs were traded – had become exceptionally valuable and needed a form of protection that was nuanced and highly specialised. Consequently, bouncers became a powerful form of local control that enabled organised crime to become firmly embedded in the infrastructure of British society in a way that the old blaggers, bandits and residents of The City Arms could only have dreamt of. But it was not only the usual suspects – violent young men with reputations to build and nurture – who were able to make money from this new market; new players with different skill sets were also keen to cash in.

Chapter 15

PEOPLE WHO NEED PEOPLE: DEALING IN THE NIGHT-TIME ECONOMY

'Best time for me without a doubt. I was working with all the top people. A lot had been in Ibiza and we knew each other, so when it came to setting up here it was easy, all anybody wanted was to have a good time. It was a time when there was no worries, and that was the E. Not only that, but people wanted to have a party, and it was a good time not just for the money, but the people.'

DEALER JASON

WHAT FRIENDS ARE FOR

Dealers in the night-time economy do not require a criminal apprenticeship or a reputation for stoic reliability proven by an extensive prison record. Individuals could fast track from clubber to serious drugs broker of 'dance drugs': ecstasy, amphetamine and cocaine powder. Friendship networks provided the most likely kickstart for a career in this area and with no prior experience of dealing, within the space of a few months, an individual could find themselves supplying a network of retailers and club dealers, yielding a profit of several thousand pounds per week.

Twenty-one-year-old Leon explained how he began dealing casually to friends during an interview in prison where he was serving a sentence for dealing ecstasy. 'It's just friends that know friends, isn't it? I could say I've sold to over, like, 300 people, but they may go and sell it over to somebody else. I didn't run it like a business, not really, it's just a friend of mine knows someone, he says, "He can sort you out," and it goes from there.' One young woman single-handedly operated a club-based business selling 1,000 ecstasy tablets and a quarter to half a kilogram of amphetamine per week. She described her function in the market as a service to others: 'It's just friends, and friends of friends, really. I'd buy the drugs I knew they would want – Es, whizz, a bit of coke, weed, what have you – people would phone in their orders for themselves and their friends, and I'd deliver before the weekend. It was simple as that. I was doing them a service. I was the go-between.'

Paul was a keen clubber in his mid-20s who, along with his friends, bought some ecstasy tablets that proved to be duds and wondered whether he could buy some of better quality outside the club scene. Paul found that he could and so bought a few for his friends. 'It just went on from there. You know, then their friends want, and their friends want and then it's just escalated, and eventually you've got other people who want to start dealing and then dealers buy from you, and it's a sky rocket before you even know it. I didn't push drugs. I didn't push drugs at all. I did a social thing for friends, and then it just got bigger.' However, for Paul, like many dance-based dealers, some drugs are beyond the pale.

'I wouldn't deal in crack, and I wouldn't deal in heroin because those are dirty drugs. They're scum drugs. You don't see people who are ravers going out and mugging people so they can get a pill for the weekend. And you see people doing crack, heroin, mugging people just so they can get drugs. I disagree with crack and heroin.'

Within a matter of months, Paul was a substantial middleman dealer, selling 2,000–3,000 ecstasy tablets per week, plus a few ounces of powdered cocaine and amphetamine, and a couple of kilos of cannabis to club-based retailers. He worked on his own, shopping for stock at the start of each week, taking orders mid-week and delivering before the weekend.

Connections to the club scene were highly valued, even at the upper end of the E business.

ALBERT: ECSTASY IMPORTATION AND DISTRIBUTION NETWORK

A Yorkshire-based club owner, Albert, was importing 20,000 to 30,000 ecstasy tablets per week, with a more limited business in cannabis and cocaine. His local distribution was handled by two employees, while known customers would travel from Glasgow and Liverpool to buy drugs on a credit basis. The financial side of these transactions was always handled by Albert but after he lost his driving licence, an old friend started working for the firm, driving to Glasgow and Liverpool to collect money which was due one week after the drugs had been received. In addition to these big customers, Albert's firm traded locally to about a dozen smaller customers, and if he could obtain one kilo of cocaine per week at the right price and quality, he could make a further £20,000 profit with minimal additional overheads.

Indeed, in the new century, cocaine powder had started to lose its exclusive cachet, becoming an increasingly common ingredient to a good night out. Further, despite the stigma often associated with its trade, for some members of the clubbing fraternity heroin had also become an essential part of a long weekend.

COME DOWN HENRY: OUNCE-BROKER IN HEROIN AND COCAINE

Henry was a Midlands-based media consultant who also ran a profitable drugs business. When still in his twenties, he had started off just selling to friends but experienced the same phenomenon that others reported of a steep growth in business once word got around. He had first used heroin to relax and 'come down' after a weekend clubbing but found that he started smoking more and more, and his drug-dealing grew proportionately.

Henry travelled weekly to London to buy cocaine from people whom he knew well and heroin from 'very wealthy drug dealers' in Merseyside, who were 'one step, maybe two down from the people who were bringing it into the country'. Henry estimated that his London-based suppliers were doing between six to ten deals of the same size as his own, amounting to roughly three kilos of cocaine, per week. His Liverpool heroin suppliers, who he had met through a friend who had given him a 'reference' as a reliable man, were strictly 'hands off' and did not use drugs. He would usually meet their courier halfway or arrange for the parcel to be delivered to him. He guessed they were selling at least ten kilos of heroin a week.

Henry never tampered with the drugs, since he was dealing

mainly to a network of friends. His typical heroin customers bought half an ounce and ounce amounts upwards and his cocaine customers bought quarter-ounces upwards. 'Towards the end [before he was arrested], it mostly went in biggish amounts to a few friends; who they sold to it was, you know, their business. I suppose it was sort of people-who-knew-people.' He contrasted this with dealers who operate a network: 'I didn't so much have people distributing for me, like some people have a little network, they have people who do jobs for them. But I was pretty much my own person.'

DEALING DELIRIUM

While the lure of the good life has always existed as an alternative to nine-to-five wage slavery, it was seldom as seductively tangible as during the ecstasy era. Rather than putting in the hard graft and coming up through petty crime, these lawbreakers quite literally turned a weekend pastime into a lucrative enterprise. However, the good times that revolved around music and hedonism somewhat inevitably morphed into a money-rich and sleaze-ripe market for cocaine.

Of course, not all villains of the modern era were focused upon youthful fantasy; others had a grittier view of drugs and the dirty business of life. For some, the old cliché about prison as a 'university of crime' remained valid. For instance, a young man from a small town in Wales was imprisoned in the early 1990s on a charge of possession with intent to supply ecstasy. While inside, he struck up a friendship with two men who were using heroin. He then developed a heroin habit and started dealing in prison. Alerted to the profitability of the drug, and with the need to fund his habit upon his release, his prison friends provided a contact with an associate in the East Midlands who gave him credit and 'sorted him out' with his personal heroin supply. From this start, he built up a heroin distribution network around his home town in Wales, selling ounces and multi-ounce deals to six or seven customers who were closer to the retail trade, maintaining his original supplier in the East Midlands.

However, not all dealers were users and increasingly, men with a traditional commercial approach entered the marketplace unencumbered either by addiction or the mystique of drug culture. For instance, a man who arranged cannabis and ecstasy imports from Holland on behalf of other people described his operation in the following terms:

> 'There was three parties involved: the man who was actually prepared to bring it through the docks – the driver – then we had the guy who was actually purchasing it – the recipient – and me in the middle. My being the middleman, obviously I didn't want the two parties to meet, because once they met that left me nowhere. Of course, I never met the actual buyer. I always met someone else on his behalf, another middleman if you like.'

NETWORKING GREG

While the intention to have a good time was never far away, there were always people with an innate talent for making money who found themselves Marbella-bound by virtue of a combination of sociability and an ability to turn a five-pound note.

Greg was a self-employed fabric trader who earned an 'above average income'. Although he was a non-drug user, he did socialise with a group of middle-class friends who took cocaine at weekends. When their supplier let them down, Greg remembered somebody who he had once met at a party, made a phone call and purchased two ounces of cocaine. Once this supplier explained how much profit could be made on a kilo of cocaine, Greg, encouraged by his enthusiastic girlfriend, commenced dealing.

He purchased a kilo of cocaine from the original supplier and sold ounces to 12 of his close friends; he had assumed the kilo would last for three months but he sold out in six weeks. He then purchased five kilos and from then on purchased ten kilos per month. By selling larger quantities to his friends, he created fresh dealing networks as they in turn were selling to friends, work colleagues and others within their circle. Although Greg continued to work in his legitimate business, he was soon purchasing 50 kilos four times a year. He had started with 12 customers and six months later, he had 200, reporting a threefold increase in demand over the Christmas and New Year party season. After several months of successful dealing, Greg joined the party and became a cocaine user.

The ease with which those wishing to dip their beaks into the drug business attracted a highly diverse crowd. For instance, in addition to middle-class cocaine users, former prisoners who developed a heroin addiction inside and young adults trying to get their friends a few pills for the weekend, I heard about a group of car dealers with no notable criminal backgrounds who pooled their resources and invested £30,000 in a one-off importation of amphetamine. To the best of my knowledge, they managed to restrain themselves – for them, this truly was a 'one-off deal' – and afterwards returned exclusively to their legal activity of knocking out barely road-worthy second-hand family saloons. However, drug use certainly equipped many individuals with an entry-level knowledge of the market, and buying and selling to friends enabled individuals to experiment with prices, contacts and suppliers before moving on to greater things, and bigger money.

Chapter 16

DEALING WITH REALITY: WORK, FAMILY, AND FANTASY

'It was a town of red brick, or of brick that would have
been red if the smoke and ashes had allowed it; but as
matters stood it was a town of unnatural red and black
like the painted face of a savage.'

CHARLES DICKENS, HARD TIMES

Despite of the global reach of the drug trade, organised crime
in Britain remains predominantly local, embedded in the
neighbourhood or 'manor' and staffed by men who often
grew up together on the same streets. In many ways, this is
an adaption of the old 'family firm' that made its money on
theft, robbery and extortion, but is far more businesslike. For
instance, Frank and Alf had known each other since they were
children, went to the same school together and played in the
same football team.

A BUSY LIFE

Having previously worked in the building trade, Alf started working for Frank when he was unemployed and doing odd jobs. He had heard rumours regarding Frank's source of income and by the time he was offered a job, Alf was also aware of the risks involved, as the man he was replacing had been arrested with £150,000 worth of drugs. The basis of Alf's work as a 'runner' was to collect and deliver drugs on Frank's instructions. Many of his customers were regulars.

For example, Alf supplied a retail-level heroin dealer who bought an ounce every one or two days. Another dealer received one ounce daily and also tested samples of heroin for Frank. One regular customer was a man who took four to five kilos of cannabis every couple of weeks plus 2,000 ecstasy tablets, while 'Salford Lennie' regularly received a few thousand ecstasy tablets. Alf usually met these customers in pub car parks or in the car parks of supermarkets or restaurants such as the Little Chef or Pizza Hut. A man called Fred took one kilo of amphetamine base every two weeks and Alf also delivered to Frank's cousin who bought ounces of heroin on a regular basis. Another man called Jay received 12 nine-ounce bars of cannabis every two weeks and Alf also used to meet Midlands-based Kaye in a pub car park every fortnight, supplying him with three to four kilos of cannabis bush and 1,000 ecstasy tablets.

In addition to these regular customers, there were times when Alf dealt with people who were unknown to him. On one of his earliest assignments, Alf met two men in a red saloon car at a designated lay-by and handed over a kilo of amphetamine paste; a few days later, he met a man in a white estate car and passed over four nine-ounce bars of cannabis.

On another occasion, he met a 'lad' from London with a 'cockney' accent who was supplied with 5,000 ecstasy tablets. Alf delivered 1,250 ecstasy tablets to a man whom he met at the Little Chef and who had a 'Scouse' accent. For these customers, 'There was never a set pattern to when I picked up or delivered.'

Alf would also collect drugs which he would sometimes deliver to Frank's or take home for storage. Although Frank had other associates, Alf was Frank's main distributor and he also sometimes acted as an intermediary with suppliers. For example, Sim regularly supplied ten kilos of amphetamine base to Frank, which Alf collected on his behalf, and which came in 2.5 kilo packets 'shaped like rugby balls and wrapped in tape'. Alf would deliver drugs and money to the electrical shop owned by Top, another regular associate of Frank's

A third associate was Frank's enforcer Vin, a local 'psycho' who was rumoured to have been involved in various shootings and who Frank supplied with heroin and cocaine. Finally, there was Will, who supplied Frank with ecstasy and cocaine on a regular basis, although this group often found cocaine difficult to source at the right price and in the right quantity.

Although Frank had regular sources of supply for most drugs, where ecstasy was concerned a number of different suppliers were used. Alf said that the first time he picked up Es was from 'three Scouse lads' that he met in a Toys R Us car park. After that, he met a man called 'Jimmy' in a different car park, and on a third occasion, he picked up 10,000 ecstasy tablets from 'two lads' in a taxi which he recognised to be from the Merseyside region. Other ecstasy deals had a more stable character: Alf picked up Es several times from Eamonn, either from a house or from a builder's yard where the drugs were stored in a skip. On a few occasions, he picked up from a man called Marty who had access to a pill press and to a tester kit for tablets. Alf had also delivered drugs to Marty's brother Zane who had access to guns and was rumoured to have been involved in an abortive armed robbery in conjunction with some 'lads' from Manchester.

'Before I knew it,' Alf said, 'I was in at the deep end.' In some networks of this type, the relationship between drug brokers and runners resembled that of colleagues or partners; there was a certain amount of 'profit sharing' and runners could set up side-lines with their own clientele. However, in this case, Frank pulled all the strings and Alf was literally steered about. 'Around Christmas,' Alf said, 'I was delivering drugs all over the place sometimes till the early hours of the morning. I was run off my feet.' This was work: reasonably well paid, stressful and illegal, but work nonetheless.

Alf would often collect drugs from Frank's father's house. Frank and his auntie would dilute heroin with 'bash' (usually caffeine) in order to enhance his profits. When Frank obtained the heroin, Alf said that it was often 'rock hard' and first had to be broken down. It was then put through a sieve into plastic boxes and mixed with quantities of the bash using other familiar kitchen implements on the kitchen worktop. When the preparations had been finished, Alf would take the heroin to his own house to be stored awaiting delivery to customers.

Family was important. Alf frequently delivered heroin to one of Frank's cousins and Frank also supplied parcels of amphetamine base to the uncle of a close associate. Some of the people with whom Alf dealt, either as buyers or suppliers, also worked with brothers or cousins. One of Frank's suppliers of ecstasy, known as 'Mad Eric', had a brother Cliff, to whom Alf used to deliver cannabis and amphetamine on a regular basis. Once, Alf was told to meet with Cliff and to collect drugs from a third party in a designated lay-by and to take them to an unfamiliar address. Frank reassured Alf, 'It'll be OK. Cliff's Mad Eric's brother, there won't be no trouble.'

COOPERATION AND CONFLICT

Drug markets are often depicted as prone to turf wars and prowled by vicious predators and hit-men. Indeed, as illegal enterprises cannot turn to the police for protection, criminals use the threat of violence to regulate the market. But violence can also be bad for business: it leaves traces, attracts police attention and invariably leads to more violence. In fact, for drug entrepreneurs and their employees, violence is something to be avoided. However, Frank was certainly not a man unaccustomed to violence. As a man with a local reputation as someone not to be crossed, he was known to have access to firearms and Alf had been required to act as courier collecting and delivering guns between third parties. However, Frank's drugs network was characterised by cooperation and harmony and run on strict business principles.

Alf described how on more than one occasion drugs had been sold to customers who weren't happy with their quality. For instance, a batch of poor quality 'runny' base amphetamine had been sold to Frank by a self-styled hard-man and body-builder known as Butch. Alf simply met up with two of Butch's men at a local pub and handed back more than ten kilos of amphetamine paste with no questions asked. On another occasion, several thousand poor-quality ecstasy tablets had been supplied to Frank. These duds were also returned to the supplier, with Frank's advice: 'I don't know where you got these from, lad, but don't do any more business with the cunt, at least, not if I'm in the frame.'

In addition to Frank, there was another major drug-dealer in the town named Percy, who operated at a similar level in the market. As free-trading entrepreneurs, both Frank and Percy found cooperation to be more practical than conflict. Alf occasionally picked up and dropped off parcels of drugs from Percy's safe house and sometimes bought the caffeine for Frank's heroin bash from him.

So, unlike the way that the drug trade is presented in the mass media, as ruthless turf wars and relentless violence, cooperation is often the norm. At times, these two busy entrepreneurs found it useful to work together in a series of linked exchanges of drugs and cash in order to supply a busy marketplace. Alf added that before he had started working for Frank, there had been another runner called Sammy, who decided to branch out on his own. Rather than regarding this as a betrayal, Frank still kept in touch with Sammy, and Alf frequently supplied drugs to him on Frank's behalf.

However, as we have seen, those involved in successful, lucrative criminal activity – and drug brokerage is no exception – often develop a sense of exaggerated personal power and invulnerability. While some invest the profits of crime in 'rational' and 'sensible' ways – for instance, Percy had bought a number of properties that he was renovating with the help of friends in the building trade – they are as equally likely to spend money with abandon, in the 'easy come, easy go' manner of conspicuous consumption. While Frank, a married man, lived an outwardly modest lifestyle in a council house, he also had a lavishly furnished house elsewhere where a girlfriend lived, and where he hoarded his collection of expensive toys, such as flashy motorbikes and jet-skis.

It was this sense of invulnerability and omnipotence that brought down Frank's drug business when he was drawn into an unnecessary conflict with the part-owner of a local nightclub. Frank had visited this venue and when the owner had thrown him out, saying that he did not want 'trash' in his club, Frank threatened revenge. A few days later, one of the doormen of the club was shot in the legs and an associate of Frank was identified as the gunman. Subsequently, his 'empire' collapsed like a house of cards. In this case, violence was a symptom of failure, disorganisation, market dysfunction, instability and inflated egos. What follows is often long years spent inside, with little more than the smell of boiled vegetables, disinfectant, shit and sweat for company.

The closer you get to the retail sector, within sniffing distance of the consumer, the less rhythm or routine there is to business, trade becomes chaotic and unpredictable, family becomes implicated, payments become unreliable, and the more likely it is that violence and humiliation are just around the next corner. What keeps the drug economy going is the fantasy of barely imaginable riches being spent in glamorous locations. This is of course a dream shared by most of the civilian population – the drug trade is merely a shortcut to a common destination, albeit one that carries considerable risks. Though, not always enough of a prospect of a reward, as described by Joey.

'The risks are too big and the money's not that brilliant. One geezer I knew was dropping off ozzies[27] for this other feller and he was getting paid £25 for each package. All right, he's maybe doing, ten, twenty, twenty-five a week, that's maybe three hundred, a monkey[28] in his hand. But he's not doing them one by one, he's always carrying, I don't know, five or seven ounces at any one time. And if it all comes on top, he's the one in the firing line, no one else, and seven ounces of cocaine, you're looking at fucking serious bird. It's not for me.'

But for some the prospect of fantasy riches and the seductive lifestyle that goes with it can be overwhelming. An importer of cannabis and cocaine described how one Friday night he gave his driver £300,000 to take abroad but 'The divvy decides it would be nice to lay the money on his bed, make mad passionate love to his 17-year-old girlfriend and photo-graph it.' When the driver took his wife out on the Saturday night, his 'girlfriend turned up pissed and showed the photos to the wife'. The driver's wife, who herself had a £2,500 per week cocaine habit, then informed Customs about her husband's business trip to Belgium and he was stopped at Dover.

After a while, even normal family life becomes drawn into the drug-dealing fantasy, particularly when dealers attempt to have their cake and eat it.

DUD

Although Dud came from a family of dockers and trade union officials, his father broke the mould by training as a butcher.

---

27 Ounces of cocaine.

28 £500.

His mother was a clerical worker and their combined salaries gave Dud a comfortable home. Like most of his mates, Dud was a conscientious objector when it came to education and stopped going to school at the age of 15, but his family provided bed, board and a bi-monthly change of trainers, and Dud enjoyed glue, dope and alcohol before segueing into life as a thief. He was a normal boy growing up in late 20th-century urban Britain.

Stealing cars and motorbikes was fun, as was a bit of casual house burglary, drinking beer and smoking dope before dealing small amounts of cannabis. 'Just spliff stuff, ounces, half-ounces, pocket money, really. I was gluing up, doing a bit of black, rolling round and doing houses. All any of us – silly kids, really – was about was getting off our faces. That's what money was for and that's where it all went.'

When Dud was 17, he stole a car and crashed it after being chased by the police. When they searched him, they found a small amount of dope and he received his first custodial sentence. This was quickly followed by the conviction of Dud and two friends for burglary. On his release, he commenced a career as an all-round thief, dealer, buyer and seller.

Marriage soon after his release from prison, along with the responsibilities of parenthood that quickly followed, led to Dud adopting a more businesslike approach to his dope-dealing and he spent a lot of time searching for a regular supplier who was willing to deal in small quantities at low prices. While still in his twenties, he and two friends stole a lorry and sold the contents to members of a family firm on the other side of London who were in the process of decamping to the suburbs. When the family firm found that the lorry was only half full, the gangsters took Dud and one of his friends into the toilet of a local pub and put guns in their mouths. After Dud soiled his trousers he was taken back into the packed bar and put on display.

However, business is business and soon Dud was working for associates of the same firm who had so cruelly humiliated him. He was a gofer, running errands before he was able to establish himself as an ecstasy dealer. He eventually went into partnership with the manager of the kind of chameleon pub that can rapidly mutate from a wine bar to an Ibiza beach bar and became the 'licensed' E and cocaine dealer. Now he was making money. He worked long hours but was able to fill the back of his mother's fridge with bricks of used notes. But by this time his wife and child had left.

A number of friends and relations had suffered downturns in their fortunes and when a cousin became indebted to a drug dealer, it created a storm of violence and chaos that overlapped with the private lives of both Dud and his business partner: 'There was a time when people were getting shot and stabbed up all everywhere. I stopped sleeping, and I was well at the gear.'

Then Dud's brief venture as part of a consortium that was funding ecstasy importation ended with him being 'mugged off' by his partners and losing everything except his car. There was nothing that he could do about being ripped off: the strong possibility of violence was enough for him to back off. 'I wiped my mouth and walked away.'

When I met Dud, he was living at the top of a high rise that shook in the wind. His second wife and children had just left him and he dreamt both of reconciling with his family and living a life of sunbathed luxury. But both dreams were just that; neither seemed likely to come true.

'I never really worked. If that makes sense, cos I am working in a way now, I suppose. I buy and sell it. Yeah, it's my business, as it is I could go out and buy anything. Lot of talk about how Es are not the thing any more and it's this and that, but people still want it. Round here, people will do anything, it's only another thing, a night out thing. The damage thing is really nothing to do with me; I don't make it so you might as well go to fucking Johnny Walker and say to him, "What about this whisky thing with all the headaches and that?" Nothing to do with me.'

Dud claimed to have money stashed at his mother's home, drove a standard family saloon car and lived on lager and takeaways. However, he wore enough cheap jewellery to suggest that inside his head there was a party going on and, like so many 21st-century consumers, straight and crooked alike, he aspired to a life of glossy leisure away from the buying, crying, dealing and stealing: 'Living in a place where at any time my girls can come over swim in the pool and that, all down to me. I could live in Cyprus or Florida, just a nice place, something with a business so I can earn without working. Just enjoy myself, drink myself fucking silly.'

I was drawn to the only photograph in Dud's sparse living room. It depicted a 1970s excursion to the seaside at Margate, where the self-conscious smiles of a group of men both young and old are framed by a slightly out of focus sign that promises 'Dreamland'.

Chapter 17

MRS POPEYE AND HER SISTERS

'There were tough, macho gangsters, drug dealers, killers, and thugs all in my neighborhood. And they were afraid of my mother. So, yeah, I know some strong women.'

STAND-UP COMEDIAN MICHAEL CHE

She had a tattoo of an eagle on her forearm, and a damp roll-up hanging from her bottom lip. Local kids called her Mrs Popeye and she lived close to a schoolfriend of mine. Whenever I visited his house, she would be standing on her doorstep watching the street and greeting her neighbours. As we kicked a ball about, our game was regularly interrupted by vans and cars stopping outside of Mrs Popeye's house to unload a few boxes and cartons, the contents of which would soon find themselves in the wardrobes and on the kitchen tables of local families. I later learnt that some of the boxes were being stored for safe keeping, while others were bought by Mrs Popeye. Her husband was an ex-docker disabled in a work accident and was seldom seen outside the pub; his wife was the one who bought and sold clothes, food and toiletries that had been liberated from the docks, local warehouses and factories. Her regular specialities were meat pies and men's nylon shirts, as well as bottles of perfume that found their way out of a factory next to an abattoir in Stratford. For a time, contrasting aromas of steak and kidney and lavender characterised a particularly fragrant corner of the East End.

Mrs Popeye was a local resource, one of many women in the area who was a conduit for cheap everyday items that made life a little easier for hard-pressed families. She was not in competition with other fences, there were no market rivalries and, as for the police, the canteen of the local police station was a vibrant hub for all manner of hookey gear. The taken-for-granted, unremarkable nature of Mrs Popeye's trade meant that she was not a target of violence and intimidation, and so never felt obliged to resort to employing security.

There were Mrs Popeyes all over the working-class city, efficiently and unceremoniously shifting hookey gear around the neighbourhood with none of the delusional machismo that accompanied so many of the little earners run by men. Indeed, along with 'Stratford's Elizabeth Taylor', who we met in The City Arms, and so many others who quietly normalised everyday skulduggery, these women were unremarkable within the local neighbourhood and largely invisible to outsiders who tended to focus upon the usual suspects.

While women have always been involved in crime, and tales of legendary female shoplifters are very much part of our understanding of the UK underworld, women remain relatively rare within this characteristically masculine enclave. Within crime groups, women tended to be viewed as victims and fair game for sexual exploitation. If they were involved in crime it was in menial, expendable roles such as couriers, with little knowledge of the full extent of the crime group's activities.

Mrs Popeye and the rest of her era of neighbourhood fences were never considered as part of the underworld. More recently, though, the decline in local stolen goods networks and the emergence of the drug trade have created criminal opportunities for women that were unimaginable within the male-dominated trades of safe-breaking, extortion and armed robbery. Although they remain in a minority, the existence of female dealers is an indication of the breaking down of the old underworld. However, while two generations ago, women like Mrs Popeye could practise their trade in a relatively open manner, independent of any man and with no consideration of violent robbery or retribution, today's female drug dealers are part of a trade that is framed by potential violence.

The inclusive scene based on empathy, sociability and camaraderie in which ecstasy was bought and consumed placed a high premium on social skills, and as a consequence, significant numbers of women became involved in the club-based drug trade. However, despite the sociability of the club scene, female dealers needed to be aware of violent possibilities.

POLLY

Polly started dealing amphetamine in her late teens around the club scene in a southern coastal town. She began in a small way but, once involved in drug dealing, her scale of operations expanded rapidly. 'Other people got to hear and it escalates very quickly. I mean, in the end, we're talking about like, a thousand tablets a week and nine ounces of amphetamine. As soon as it started, phew, it got out of control, really.' Polly paid £450 for nine ounces 'pretty pure', with which she used bulking agents, selling for £250 per ounce. Her outlay of £450 yielded a profit of approximately £4,000. In addition, she was also buying batches of 100 ecstasy pills at 75p to £1 per tablet, which she sold at £3 to £5 per tablet, depending on how well she knew the buyer.

Although she was making serious money, Polly still felt vulnerable and in need of protection, which she got by reaching an agreement with a club owner for 'exclusive rights' in his establishment. She was already paying off door staff and bar staff in drink and drugs, so it was a natural progression to formalise the arrangement. This arrangement with the club owner cost Polly £500 per week and although she was now a protected mid-level distributor with an established clientele of dealers, she could not resist selling retail, directly to punters. She would regularly carry 200 tablets per night into clubs. 'I was greedy,' Polly said, 'out of my depth.' Which is why her interview was carried out in prison.

YVONNE

Physical protection is not always purchased, it can be more subtle and linked to relationships. In Yvonne's family, there are four women of working age living within 400 yards of each other in three flats on a housing estate that has been disrupted by owner occupiers and the prospect of regeneration. Combining child rearing with increasingly desperate attempts to get an education, the two youngest women live together, while Zena, who was widowed in her fifties, spends most of her time minding her grandchildren. Her eldest daughter, Yvonne, is a grandmother in her late thirties who buys kilos of cannabis from a male ex-partner and is the main source of income for the entire family. All of the kids are well dressed and the three homes clean and well furnished. Yvonne has created a silo of self-respect, discipline and well-being against a fragmented, uncertain backdrop that features a distinct scarcity of successful men and a paucity of employment opportunities for women beyond the fast food and cleaning sectors.

As an enthusiastic teenage smoker, Yvonne learnt about the cannabis trade from the bottom up. She first sold to friends and collaborated with the father of her eldest child, a man who was involved at the edges of an importation network. Her current male partner is not involved with her business but Yvonne is connected to a trading network that features a number of well-known violent men, and this association with traditional violence is an essential component of a business that she runs discreetly in between school runs and shopping for food.

MOIRA

Moira's incompetent boyfriend provided a fine education in how not to deal illegal drugs:

> 'A lot of people who are in that line of business, they also take in the merchandise as it were, so that doesn't exactly help for a clear head. I'd go and do the money side of it, or hold the money and stuff like that. I used to do kilos of dope which is what I still do. Coke makes

a lot more money and most people do that these days, most people do that for better return as the saying goes, but I prefer to do just straight-forward dope, I find that it's just a bit safer. People are addicted to coke, so you're more likely to have trouble with other people because it's like a much heavier drug to be dealing with than it is with dope.'

Moira's humdrum routine stoods in stark contrast to popular images of drug-dealing: her world is removed from both inner-city sleaze and jet-set glamour. In addition, she despised her customers, identifying mutual distrust as the crucial instinct that drove her successful enterprise.

'Well, a lot of it's just waiting around and you spend a lot of time on the phone. People are ringing you up saying, "I want this, I want that". Then you'll be ringing other people to see what's around or you might know that something's going to be happening in a week's time and you've got an order in for that, and then it's like keeping ringing up finding out what's happening. And then you've got to have your money ready, to go and sort it out.'

There was no complex code of conduct and she avoided the typical arcane boys' games of her work.

'Well, it is a business, it's like any sort of business. A lot of people who do dope have a set lot of customers who'll always buy from them, and that's what they'll do. I know people I sell to, they've got a set lot of people who they'll maybe give out five ounces, six ounces, whatever to them and they have almost like a set order with people. I don't think people realise how many people smoke regularly, continually, and always have to have a supply because it is definitely a most common thing.

'It's not at all glamorous, in fact it's really boring. It's a lot of a waste of time and you have to deal with a lot of dickheads all the time. If somebody can rip you off they will do. Selling you under, selling you shit, giving you a taste of something then selling you something different, taking money and not coming up with the goods. If you sell short weight that's the traditional way of doing it. You can mix them up, there's ways you can make hash go further, it's fucking hard work, it's not worth the bother I think, but people do it. Or you could sell just slightly short, that's why you should always take your own scales, but again that's a dangerous thing to do because if you're walking the streets with a pair of electric scales it's kind of hard to explain what you've got them for really.'

Moira was always smartly dressed and used her femininity every bit as blatantly and efficiently as armed robbers use their masculinity to ply their trade. Importantly, she turned around and exploited the assumptions of incompetence that her male customers made regarding a woman's business acumen and appearance.

'I get away with a lot more because the way I look, the way I dress, the way I carry on my life is not the sort of way that anybody would think that was particularly dodgy. They [men] think they can get one over on you, which is an advantage in a way, because they do treat me like I'm a bit dumb occasionally, which is quite funny because I'm not, but that's quite a laugh because they do under-estimate my intelligence at times. Cos they think they're dead smart about the money, and that's when I manage to get one over on people because they think that they're pulling a fast one, and in fact I end up turning it round the other way and saying, "OK, well I'll have this for that and this for that." And it ends up actually I'll have knocked a oner off the deal and still getting the same money, and it's only when they've agreed to it and they'll go, "Oh hang on a sec," and of course they've agreed to it and you just say, "Oh well, blah, blah," and get the money out. Getting the money out usually settles the deal.'

But there are some practical disadvantages to being a woman in the drug trade, which made it difficult for Moira to completely exclude men from her enterprise.

'I have a partner who is a man; you have to, you can't deal on your own as a woman. It's not safe, you have to have somebody with you, you could get ripped off and it's just not safe. You have to have a bloke. Certainly, people get to know that you've got maybe money, or gear at your house and you're likely to get held up or robbed, or taxed as they say. If you're quite good-looking you can appeal to various people's whatever and get away with stuff like that. Just like being really nice and looking nice gets their guard down a bit.

'It's up to you to protect yourself from a dodgy deal. It's up to you and if you can't protect yourself from that, well then, you're a mug and that's your problem, it's not anybody else's problem and that's the way it runs. It's not a glamorous business, there's nothing glamorous about it, nothing goes on in posh hotels, nobody meets under clocks in stations, there's nothing like James Bond, nothing glamorous about it at all. Maybe if you get into top level it is because you've got a lot more money, but it's not glamorous so maybe dealing with a woman is a bit more glamorous, I don't know.'

Even her dealings with the police involved the manipulation of gender stereotypes.

'Well, yeah, I have had a couple of near misses. The worst one was when I got stopped in the car and I had actually got somebody with me who had a lot of form, and they were going, "Is this your new bird?" and cos he's such a fucking arsehole he's going, "Oh yeah, yeah." They've asked me what my name is and I've given them a name and they're checking through the car and of course I've got some stuff in the car. Normally I wouldn't have somebody around but it was a contact and we were going to somebody else's friend so we're going in the car.'

Moira had four kilograms of dope in the boot of her car.

'Anyway, we're in the car and they're giving him a load of hassle and making him take everything out of his pockets and everything like that and I was thinking, "Oh fuck, they're going to start looking in the back of the car." But it was my car and so they were trying to ask me how I knew him and everything, and the stupid bastard said I was his girlfriend. I'm going, "He's lying, I'm not his girlfriend, I've just been out on a date with him a couple of times." They're going, "Do you know who he is?" and I said, "Oh no, I just met him in a pub." They're giving me all this and I start doing all the really Miss Innocent.

'Fortunately, this sort of fatherly copper said, "You do realise who he is, don't you?" and I'm going like, "No, no, has he been in trouble, then?" and he's going, "Oh yeah, he's got form as long as your arm," and I'm going, "Oh God, my mum will kill me!" I'm practically crying, you know, and I turned round to him and goes, "You're not getting back in my car, they've just told me that you're a big nerd." And he's going, "What, you what?" and I'm going, "You told me in the pub that you were in business," and getting really hysterical. So of course they don't want to have a hysterical woman so they're going, "All right love, all right." So I'm going, "Can I go now, can I go now?" so they say, "Oh yeah, of course you can." So I just get in the car again and drive off and he's left standing on the pavement.'

Untroubled by the criminal justice system, Moira eventually made a decision to get out of the drug business and travelled the world before settling down on an exotic island and starting family. Eventually, she entered a profession that enabled her to engage with disadvantaged youth. Not exactly your usual demonic drug dealer. But then, few people are.

In a development that finds parallel in the legitimate world of work, where much traditional male labour has become redundant, there are now opportunities for women that were unthinkable in Mrs Popeye's era. While the drug business is far from an equal opportunity employer, female involvement in the drug economy has grown, the door to dealing networks has been wedged open and new horizons have emerged.

Chapter 18

A PLACE CALLED ABROAD

'Globalisation is not only something that will concern and threaten us in the future, but something that is taking place in the present and to which we must first open our eyes.'

ULRICH BECK

'At the moment, everybody wants to have a Turk on the firm.'

SERIOUS ORGANISED CRIME AGENCY OFFICER, PERSONAL COMMUNICATION, 2006

PIRATES

The Rotary was an old pub where most evenings two Eastern European men in their thirties would sit drinking in a corner while selling leather belts and bags, cannabis and counterfeit DVDs. The leather goods were snide – counterfeit versions of expensive designer products – and could be purchased for the same price from a stall in a nearby street market, but the dope transactions, which were rare, were conducted after a nod and a wink and a short walk to the gents. Generally, it was hard to regard their enterprise as a serious ongoing concern and one local, watching with bemusement as the two men plied their trade, shared my reservations. 'Last week, those cunts had DVDs, all old like *Pirates of the Caribbean,* and all that at double what the Chinese geezer does of a Friday. I can't see what they are earning out of it.'

There was nothing strange or particularly deviant in these two men far from home retailing cheap leather accessories and small quantities of cannabis. Their 'bit of business', knocking out dodgy gear in a backstreet boozer, is a time-honoured activity that is a mark of belonging, earns status, self-respect and a few quid, and is nothing too dramatic – merely a variation on the 'little earners', 'parcels' or 'lorry loads' of previous eras. Times change and the 'Chinese geezer' selling DVDs has almost replaced the traditional shellfish vendor who once toured the pubs on a Friday night. In addition, the Rotary pair are not dissimilar to the exceptionally polite group of young West African men who lurk around the train station supplying cannabis to a significant portion of the local student population, or the super-reliable Polish coke dealer who can always provide a livener should the effects of one-too-many pints of cooking lager become a problem. However, when you eventually get home in the early hours don't slam the front door as the Pole is also your next-door neighbour and he has an early start driving down the A13 for his day job as a plasterer.

The market for recreational drugs has merged seamlessly with the demand for cheap goods in areas where the legal and illegal have traditionally intermingled, and the boundaries of right and wrong are constantly being negotiated. The demise of local industries and the flight to the suburbs has not eliminated 'ducking and diving' but enhanced it with aspirations for a lush life cut from extreme poverty, with an edge honed in war zones or in regions of the globe boasting valuable illegal harvests ripe for export.

British cities emptied out by industrial decline and an exodus to the suburbs now house a cosmopolitan population boasting their own businesses, places of worship and social centres, and like the men and women that they have partially replaced, some break the law.

A TURK ON THE FIRM

Baz came to England as a child and as a young man, he took over the family kebab shop when his father returned to Turkey. As a heavy gambler, and with the kebab shop in decline, Baz was deeply in debt when a fellow gambler came to his rescue. All Baz had to do was to store a parcel of heroin, an arrangement that soon became regular, and he would be rewarded by a payment of £4,000–£5,000 per parcel. Baz was a 'clean skin' – he had no criminal background and was therefore less likely to attract police attention. He was able to graduate to seeking out customers before becoming a driver for a key London distributor, driving to meetings and interpreting for him.

The money was good and within a couple of years, Baz had progressed to coordinating the distribution of 150 kilos of heroin in two London boroughs. Soon he was travelling every two months to Turkey, meeting with lawyers, politicians and border control police. Every three to four months, Baz would go to a meeting at a night-club that was also attended by competitors where strategic information concerning prices, informants and non-payers was shared. In the two years before he was arrested and imprisoned, Baz estimated that he made £400,000.

With no criminal background, Baz had joined an ongoing enterprise and worked his way up to a position of well-paid responsibility. In his case, his ethnicity promoted trust with a group of entrepreneurs who were connected to a lucrative crop on the other side of the world. Across the globe and along established trade routes, people like Baz help to move the product along to its final destination where it is consumed. The fact that these networks are transnational should not divert us from the fact that at each point in the transportation of contraband, whether it is drugs, guns or human beings, there are people like Baz linking similar people in cities home and abroad. While outsiders still have a value to criminal entrepreneurs, horizons have broadened and those with connections to that mysterious place called 'abroad' are particularly valued. If it is good for profits then there is no need to exclude anyone on the grounds of ethnicity and in modern cities around the world, multi-ethnic networks thrive as displaced people come together to make money.

CROSSING BORDERS

Osman, a Turkish clerk who had been a UK resident for five years, teamed up with Mar, an African, and employed a retinue of British South Asians and more recent arrivals from Pakistan to distribute cannabis purchased from an established British firm of importers. Based in premises owned by an unsuspecting Turkish landlord, they also manufactured and distributed amphetamine sulphate, while Mar worked with another Turk, buying, 'stepping on' (bulk up the weight with additives) and distributing cocaine. One of Mar's customers was a British man married to a Spanish citizen who ran a clothing manufacturer that employed Asian and African women off the books. Her husband, along with two African men who delivered clothing for the sweatshop, was arrested for dealing ecstasy. When the case finally came to court, a cluster of legal companies and over a dozen British bank accounts, along with accounts in Spain and Africa, were discovered.

In 2005, as part of a series of cases that jailed 60 men and women across the Caribbean, France, the USA and the UK, a London-based group whose members were from French Guiana stood out for the complexity and extraordinarily lucrative nature of their operation. They gave single mothers £10,000 to fly to the Caribbean, where each one was given three kilos of near-pure cocaine hidden in resealed rum bottles, vases, shampoo containers or toothpaste tubes. They were then flown back to Paris or Amsterdam where they were guarded overnight before travelling to London by coach, ferry or Eurostar. Each trip was made up of up to three couriers, who were unaware of each other. The same crime group used a parcel courier company to send drugs through the post. These packages were sent to non-existent addresses and intercepted by a worker at the parcel company who then extracted the cocaine and returned the packages to the depot as undelivered. Meanwhile, the cocaine was converted to crack in the kitchen of a rented East End house.

Eventually, police seized the group's properties in the Caribbean and Africa, while in London they discovered Cartier and Rolex watches, diamond jewellery, designer clothes and large quantities of cash. In court, it was claimed that over a two-year period, the group made £3m per week from importing cocaine and producing and selling crack. A total of 14 people were sentenced to a combined total of 178 years imprisonment.

All of this could be bemusing for old-school white villains pining for the days of Empire. In the nineties, I learnt of an armed robber who, on his release from prison, invested what remained of his ill-gotten gains in a part shipment of cocaine via a Turkish contact that he had made while inside. The ex-robber, who had been incarcerated for over a decade during the rise of the 'powder trade', was mystified when his new Turkish partner bought from one firm of Jamaicans and sold most of the consignment to another group of Jamaicans. Crime is a global game but it is played out locally.

Of course, this case of non-Brits making big money was exceptional and we need to be careful how we categorise people. Not all Eastern Europeans residing in UK cities are members of the Russian mafia or running prostitution or drug-dealing operations, and far too often when a Black man, whether British or from overseas, commits a crime he is described as a Yardie, or in terms that highlights the fact that he is not white and exaggerates the crime of which he is accused. Indeed, generally newcomers join in with local working-class populations who are part of a rich cocktail of migrant histories going back many generations and featuring many forms of ducking and diving, some with links to 'the old country', wherever that is.

In the tabloid press and the outside smoking areas of Britain's boozers, the names most likely to be linked to organised crime, regardless of the extent of their actual abilities or significance in the crime business, are usually foreign. There is nothing new in this: during previous eras, blame fell on so-called 'white-slaving Jews', 'opium-dealing Chinamen', 'Black drug dealers' and 'Mediterranean pimps and ponces'. However, we live in a society that is complex, cosmopolitan and driven by entrepreneurship, and while Jewish, Chinese, Black and Maltese members of that society were, like every other community, never entirely blameless, the relationship between ethnicity and crime is far from straightforward, and UK criminals have been among the most enthusiastic fans of ethnic stereotyping.

A JOCK ON THE FIRM

Traditionally, theft and stolen goods networks were at the very core of criminal culture, particularly in cities boasting a major port. As the economy began to recover after the Second World War, the interchange of goods, services and people between cities became more common. Meanwhile, as discussed earlier, the police continued to be organised on a local basis with very few effective links between individual police forces until the mid-1960s, when the Regional Crime Squads were formed. The plethora of police forces in the UK meant that if goods or people were transported across their boundaries, there was little chance of detection. For instance, Glasgow was a supplier of stolen goods to London's voracious marketplace during and after the war. This was a time before motorways and cheap air travel, and before many people owned a car or a telephone, so in this sense, Glasgow might as well have been Greenland: it was in every sense of the word a foreign place.

Markets established during the rationing of the Second World War and the post-war period resulted in Glaswegian thieves building valuable individual reputations for themselves, particularly in the West End of London, where both licensed and unlicensed premises cashed in on the post-war consumer boom. Scotland was of course the centre of whisky manufacturing and a lorry load of whisky stolen in Scotland had a warm welcome waiting for it in London. Many of London's pubs and clubs were connected to networks of theft and extortion with bases all over the working-class city, and these key connections between Glasgow and London matured along with the status of a number of the key players.

ANONYMITY AND SAFE HAVENS

During the 1940s, 1950s and 1960s, the reliability of some of the Glaswegians associated with networks of theft was matched by the value of their anonymity in London, and a number were employed to collect and transport illegal proceeds from businesses across the capital. Indeed, they were anonymous both to the police, who lacked anything resembling a national database, and to rival London villains, who tended to only be familiar with the usual suspects. Scottish couriers and minders had a reputation for being stoic men of violence and a number became involved in robberies, albeit initially as employees of established London firms. As Stan, an ex-thief and club manager told me, 'No idea how they got connected. They turned up and went to work. Yeah, [there were] rumours about who they were and who they was with up north and what they had done. [Arthur] Thompson came up. To be honest, he is the only Jock [villain] I heard of.' Arthur Thompson had been a regular visitor to London in the 1950s and went on to become a dominant figure in Glaswegian criminal circles.

By the mid-1950s, the Glaswegian criminal in London

was regarded as a somewhat exotic beast: a highly prized, dependably violent alien. As Bob, an ex-thief who frequented London's night spots in the 1960s, explained: 'A lot of firms used to like a Jock on the firm . . . They was heavy, very heavy . . . minding, bit of debt collecting. Very heavy, solid, reliable geezers.' As Jimmy Boyle explained, 'The English guys recognise that Scotland produces good heavies and that is why they have so many on their firms.'

Glaswegian gangster and robber Victor 'Scarface' Russo was Albert Dimes' cousin and a key player in the Jack Spot vs Billy Hill conflict in mid-1950s London. There was also 'Scotch Jack' Buggy who had arrived in the UK as a member of the American Forces, settling in Glasgow before travelling to London and becoming involved in a wide range of violent crime, in particular extortion. While serving time for a shooting incident, which bizarrely involved the singer Shirley Bassey, Buggy befriended Train Robber Roy James; on Buggy's release from prison he set out to recover the robber's share of the loot, which had been stolen. In 1967, Buggy's body was recovered from the sea off the south coast.

On occasions, criminal craftsmen with highly unique methods that made them easily traced by local police were brought into London where their modus operandi was not recognisable. For instance, safe-blower Paddy Meehan, who in the 1960s was the victim of a controversial miscarriage of justice in Scotland, travelled down south to work for a London firm and the Krays allegedly employed Glaswegians as itinerant gunmen before they were whisked away back north.

The Kray twins were particularly taken with the kudos of having a 'Jock on the firm' and they recruited Glaswegian Big Pat Connelly in addition to two natives of Edinburgh, 'Scotch'

Jack Dickson and Ian Barrie, as minders. As Paulie, a one-time lorry thief and professional fence explained: 'The Krays had a couple. Lovely fellas, respectful, good company. They used them for debt [collecting] and they liked them to be around them in the clubs and pubs. Bit of show, like.' Yet until they began consorting with the Krays, the combined criminal record of these three Scottish imports amounted to just one conviction for vagrancy. However, after joining the Kray firm, Connelly, who acted as an emissary between the Krays and Glaswegian villains, was convicted for five offences between November 1957 and February 1968 for receiving stolen goods and possession of a firearm. Barrie was found guilty of murder in 1968 and was sentenced to life imprisonment with a recommendation that he serve at least 20 years and Dickson turned Queen's evidence and was rewarded with a token nine-month sentence.

Before EasyJet offered a cheap and quick passage to a safe haven in Amsterdam, Spain or Cyprus, numerous Scottish criminals were offered sanctuary in London. Of these individuals, Jimmy Boyle, who went on to become a renowned author and sculptor, was the best known: 'We had a strong friendship with the Kray twins in London and we would go down there to the big fights or to get a few days away from the Glasgow scene. Whenever we went to London, we were made most welcome by the friends that we had there.' In 1967, Boyle came to London to be looked after by the Krays. Wanted in Glasgow for assault and murder, he was eventually arrested in a pub in Stratford.

In the early- to mid-20th century, when most people seldom ventured far beyond their local neighbourhoods, it was relatively easy to create a violent bogeyman from myths surrounding another part of the UK. However, with the rise in car ownership and cheap flights, the 400 miles between London and Glasgow are now covered quickly and easily. Glasgow has lost its mystery and a Scottish accent is not quite as exotic as it once was.

EMPIRE OF THE SUN: BRITS ABROAD

From the 1960s onwards, generations of Brits became accustomed to cheap holidays and air travel, and progressed to investments in bars and apartment blocks in the Mediterranean, Florida and beyond, and dabbling with sex tourism and drug cultures in Africa and Asia. British villains are merely part of this shift, and their overseas careers have been spectacular. But apart from investing in obvious places such as southern Spain, the Canary Islands and Thailand, and there are key players in modern-day pirate havens such as Amsterdam and Pattaya, which host thriving criminal communities from across the globe as well as those on the missing list, fugitives and villainous visitors seeking relief from the various forms of grief that are part and parcel of criminal life.

When law enforcement interrupts the world of illegal entrepreneurs, the results are relatively predictable. If you don't find yourself in a pub celebrating the stupidity of the straight world with multiple pats on the back and a strippergram powdering your nose, then you will be waking up behind the door with a soap-dodging heroin addict who farts all night. Alternatively, when deals go wrong, debts increasingly go unpaid or the punter that you ripped off has a psychopath for a cousin, going missing is always an option. In a world ridden with gossip and rumour, the mere suggestion that somebody has 'gone missing' conjures up an endless list of possibilities. For example, weighed down on the sea bed off the Sussex coast, under six foot of Essex marshland or an added ingredient to various pork products. Or the 'missing' may be living a life of barely imaginable luxury on a faraway beach of fleshy delights and fruity cocktails. Either way, it is another country. However, a return from the 'dead', or even from Benidorm, was not uncommon, as cheap airfares, second homes and business interests abroad created previously unimaginable opportunities for 'going missing'.

EL PLUNGER

With a liking for customised Ford Escorts, white wine and other people's money, Stevie was, back in the eighties, a fresh-faced 'Jack the lad' who progressed through an impressive list of self-employment, including kitchen and carpet fitting, carpet cleaning, office cleaning and double glazing installation. The problem with Stevie was that he was useless. If you hired Stevie, late starts and early finishes were supplemented with no shows and distinctly amateur levels of workmanship. Stevie was part of a group of friends who were picking up crumbs from the emerging ecstasy market, and in the early nineties, when he followed the pharmacology to the Canary Islands, he left behind a pile of debt and a lot of sub-standard home improvements.

And then, around 1995, Stevie went missing.

Rumours of unpaid debts to gangsters were soon circulating around pubs in East London, rapidly followed by allegations that he had been murdered. Of course, the gangsters were foreign. Stevie was consigned to the missing list and it was not long before speculation concerning his fate had faded as a topic of conversation.

However, a few years into the new century, Stevie was once again the subject of gossip as rumours of sightings at Essex-based family funerals abounded. Eventually, the gaunt figure with skin the tone and colour of a well-worn horse saddle, who was driving nothing more noteworthy than a hired French people carrier, was approached by an old friend while drinking in a pub garden. Stevie was back in the UK for one of his regular visits to his mother who was living in a suburban care home. Stevie, apparently unmolested by gangsters, was now 'doing well' and displayed a business card proclaiming his new profession as a plumber serving British ex-pats unwilling to trust their pipework to the vagaries of local Spanish tradesmen.

Most people who make their money from crime got into the business because the money was good and the hours were even better. Their motivation is not complicated: they like to dress well, get drunk, use drugs, drive nice cars and live in luxurious accommodation – the trick is to claim the prize without paying the price. Sunshine just puts the cherry on the cake. In this respect at least, they are largely indistinguishable from the bulk of the non-criminal population.

DOING WELL

In a backwater of suburban London, 13 men gathered quietly outside a car dealership in the early dawn to take a minibus to the airport. Aged between their early thirties and late fifties, the men were dressed in a variety of casual styles, ranging from Dolce & Gabbana to Marks & Spencer with a number of obvious diversions to TK Maxx. All of these men were Londoners: two were born in the Caribbean and came to London as children while four others are also Black British, their parents arriving as part of the Windrush generation. The early morning conversation was generally confined to some muted piss-taking regarding one of the traveller's 'distressed' Adidas holdall. On arrival at the airport, there was some loud abuse for Jason and Kenny, two of the older travellers, who admitted to feeling sick.

Following security and passport control, there were lagers all round and by 7:45am, most of the group were engaged in a sit-up competition, with the loser buying a replacement for the sweat-sodden top worn by the minibus's driver. He returned with a white Nike T-shirt, accompanied by a group of drunk office workers from Basildon who were heading to Tenerife on a hen do. In response, Quiet Charlie was pushed to the fore and soon a mock wedding ceremony had taken place between the softly spoken builder and the prospective bride. The ceremony was presided over by thrice-married Bobby, who officiated with a copy of a *Motorsport* magazine in one hand and a pint of Carlsberg in the other. An uneventful flight was marked only by a dozing member of the party who was reprimanded by an irate flight attendant who insisted that he stay awake while the obligatory safety instructions were read out.

All of these men had 'done well', having acquired a lifestyle that the middle classes once claimed for themselves. Most were widely travelled and several owned properties in southern Europe, USA and the Middle East. They were exceedingly at ease with the world having made their money grafting on building sites, and buying and selling property, cars and drugs.

Soon after arriving at their beach-front hotel, they visited the jet-ski concession and obtained supplies of coke. Jerry the Plumber was irate: he doesn't like drugs and told anyone who would listen that he 'doesn't believe in them'. But he was a long-time believer in alcohol and at the evening meal it was clear that he had enthusiastically imbibed from the bottle of whisky that he bought 'for the room', sharing it with a large, sweating used-car salesman. During the meal, Jerry loudly accused anyone who was having a good time of using 'that coke shit' and later made a comment about 'suntans' to Stanley, whose mother came from West Africa and his white father from London. Stanley had an upper body honed from two decades working as a scaffolder but after two more suntan remarks and a Frank Bruno reference, he decided to contribute in his own special way to 21st-century race relations. He sat on the plumber's lap and stuck his tongue in his ear. It worked a treat. The humiliation was enough and by the time most of the party had moved on to a club, Jerry was back in his room alone, going solo with Johnny Walker.

The next day, two of the party visited some property investments whose value had recently plummeted and another, who I later learnt was in league with corrupt council officials in a suburban property scam, spent the morning with estate agents enquiring about buying 'a little bolt hole away from the coast. Something off a little village square near a nice bar'. Another member of the party, who had made money from cannabis importation two decades earlier and had served at least one prison sentence for receiving stolen goods, wept into his lunchtime lager as he told a builder with sunburn about his attempts to adopt a child. As the sun went down, a self-employed lorry driver tried to pick a fight with the hotel's Eastern European security staff and was sick in a paddling pool. By the end of the trip, alcohol, drugs and golf had contrived to create a self-congratulatory, hedonistic bubble where notions of what was legal and illegal seemed vague, pompous and utterly irrelevant.

For these men, making money and lavishly spending it was normal, and if you have to ask where the money came from, you are missing the point. They are part of an affluent culture of entrepreneurially minded people who refuse to be intimidated by this weird place called 'abroad', which, let's be honest, just aint foreign any more. Because huge chunks of our planet have been transformed into marketplaces as well as playgrounds, men and women whose parents gave their lives to factories, mines, docks and mills are now familiar with the benefits of investment in Northern Cyprus, local taxation in Croatia, building regulations in Andalusia and much more. They no longer squint at the unfamiliar glare of the sun. They belong, for this place called abroad is no less 'real' than the place that used to be called 'home'.

JACK

Jack never really got over wanting 'to be like the cool boys in school' but in his early twenties he found himself barely scraping a living near the bottom of the white-collar food chain. He lived for the weekend, consuming a conservative 'cheeky half' (of a gram) and dabbling in dealing. He bought an eighth (3.5 grams) and stepped on it with herbal remedies or sinus-clearing tablets to make it up to 4 or 5 grams before selling to the notoriously non-discriminating retail powder market. Jack did not want to live at the bottom of both the criminal and non-criminal worlds and his frustration came to the fore every Friday when he watched from his office while affluent diners arrived to lunch at a fashionable restaurant nearby. After a meagre lunch, Jack would return to his desk, then, just before he left work for the weekend, he would enviously watch the happy sated diners leave the restaurant. This was the lifestyle that he so desperately craved.

Jack gave up work and embarked upon a month-long holiday to Spain that lasted for four years and changed his fortunes. He met Reg, an ex-pat British villain who gave him an ounce of cocaine to sell. Jack made quick work of selling the coke and Reg was so impressed that he refused his slice of the profit. Their partnership was sealed: Reg provided the product and Jack honed his skills as a salesman, selling cocaine to enthusiastic holidaymakers who were charged according to their nationality. For instance, Swedish tourists were charged £60 per gram, which at the time was £20 over the going rate, while British ex-pats received a special discount of £32.

Eventually, Reg asked if Jack had any contacts in the UK who might be interested in buying kilos of cocaine. Soon, Jack, who would never see the drug, was organising five to six deals a month of 4 to 5 kilos each, making a grand on each kilo and receiving the money from his contacts in London via a Western Union wire. This was, Jack admitted, taking a big risk. 'If something goes wrong you have a huge amount of money to pay – people don't care if your guy got nicked with the drugs, you still owe for the money, everyone knows the risks they are taking.'

Their operation quickly expanded and Jack moved back to London to run the British end. In Spain, Reg dealt directly with a community of Colombian 'retirees' who imported the drugs to Spain by boat from Colombia before storing the drugs and smuggling them to London, at which point Jack took over, supplying clients in the north, south west and Midlands, most of whom were connected to Reg. At Jack's insistence, the couriers, who were carrying up to 10kg of cocaine in 'a pikey Nike bag', wore a thin pair of gloves even in the summer to avoid leaving any forensic evidence and were paid £500 to deliver the drugs to a customer. Always travelling by black cab in London and taking the train around the country before checking into a hotel, Jack would provide a phone number to arrange the drop off and the customers would deliver the money to London the following day. To collect the money, a second worker was paid £250 a day and worked most days travelling around London in black cabs, delivering the money to another man who was also paid £250 a day to count it. An elegantly dressed woman was also paid £250 a day to collect the money from the counter and, using a Louis Vuitton bag, deliver it to the Colombians, after which it would find its way to Spain. The same woman would then deliver Jack's profits to another house and, an hour later Jack, came to collect it. The profits would be split 50-50 with Reg, who every three weeks would send couriers to the UK to collect his share, strapping the cash around their waists.

Although he had been inspired by the lure of the high life, and he admitted to spending £8,000–£9,000 taking groups of people on nights out, Jack kept a low profile. His flat was rented using a friend's name; he had a car, but nothing more extravagant than a BMW and employed a driver who 'wasn't exactly security' but happened to be large. He also had a nice watch, preferred vintage clothing to designer labels, but would give money away 'to any half decent sob story'.

Jack emphasised the importance of staying calm, keeping the money, drugs and employees separate, and having as many links in the chain as possible. However, his arrest shows that he was unable to stick to his own rules. When a client from a big northern city wanted 10kgs of cocaine, Jack had no staff available and so, going against all of his own rules, agreed to pass over the drugs and pick up the money himself. Jack told the northern contact to ensure that the courier 'fitted in'. When the courier arrived with the money he was a very large black man. 'It was a joke – kids were staring at me and him walking down the street together.' They went for lunch at midday to wait for the Colombians to deliver the drugs and at 5 o'clock when the cocaine eventually arrived, the courier was drunk and made a clumsy bag handover 'like in the movies' before heading off with the drugs to catch his train back north.

At three in the morning, a telephone call from Jack's northern clients relayed the news that the courier had not caught the train but had been arrested at Euston Station. Jack immediately left his home and checked into a hotel for a month, living on room service. When he returned to his flat, he became convinced that he was under surveillance and decided from then on only to come out at night. Incredibly, Jack believed that if he stopped dealing the police would think that he had learned his lesson and let him off. He was arrested when he attempted to board a ferry to Holland.

Jack's criminal career was defined by two lunches: one inspired him and the other led to his downfall. But his overseas adventure made him a lot of money and he became adept at working between foreign criminals operating transnationally, old school British villains and drug trade impresarios operating in a range of British cities. As he explained, 'It's a very simple business if you have the balls to do it.'

Brits go abroad and non-Brits come to Britain. Interconnected globally by a quest for money, criminal careers are no longer limited to home fixtures; there is real money to be had from investing in away days and while these adventures are not for everybody, the opportunities on offer are not to be sniffed at. Clearly the British engage with money-making opportunities wherever they hang their hats, but to make the most of them it is necessary to be able to move goods undetected around the UK as well as across the nation's borders.

Chapter 19

TRUCKS AND BOATS AND PLANES: TRANSPORT

'Lorry loads of legit gear was coming in with the drugs
stuffed in it. The driver goes for a walk comes back and
there it is all whacked away in the furniture or whatever.
On the boat and through, and we had these stop offs for
unloading the gear. Driver goes missing again, comes
back and makes the proper legit drop off. He never sees
a thing, it never gets talked about to him and he gets
a monkey or a grand top for a bonus.'

**TOMMY, AN ODD-JOB MAN IN A
DRUG IMPORTATION BUSINESS**

As the age of the entrepreneur dawned in the 1970s, and
bargains and desirable goods were often to be had in another
manor, another town or from a different continent, the question
of transport naturally became key. This new game of pirates
required people with an understanding of the road haulage
industry – its depots, routes, loading methodologies and
markets – and that came at a high price. Information concerning

who was buying what and from where was not easily obtained, and so those individuals who operated as brokers were aware that their knowledge of vital details regarding cargoes, routes and financial alliances was worth money.

SAM: TRANSPORT FOR LONDON

As the only son of a greengrocer, Sam was accustomed to early morning starts on relatively empty roads and London's wholesale markets provided an apprenticeship for a young man with a natural talent for making contacts. At school, he found academic work and charming the teachers easy, but he quickly understood that a ready smile and a box of cabbages were likely to get him further than a clutch of O levels, so he stopped going to school at the age of 15. In the smoky banter of the early morning market cafes, he learnt who could be relied on for an extra hundredweight of King Edwards or a sack of carrots, or which of the market porters had some jewellery to sell. By the time he gained his heavy goods licence in his late teens, Sam was a well-connected young man and as his family's fruit and vegetable business gave him a very good reason to be driving around in the dead of night in a large lorry, he became a popular night-time purveyor of stolen goods.

Over the years, Sam continued to be a reliable and efficient networker across the heavy goods and criminal fraternities: his contacts spread across London and up to the port cities of northern England. It was only a matter of time before he became connected to the cannabis trade that was overwhelmingly dominated by white villains and their colleagues in the haulage industry, bringing in loads via roll-on roll-off ferries. He served five years in prison after his business premises were raided and a recently arrived consignment of ecstasy was found but he remained a vital cog in a number of networks, some of which linked to contacts that he had first made as a youth.

Sam set up deals, found drivers and transported part-loads and multiple kilos around the M25. Sam was valued in particular for brokering deals on behalf of players who were keen on maintaining distance from their investments. Sam enabled villains with violent reputations to fade gracefully into the background and become back-seat investors in both the importation and middle market of a number of illegal drugs, as well as tobacco and alcohol. Sam could pick up and deliver loads or part-loads, organise trade and negotiate prices. This, along with finding vehicles, drivers, buyers, sellers, storage facilities, safe houses and the nooks and crannies of car parks where the CCTV cameras no longer worked, were all part of Sam's extensive skill set, a skill set that is highly adaptable to accommodate various markets. One Saturday afternoon on my way to a football match, I saw Sam standing next to a transit van staring at the metal grill of an off-licence's door, half a dozen slabs of lager next to his feet. He appeared agitated. 'Does he want the fucking lager or what?'

CHARLIE: JUST WALKING THE DOG

Charlie possessed a similar skill set. At the age of 20, he took over his brother's newsagents, which along with their father's transport company, sat at the core of the family heroin distribution business. In an interview conducted in prison, Charlie explained that his family worked exclusively with one supplier, who he described as a partner. With four main customers, they were buying 10–15 kilos a week from this supplier, who imported via Liverpool and Dover in trucks with concealed compartments. With the family's transport firm behind him, Charlie's role was to take responsibility for security and anti-surveillance. He would personally observe the exchange of drugs by surreptitiously walking his dog nearby. He was also concerned with setting routes for the transport of the heroin and paid particular attention to the general appearance of the four men and women who worked in his drug operation, paying them salaries, and stressing the need for a moderate, low-key demeanour.

Knowledge of haulage, of how the business works and especially its vulnerabilities have provided a solid bedrock for many careers in skulduggery and new recruits were constantly being sought out. For instance, one haulier involved in the drugs trade reported that his boss would identify a firm in financial trouble but who still had regular consignments coming into the country and would then offer them a deal so he could use their legitimate consignment as a front to enable drug importation. Transport was the key to a successful enterprise and key personnel commanded high wages.

However, lorry drivers were not the only individuals with legitimate occupations who were valuable to drug importers.

DENNIS: THE AIRPORT CLEANER

Dennis had been an airport employee for over a decade before he progressed to become a manager of a group of aircraft cleaners – a job that required security clearance and gave him access to most areas of the airport. When a local man asked him where parcels of cocaine powder might be hidden on aircraft arriving from South America and the Caribbean, Dennis was happy to help. He highlighted a flaw in the airport's security system: there were no checks on staff driving off the site. He was paid £20,000 for this information and from then on worked as a watcher, observing flights from South America and reporting any unusual Customs activity.

As the cleaning teams were the first people to board any recently arrived aircraft, it was only a matter of time before Dennis progressed to removing the drugs from their hiding places before transporting them out of the airport. Dennis and his associates were soon turning 10 kilos of cocaine into 20 kilos by changing its purity from 95 per cent, to around 40 per cent. with 'any white powder', such as bicarbonate of soda, novocaine or mannitol, before repackaging and selling on.

Dennis was clearly ambitious and used his crucial position at the airport to progress his career by developing a more strategic and profitable role. Other drug market workers utilised air travel in a different manner, managing couriers in a very hands-on fashion.

RON THE MANAGER

Ron was in his mid-fifties and ten years into his retirement from the police force when he first became involved in the drug trade. He was tasked with managing a cocaine importation operation based on couriers from the Caribbean, and the recruitment of personnel was a crucial part of his role. In a prison interview, Ron detailed how he identified white middle-aged men who were short of money and 'needed a holiday' as potential couriers among the clientele of the casino where he was a regular punter. He would befriend the gamblers and over a period of time introduce the prospect of a free holiday in the sun. On acceptance of the deal Ron made all of the travel arrangements, purchased the airline tickets, provided the suitcase and handed over a generous amount of spending money, before instructing the courier to 'behave like a normal holidaymaker, don't draw attention to yourself, basically enjoy your holiday'. Ron's job was then over until the holidaymaker returned with an identical suitcase containing cocaine.

Ron explained that on the successful arrival of a consignment he would relieve the courier of the case at the airport and carry the drugs to his bosses, waiting in a nearby car park, who would take the bag away, remove the drugs and return to the airport an hour later with a number of shopping bags containing £12,000 in cash. Ron would take his £5,000 fee, and pass £7,000 to the courier, who had enjoyed an all-expenses-paid two-week holiday.

Another example of Ron's management role involved a successful cocaine courier being employed to recruit couriers herself, which she did, mainly from the local prostitute community. This method is common and many inmates of British prisons who received long sentences were little more than bit-part players in drug-trafficking operations, for couriers are expendable to dealing networks. One dealer estimated that one in four couriers using aircraft were apprehended and research indicated that lorry drivers transporting drugs had a far better chance of making crime pay than drug couriers.

However, some individuals were able to successfully develop even more highly specialised transport roles within the drug importation industry – like Tommy's – very similar to those of logistics experts working in legitimate markets.

TOMMY

After a 20-year army career, Tommy drifted for six years trying various jobs before a friend in the drug trade paid him £1,000 to work on a 'money-out' trip, delivering money out of the country, either to suppliers or as part of a money laundering operation. Predators were targeting these money-out trips, robbing couriers and as an ex-army man, Tommy was regarded as a suitable employee. Over the next six months, Tommy regularly delivered money to an address in France and learnt enough about the drug trade to branch out, using the logistics expertise that he had acquired in the Army. As an independent contractor, he specialised in organising the transport of anything except heroin and people across the Channel, warehouse to warehouse.

Tommy dealt with large loads transported by vehicle, for instance 100kg of cocaine or 120kg of amphetamine, while foot passengers on ferries 'walked through' small loads such as 5kg of cocaine. The price for moving 1kg of anything across the Channel was £2,000. Tommy took £500 per kilo and the rest was spent on his staff. To put this into context, he would charge, based on the year of his interview, £200,000 to move 100kg of cocaine valued at £4.5m, giving him a personal fee of £50,000.

Whenever possible, Tommy recruited ex-military personnel and unsurprisingly spent considerable amounts of time making sure potential recruits were genuine and committed to working in the drug trade. He paid his staff a salary and even though the drug trade from mid-December to February was slow, 'everyone gets paid and for holidays'. Tommy always expected to be arrested at some point in his career and built financial provision for that event into the fees that he charged. He also applied this principle to staff and when two of his personnel were arrested and imprisoned, their families continued to be supported.

After receiving a coded message, Tommy would attend a face-to-face meeting with the wholesaler where they would discuss details, in particular the nature and size of the load, and the timing of the deal. In Tommy's operation, few people actually knew each other and face-to-face meetings were rare, but with expenses paid up-front, Tommy would develop a plan and brief his personnel before agreeing the details of the pick-up and final destination with the wholesaler. Tommy would then rendezvous with the driver and supplier and make final arrangements for shipping the illegal freight, ensuring that he was never actually present when the consignment was loaded. He was meticulous in ensuring that even in the event of being searched his loads seemed entirely legitimate, with the drugs imported as part of a load often bound for wholesale fruit and vegetable markets or hidden in consignments of frozen fish. Tommy would then travel to the UK and, after confirming the unloading details, wait for the lorry to disembark then proceed to a prearranged location near to the final drop point. Tommy would meet the wholesaler and receive his fee before phoning the driver with details of his final destination point, and then meet the driver at another location to pay him off.

When restricted to plundering their own manor, professional criminals were clustered into tight-knit communities within the urban underworld and venturing outside the neighbourhood was an exceptional and ambitious adventure. But as the ability to move goods, money, even people across cities, countries and continents became the key to real wealth, a knowledge base and skill set within the world of haulage and transport was consequently as valuable as knowing how to disable an alarm, drill a safe, or intimidate bank staff had been during previous eras. Modern day criminals, if they are to thrive, have had to learn to think outside of their local boxes, nurturing relationships between players residing in different parts of the UK, as well as different parts of the world.

Chapter 20

SMOKING AND THE BANDITS

'Some were making money, others were getting cheap fags, everyone's a winner. None of the people I knew saw this as criminal, what the fuck's criminal about providing cheaper stuff than what's already out there?'

GEOFF, TOBACCO BOOTLEGGER

The owner of the newsagent's had a reputation for surliness and so local shoppers tried to restrict their purchases to newspapers, magazines and soft drinks from the refrigerator. If they had to ask for something from behind the counter – for instance, a phone card or twenty Benson & Hedges – the newsagent would call them a 'cunt' under his breath, before tersely selling the goods. The one exception was if the shopper asked for 'Albanian Marlboros'. This code triggered the shopkeeper to bring out from below the counter a range of apparently conventionally branded cigarettes that appeared identical to the glossy packets that lined the wall behind his head. The only obvious difference was the price.

JASON'S FIRM

Jason started his bootlegging forays from Southshore into France in 1998 when he recruited family members, friends and acquaintances as day trippers to act as his 'mules'. Offering free coach trips on Channel ferry crossings, Jason provided his mules with money and shopping lists of cigarettes and tobacco to purchase in France 'as their own goods'. They were paid in cash, handing over their purchases to Jason on the return trip. He explained the procedure:

'These runs were known as the pensioner day outs. Most of the people on the coaches were old folks and doleys[29] wanting to make some extra money. They were all told: "If you get stopped and your bags get pulled, admit it's yours, you've bought the cigarettes and they're for your own personal use and let Customs keep them. You'll still get paid and no one's going to get into trouble." The ferries were full of coaches where the same racket was going on. It was just a laugh, really. No real effort required, hardly any risks associated with it at that time, just me driving the coach with a load of pensioners having sing-songs and playing housey.[30] The people were just having a laugh and a drink, getting a free run out to France, filling their bags up with fags and baccy and then handing them over to me once we got back to England.'

---

29 Benefit recipients.
30 Bingo.

Jason's right-hand man, Geoff, explained:

'Everybody wanted cheap fags and baccy, fucking
everyone, and there was just never enough of the stuff
to go around. When Jason started doing the ferry runs,
he couldn't get the stuff in fast enough. He'd have five
or six grands' worth of tobacco from the ferry runs
in one day, the next it's gone – sold out, vanished.
See, the word was getting passed round, friends and
family and everyone – I mean fucking everyone –
wanted some of the action, cos everyone was getting
something out of it. Some were making money, others
were getting cheap fags, everyone's a winner. None of
the people I knew saw this as criminal, what the fuck's
criminal about providing cheaper stuff than what's
already out there?'

Jason made a remarkably ambitious move: from a base in
eastern France, he employed six British drivers to make
smuggling runs into Luxembourg in locally hired cars with
the seats down so that, including the boot space, each car
carried 100,000 cigarettes. Jason rented one floor of a small
French hotel to provide accommodation for his drivers with a
room set aside to store the contraband. Soon a steady stream
of professional UK bootleggers aiming to evade UK tobacco
levies realised that Jason's cigarettes were significantly cheaper
than the French and Belgian alternatives and formed a queue.

'I had such a flow of punters turning up it was difficult
to keep stocked. Phone calls day and night. "Jason,
I need 40,000 fags, 300 packs of baccy." I had four

mobile phones on the go at all times, it was that busy. I was spending, on average, £20,000 a week, I had six English lads going over the borders between France and Luxembourg, filling the cars up, driving back to the digs, dropping off the goods and then turning straight round to go and fill the motors up with fags again. So I'm paying for hotel rooms, renting six big French cars, spending 20 grand a week on the goods, paying the lads a grand each, tax-free, on a weekly basis and on average I'm making nine grand clear profit a week.'

Evading both French and British excise duties, Jason co-ordinated a well-organised, efficient and highly profitable smuggling operation. Here he explains the market niche that he was exploiting:

'The Adinkerke [Belgian] hypermarkets were full of Brits buying nothing but fags, baccy and booze but Luxembourg was cheaper, less tax. You see, in games like these most people don't see the wood for the trees. They just want to get in quick, make as much money as they can in as short a time and with as little work and overheads as possible. Take the money and run. Usually pretty sloppy with no real investment, no plans.'

In Europe, the further east you travel, the less excise is charged and the cheaper the goods, and Jason aimed to capitalise on the price disparities between neighbouring countries. Importantly, by buying in Luxembourg and selling in France to

British buyers, Jason was able to evade the attention of British law enforcement. Geoff worked with Jason for the duration of the operation's five-year lifespan.

> 'We're running over the borders [between France and Luxembourg] loading up with the fags and then hammering it back to the hotel. In hiring French motors, if the cars get seized by the French [Customs], "It's not my motor, is it?" French Customs would have to return it at some point, back to the hire company we got it from. We also knew that French Customs were sometimes pulling cars with UK licence plates, so to avoid that risk we're using motors with French number plates. If I got pinched crossing the border, I'm going to say that the goods were mine and for my personal use only. If I'm over [the national 'duty free' limit] I'd have said, "You can keep 'em mate, I aint paying yer fucking tax, you have 'em." But see, the French and Luxembourg Customs were a lot more lax than our [UK] Customs because they had a different set of rules, see, and word had it that they didn't really give a shit.'

Jason added:

> 'We're avoiding smuggling the stock back into England because we're selling it on in France to the English. If they get tugged[31] at Southshore or wherever, the stuff simply gets confiscated, no questions asked, really.

31 Arrested.

Essentially, we've done our bit and made our money, everyone keeps their mouths shut. If someone gets done I'm no worse off as the money's already changed hands, so it's someone else's loss. Basing the job to start in Luxembourg, then selling the goods on in France, cut me loose from English Customs. For those who were unfortunate enough to get nicked, they never said a word and I've been told that they [Customs] rarely asked too many probing questions.

'The odd motor or two might get seized by Customs and that was all part of the risk, but most of the lads I was selling to weren't driving over in top-drawer vehicles, they left them at home and came over in vans, which were sound enough under the bonnet but you'd be lucky to get 250 quid for it if you'd tried to sell it. See, the lads I was selling to weren't the type of bootleggers on chancer day runs across the Channel. These lads were usually business types, players of sorts, with a fair bit to lose but who knew the game. My biggest threat came on the French side. But we did everything that we could to distance ourselves from being caught. Look, in five years of trading we never got pinched, not once by either side. That speaks for itself, don't it?'

This was a smart, risk-averse firm who were discreet, avoiding flashing the cash in a coke-fuelled world of champagne and strippers, and the routine nature of their business ruled out the extremes displayed at certain levels of the drug trade. Jason employed 'touts' who found customers trading at wholesale level in the UK and who were willing to take the major burden of risk by coming to France, loading up, and taking their chances in avoiding Customs and Excise at English ports. The pensioner day-outs into France continued, this was for his 'friends in the north', who would travel to Southshore in vans and minibuses on a regular basis, fill the vehicles and return home to sell on the contraband to customers scattered around the north of England.

Graham, an associate of Jason's explained:

> 'The flat was a property investment, just an empty flat he was waiting to do something with, really. Anyway, that flat was filled to chest height in every room with cigarettes and rolly tobacco. If it had caught fire and gone up in smoke half of Southshore would have gone down with lung cancer, there was that much of the stuff in it. All these mad northerners would land in vans and that, every couple of weeks or so, and it was like feeding time at the zoo when they landed here. They went mad for it. Couldn't get enough of the stuff, cos them northerners – they do like a smoke you know – and they were running down here in droves all of the time.'

COMMODITY-HOPPING

Many smuggling groups alternate between the importation of illegal drugs and less risky commodities such as tobacco and cigarettes, a process known as 'commodity-hopping'. This is particularly attractive if you consider the UK's sentencing tariffs, which are far more lenient for illegally importing cigarettes and tobacco than they are for the same value of illegal drugs. The importance of flexibility cannot be overestimated; for instance, one cocaine importer discovered that he was attracting police attention and seamlessly switched to the large-scale importation of contraband cigarettes. Subsequently, he shifted again, this time to buying huge quantities of an everyday domestic detergent product from Belgium, where it was considerably cheaper than in the UK, importing it and selling it across the south-east. It's all money.

SEIZURE

There has long been a powerful tobacco industry lobby in the House of Commons and it was just a matter of time before Customs and Excise focused on the smuggling and bootlegging of cigarettes and tobacco. Both the contraband and the commercial vehicles carrying them were seized, 'even if this is the first time you have been caught'. While this impacted on small-scale bootlegging, initially high-level commodity-hoppers were prepared to take their chances, for while the van and goods would be seized, nothing below one million cigarettes seized resulted in a prosecution, so for the professionals this remained a high-profit/relatively low-risk business.

However, eventually the government's strategy in targeting the bootleggers did impact Jason's business:

'They [Customs and Excise] began seizing everyone and his dog's motors. For years, we'd all got away with it and then, BANG, I've now got lads whining down my mobile to me, "They've taken the lot. 100,000 cigarettes fucking gone, and the bastards have seized my motor." I had loads of sob stories like that, one straight after another. I realised that the longer this went on, the more chance that people might start opening their mouths and begin telling tales about me. It was time to get out. They weren't fucking about anymore, so we shut it down in three days.'

The threat of violence was also a factor in his decision.

'Towards the end of it all, some nasty pieces of work starting getting in on it, and these were very violent men. People were getting ripped off, were getting taxed on the stuff they were smuggling in by serious villains, and stock was getting nicked. For something that started out as a pretty laid-back business with only the law to look out for, we heard about people being beaten up and threatened with guns. So at the same point in time you've got Customs seizing goods and motors and then seriously violent men robbing whatever they weren't picking up and taking the rest of it. Killed it off for me and I thought "Fuck it, I'm out."'

The focus on smaller-scale bootlegging firms and individual cross-Channel shoppers amplified the risks both for those operating at Jason's level and for mere nicotine-addicted bargain hunters. Consequently, cargo containers were increasingly used by the more committed sectors of the criminal fraternity, along with bootlegging alternatives, such as passenger flights. For instance, in 2004, a flight returning at 1am on Christmas Day was targeted by HM Customs and Excise and over two million cigarettes were seized from 21 passengers – approximately 100,000 cigarettes per arrested passenger. A Customs officer explained, 'These individual bootleggers were in fact mules for a bigger operation and were smuggling the cigarettes for an organised criminal group.'

Jason's firm exploited a market that is barely different from the legitimate version and his role as a supplier to the 'white van trade' was the result of price discrepancies within the European free market: cheap in the east, expensive in the west.

JAKE'S STORY

As a skilled building worker sub-contracting his skills to property developers in London, Jake had succeeded in providing a decent standard of living for his family and paid what he felt was a high tax bill. While he had never visited mainland Europe, he had holidayed in Florida and Dubai and once went on a stag weekend to Dublin. Although he always voted for the Labour Party, he seemed to pine for the Thatcher era. He sometimes played golf at the local municipal course.

'My views on crime? With kids [as a father], you are going to be anti-drugs. I never did them and I know nothing about them, but they are bad. We have worked on places that have been used by druggies and I don't think you can imagine what their lives are like. My aunt, who is the only one of the older generation left, lives in a flat, one of them warden-assisted places. She has been burgled. Shocking really, so I am glad we live out of it a bit. Having said that, you get trouble round here more and more.'

While working on a central London building site, Jake employed a young electrician who sold bootlegged cigarettes to the site's large workforce. 'I can't remember the prices, I don't smoke so it wouldn't mean much to me. But they was cheap and it was upfront cos it's hardly criminal – the only ones who are suffering are the smokers and they are going to get sick anyway, whether they pay full price or not.' The electrician and his cousin travelled to Belgium every few weeks to buy cigarettes legitimately at hypermarkets and illegally sold them to friends and acquaintances without paying the excise duty. When the electrician left to work on the other side of London, many of the electrician's customers continued to arrive at Jake's place of work looking for their cheap supply. 'I just went back to this sparks[32] and told him that he had a lot of customers looking for him, and he gave me these big old sleeves of fags to go into work with.' And so, law-abiding non-smoking Jake entered the world of retail contraband. By now, the two cousins were working hard across both Belgium and French hypermarkets, varying their routes and buying patterns before they found a wholesaler 'who was doing loads of legit booze for the coach parties and that. He put them onto really cheap fags, really cheap, wholesale it was so no tax.'

Now the cousins, and Jake, had taken a big step up from bootlegging – where local taxes are paid before importing and selling the goods to consumers who benefit by not paying UK tax. In the eyes of the law, Jake was now a smuggler and, along with his two partners, started bringing in lorries with large amounts of cigarettes hidden among legitimate loads. 'Our drivers was always picking up in France but the fags come

---

32 Electrician.

from Spain, all the usual brands that you get in the shops.' Jake's job was to find customers, and both entrepreneurially minded individuals as well as legitimate retail businesses clamoured for his business. While maintaining his day job, Jake was soon spending many hours talking to potential customers on the telephone.

When the smugglers obtained access to warehousing facilities on an industrial estate adjacent to a firm who operated 24 hours a day, their business was able to merge seamlessly with their legitimate traffic both day and night. They found it easy to recruit lorry drivers who were picking up legitimate loads in continental Europe. Jack's main problem was money:

> 'I had dough in the fridge, the freezer, behind kitchen units. See, for somebody like me, used to earning enough to look after the family, having bricks of tenners passed to me was – it sounds strange I know, but I didn't always like it. I never put a total on it. All the phone calls did my head in, I am no businessman, it felt kind of serious. Well, I did start to think about what might happen if it all came on top. The family, kids, mortgage . . . The other two were so well at it I could never say to them, "Hang on, my bottle's going." It just went off on its own.'

Each load carried a minimum of a million cigarettes.

> 'Take the driver's chunk of a grand and a few quid for rent and extras and we were splitting 60–70 grand three ways.'

This trip was made three times in six months and then a buyer was arrested for receiving stolen goods, setting in train a series of arrests for non-smuggling offences. The smugglers ceased trading and when Jake told his partners that he wanted to retire from the smuggling business, the cousins became aggressive, demanding money to pay for what they claimed were outstanding overheads. 'They came on a bit strong with me. Nothing happened but I'm worried about my kids and what might happen. So I was not getting into it any more, and that was that. I give them some dough for the lock up but I was out. They went back to buying from the supermarkets, so I heard.'

The only time that I heard Jake swear was in response to me asking if he had ever considered himself to be an organised criminal:

'It's fucking daft to even think about what we were up to as being anything more than a bit of a scam, a bit of tax dodging, really. There is a piece in one of the papers about how footballers avoid tax by making themselves into companies. Our thing was harder work than that but it's just accepted by most people. If fags was illegal I could see it but you can buy them anywhere. Having said that, my eldest smokes and it worries me, the health issue.'

The tobacco trade brought players into the business who were otherwise law-abiding citizens. As Jake said, cigarettes or indeed alcohol are everyday items available on supermarket shelves, so making these admittedly damaging items a little cheaper for eager punters does not seem particularly criminal. Just another scam, like Charlie Nails and his recycled sweepings, it's a little earner that allows a rare ray of sunshine into life in the city. Just so long as you don't go too far. For above and beyond the friends and neighbourhood-based trade, there are higher stakes and bigger risks.

Chapter 21

'I CAN GET IT WHOLESALE': GETTING INTO A BUSINESS LIKE NO OTHER

'People used to think I'm the boss but I said to myself, they should see some of the blokes who I'm dealing with, a bloke who I'm giving 70 grand to twice a week and I'm not his best customer.'

WAZ, HEROIN DEALER

Entrepreneurs like Jason needed to be flexible and willing to mutate: when the smuggling business became difficult he shifted his attention to counterfeit cigarettes and tobacco, buying from a wholesaler in southern England who imported container loads directly from China and eastern Europe. In addition, Jason worked with an army of dealers whose business it was to shift the product a little closer to the consumer. However, as the counterfeits routinely contain pesticides, arsenic, rat poison and high levels of nicotine, 'beating the revenue' feels a little less of a social service carried out by bold outlaws, as loss to the exchequer is replaced by an even greater loss of life than that instigated by their deadly legal counterparts.

But there is money to be made from addiction and purveyors of both legal and illegal alcohol and tobacco should be considered on a continuum of harm along with usual suspects such as heroin dealers. Often considered as being among the most harmful product on this continuum, and also containing quantities of deadly adulterants, heroin has a mark-up from production to the street of over 16,000 per cent and the businesses that make up the vital link between importation and the street, the wholesale or middle-market sector, have become embedded into the UKs illegal economy.

As the demand for heroin is relatively stable, dealers enjoy a measure of predictability. Given the money at stake and the heavy price to be paid for failure, trust is highly valued. Consequently, the core membership of heroin dealing networks tend to be small, comprising no more than four or five people, with dealers placing a high premium on relationships with family and friends. Networks are often tightly bonded groups of individuals with relationships going back a long way – whether in terms of kinship, coming from the same neighbourhood or growing up at school together. However, if these qualifications regarding kinship and friendship are met, there are few barriers to entering this business. A desire to make money and a willingness to break the law is all that is required.

DEE THE FAMILY MAN

In the mid-1990s, Dee joined the family business that his uncles had formed a decade earlier and quickly proved his worth by buying a kilo of heroin and selling it in two months. He soon progressed to collecting from his supplier once or twice a week, storing the drugs in his house and car and selling between nine ounces and a kilo per week to over a hundred users and dealers. After only three months, he employed four men of Afghani and Turkish origin, stressing that coming from the same community engendered a high degree of mutual trust. A supply of high quality product, along with a good line of credit with the wholesaler, enabled the business to expand and soon his suppliers were delivering the drugs by taxi to a series of safe houses where the heroin was bagged and sold. Dee's solicitor, although ostensibly employed to defend his runners if they were arrested, also passed on details pertaining to other cases, including police activity and forensic test results regarding the quantity and quality of his other clients' drugs, who were Dee's competitors. Dee shrewdly invested his profits in rental property and a post office, along with contraband cigarettes and alcohol.

While British prisons increasingly warehouse individuals suffering a multitude of social, medical and mental health afflictions, prison is a fine source of knowledge for individuals who have failed in other criminal endeavours. Even those imprisoned for reasons unrelated to drugs might educate themselves on this topic while inside.

WAZ

While serving a sentence for living on immoral earnings, Waz learnt about the profitability of the heroin business by paying close attention to prison dealers. 'All I could see was pound signs; it was just too much money to let it go. So I started when I came out.' Commencing as an ounce dealer, he was making £300 per day, but he was ambitious and soon moved on from trading in ounces to buying and selling five kilos per week, a trade based upon an arrangement that gave him one kilo on credit for every kilo that he bought with cash. The four women that he employed received £1,500 per week for collecting and delivering parcels to customers who were old friends and family members in Manchester, Southampton, Bristol and London. Crucially he was not a heroin user and while he also traded in small amounts of cocaine, this was mainly because he liked to smoke crack 'as a treat'. Although his heroin business funded a lavish lifestyle, he was well aware of his place in the dealing hierarchy. 'I never liked to think of myself as the boss. People used to think I'm the boss but I said to myself, they should see some of the blokes who I'm dealing with, a bloke who I'm giving 70 grand to twice a week and I'm not his best customer.'

Prison was an even more vital hub for those locked up for drug related offences and the quality of the contacts made in prison can be high and often of an international nature, thanks to the increasingly cosmopolitan UK prison population.

ERVING THE PRISON SCHOLAR

In the late 1970s, while serving a four-year sentence for fraud, Erving dabbled in cannabis dealing, but paid close attention to the market in heroin. Although he knew little about the business, friends of his wife were addicts and, on his release, and with his appetite whetted by his prison dealing, he soon commenced selling £10 bags of heroin. However, he became dissatisfied with his erratic supply and, while hindered by not being a heroin user, he spent a great deal of time seeking reliable suppliers. Once this was achieved, Erving, who described himself as being 'quite ambitious', soon had several dealers working for him and moved up to buying ounces before once again his supply went 'haywire'.

But Erving worked his way back and within 18 months he was buying 2–3 kilos of heroin and selling to old friends at a 40 per cent mark-up, who in turn sold on to their own networks of users. After working with a group of Asian heroin importers, Erving made a huge career leap by flying to India to meet contacts who were networked with his Indian/Pakistani connections back in the UK. In an attempt to 'cut out the middle man to cut costs and increase quality', he flew to India twice, buying consignments of eight kilos of heroin. The Indians transported the drugs to the UK and the suitcase full of heroin was picked up by a courier from a pre-arranged address. Eventually, after a period of success, the courier picking up the suitcase was arrested and subsequently informed on Erving.

He served his sentence and promptly returned to the heroin business, overseeing the importation of kilos of heroin concealed in passenger luggage flown to Europe from India. However, a courier failed to pick up the drugs from the airport in Belgium and Erving had to make the pick-up himself. The courier had been arrested at the airport and the police were waiting for Erving.

The six years that he subsequently spent with Kurdish and Turkish traffickers in a Belgian prison raised Erving's education to another level, and within a fortnight of his release he was working with some of his new Turkish contacts, this time importing hundreds of kilos. The drugs were brought from Turkey to Belgium, leaving Erving to coordinate the final leg to the UK, supplying customers in Scotland and the north-west of England.

Jail time provided Erving with the knowledge to engage with a higher level of enterprise: a prison sentence was the price that he paid for this education. Given the number of convictions that he accrued in his career, however, his persistence was remarkable.

STAN THE QUICK LEARNER

Unlike Erving, Stan was an enthusiastic consumer of the product he sold. He had used cannabis from the age of 14 and cocaine from 18. His family had been importing heroin for many years and he had accrued a general knowledge of the business through his own drug use as well as 'hearing things' from family members. Aspiring to a nice lifestyle, he began buying ounces of heroin and selling it in £10 bags when he was 17 years old, and in just six months was purchasing kilos (36 ounces) of heroin and selling ounces. Initially, his customers were addicts, but Stan gained access to their dealers and in turn was introduced to their dealers and converted them into his customers. When he commenced purchasing larger quantities, he transferred the £10 bag business to someone else, who in exchange agreed to purchase ounce deals from Stan. Aged just 18, he spent just under two years in prison for conspiracy to import but on his release began purchasing 5 kilo parcels, before quickly progressing to buying 350 kilo loads from various importers. These operations involved one car to transport the heroin and two additional vehicles providing a protective shield, specifically to 'ram the police off the road' in the event of interception.

Stan's 20 to 30 customers were from all over northern England and included 'suit and tie types' as well as trusted friends and business associates who 'knew the rules'. The four people who worked for him were paid £500 a week, delivering drugs, collecting money, providing surveillance at handovers and occasionally 'cutting' the heroin. The iron rule for Stan, as for the majority of drug entrepreneurs, was to 'keep the drugs and money separate'.

Entrepreneurs running legal commercial concerns are attractive potential partners for traffickers as they have access to premises, cash flow, transport and other vital infrastructure of an ongoing legitimate enterprise into which illegitimate money, goods and labour can blend. Most importantly, proven entrepreneurial competence within legitimate business signals that an individual is willing to take a risk for profit, he is game and, as in the old underworld, being game is crucial.

STEVE THE BUSINESSMAN

As a businessman running a legitimate enterprise, Steve considered that the qualities demanded by the drugs trade to be the same as in any other business – integrity, reliability and trustworthiness. He took the training of his employees seriously, equipping them with the necessary knowledge and skills by passing on his own experience. Steve only ever worked with small units of four or five people and, although he acknowledged that trust was important, it was vital that the members of the unit were not so close that they could be connected to each other if caught. New staff would be inducted into the enterprise by initially performing easy tasks, for instance, organising a drop-off or a pick-up, before moving on to more responsible roles. Employees were paid on a commission basis and if they performed particularly well they were rewarded with a bonus. Steve did not work with close friends and considered that the unreliability of drug users made them unemployable.

All communications with customers were disguised as part of his legitimate business, which was carried out over the phone. Steve never employed storers but took responsibility for this role himself, burying the drugs in the ground. Although he did lose some drugs in this way to theft, he felt that this was a reasonable price to pay, as if the drugs were discovered they would be especially difficult to track back to him. Steve took responsibility for sourcing the goods before selling directly to upper-level dealers, while a close associate handled the finances.

One of the most pervasive cliches of the drug trade is that all members of the drug dealing community are intrinsically violent. The reality is more nuanced. While violence certainly is an ever present possibility, not everyone can be typified by latent blood lust. Steve was never involved with any violence, he abhorred it and, although he did on occasions feel intimidated by buyers, if he did trade with people who had violent reputations, he would only deal small quantities until they proved their trustworthiness. If he was ripped off he put it down to experience and avoided any conflict.

As another dealer eloquently explained:

'It all depends how you conduct your business. I've seen people going on, "You fuckin' this, you fuckin' that, don't let me down or else blah, blah, blah." All we used to say was, "Listen, here's what. You let me down then you don't get it again." Simple as that. Don't even come knocking on the door. But none of this

"I'll threaten to do this or that" . . . That's what makes people more on edge, and if they're on edge they can do silly things. They always say don't be scared of the hard man, be scared of the frightened man. So try to keep people sweet, I see as the best way.'

JOEY: TOO MUCH JUNKIE BUSINESS

Joey was a 33-year-old who had been involved with drugs for half of his life. His local pub was a retail hub for a wide range of drugs and, as a regular, he was eventually asked to deliver heroin, amphetamine and LSD to various locations, for which he was paid generously. His employers would put the drugs in a rental car and Joey was told to pick up the car and drive it to a location where he would leave it for someone else to collect. Joey would arrive early to collect the car and check the surrounding area for police. However, 'Sometimes it doesn't feel right,' and he would walk away.

Joey quickly progressed and by the age of 23 had set up his own business buying kilos and setting people up to sell for him. He had a close business associate who was also a good friend and they moved around the country drinking in pubs and talking to people involved in the drug trade before setting up a trading base. When they left an area because 'things were getting on top', they would first set up a dealer to take over the business, passing on their clients and supplying them with an eighth of heroin and 'build up from there'. If the fledgling could prove that he could pay back the cost of the eighth, Joey and his partner would supply him with a larger amount.

The closer to retail, the more likely that dealers will be users and addicts. While the chaos of addiction merges all too well into the street dealer's toxic lifestyle, at the higher levels, with complex arrangements in a constant state of flux, addiction is a bad fit. At around the age of 25, Joey had become a daily heroin user and four years later, he had a £2,000-per-week crack habit. When he became addicted, Joey lost his reputation as a competent dealer; he was no longer reliable and resorted to robbery and burglary to fund his habit. He was arrested in a car he had stolen.

The men whose words I have included in this chapter were not members of some glossy mafia conspiracy, but independently minded traders who had to be extremely light on their feet in order to adapt and exploit opportunities. The ethnicity of individuals linked to parts of the world where drugs are harvested or processed are particularly relevant, offering opportunities that are attractive to newcomers as well as the usual suspects.

The cost of a 0.1g bag of heroin is approximately £10 and although according to the Home Office, only 0.1 per cent of adults aged 16–59 in England and Wales had used heroin in the last year, opiates are responsible for 80 per cent of drug related deaths in the UK, which has the largest reported opioid-using population in Europe. The UK opiate market is worth £3.8bn and among British drug users, heroin users have the highest average annual spend of £12,500.

By the time that they were interviewed, all of these dealers featured in this chapter were of course prisoners, the majority of whom considered themselves to be 'unlucky' to have been caught. 'Being unlucky' is of course the convicted villain's equivalent of the schoolboy's 'My dog ate my homework' excuse. Though of course for Joey, his luck disappeared into his arm.

EPILOGUE: THE BUSINESS

'Life is nothing but a competition to be the criminal rather than the victim.'

BERTRAND RUSSELL

Getting on for 70 years since that smoggy day in Plaistow, I found myself in a bar in Essex with a group of men aged from mid-fifties to early eighties who wistfully stroked their fading scars while carrying out a roll call of those who are no longer with us, 'doing a ten' or living in Lanzarote. These men were all born and bred in the East End, most wear heavily branded leisurewear and, mid-afternoon on a workday, with the lager in full flow, they were keen to outdo each other with tales of saucy skulduggery from the good old, bad old days.

One man who I had not met before plugged into a 'the older I get the better I was' riff by telling me a story of how he had once faced down a violent drunk who had threatened him, going on to exclaim that, 'I don't know what it is about me, but people do find me intimidating.' When he left the table to visit the toilet, one of his friends who had overheard the boast said, 'Take no fucking notice of him. I have known him all his life and he aint had a fight since he was about nine.' Another companion explained that, 'The most intimidating thing about him is the hair growing out of his ears.' But take away the green screen of fantasy onto which they project their lives and many of these men were dealing with issues that would have been unimaginable to their young selves.

They have reached an age when funerals outnumber weddings, half a century or more of booze and fags are catching up with them, and old faces from the days of tight shirts and demi-perms regularly go absent without leave, with or without a Charlie habit and a 30-year-old trainee beautician on their arm. These men have either done well or were working very hard to look as if they have, and despite their camaraderie, they remain competitively materialistic. When one of the drinkers proclaimed that a friend was now driving a Porsche, they all eagerly interrogated their telephones before gleefully reporting that the vehicle was over 20 years old and worth less than £5,000. The sports car enthusiast had been put back in his box.

While most of these old boys shifted to the suburbs long ago, they are regularly drawn back to the streets where they made their names and where, in their youth, they learnt their trades, the art of a moody deal, or both. Back then life was simple. As far as skulduggery was concerned, unless it was 'your turn', the local Old Bill seldom got involved as long as you tidied up afterwards. And if that didn't work, there was always an envelope tucked behind a cistern in the gents. Apart from the odd hillbilly feud between families, serious violence was usually limited to the activities of the respected and much feared Faces, who displayed an enthusiasm for firearms, but 'only hurt their own', firing the imaginations of both villains and civilians.

Increasingly over the years, conversations have become pock-marked with worries of children and grandchildren being 'on the gear', and as those three words hang in the air, the beer and the bullshit evaporate. There is seldom any follow-up chat, just a rueful shaking of the head. Shame, regret and incomprehension are left suspended between these men who, for all their Jack-the-lad bombast, find many aspects of the world that they have helped create both frightening and utterly mystifying. After badly beating two debtors, both the cocaine-dealing son-in-law and grandson of one man were now serving serious time together. When I was introduced to another drinker's grandson, I barely recognised him from the talented footballer and keen kick-boxer I had met just a few years earlier. While reasonably well dressed, there was an exhausted hollowness to his expression and when he said his goodbyes, it was in a voice reduced to a faint monotone. We all avoided eye contact while his heartbroken grandfather got the drinks in.

Sitting to the edge of the group was a sallow-skinned man in a black three-piece suit, black tie and shiny black Oxfords, who took discreet, economic sips of his lager. His deep-set eyes deflected the enquiring gaze with a slightly off kilter stare and he oozed mordant threat. The group wondered who he was. A gangster? A middle-aged predator reaffirming an ancient territory? There was no doubt whatsoever that this was an agent from the underworld. It took almost two years before regulars discovered that this wraith-like man was actually an undertaker's assistant taking time out with a beer and a bag of nuts. Criminals don't look like they used to. As one admirable individual who had used education to leave the life behind explained to me, 'Now when you get somebody who is a Chap gets shot, look in the paper when they nick who did it. Nobody would have heard of him, he won't be a Face, it'll be some young boy with no record whose been bunged a few quid and given a gun.'

Nowadays discretion is the key and it is only the dinosaurs of the old underworld chasing another book contract who encourage publicity. Of course, a few smart villains have managed to enter a form of retirement that does not require 24-hour security, but they are essentially consultants providing advice and settling disputes for a price. As one London-based ex-armed robber explained of a sociable and exceedingly smart Face: 'He would never get at it himself, not any more. But he is always helpful to people with a problem. He knows everybody, very dependable and good company.'

Thanks in no small part to the prison system, these highly valued men have connections all over the UK and among the ex-pat community in well-established outposts of skulduggery in Europe and beyond. Importantly, these same Faces are able to lend their reputations to legal activities such as security and debt collection, and in the case of the latter, they can find themselves competing with other retired Faces whose reputations carry considerable clout, even within discreet alcoves of the corporate world.

This book started off in the smog of 1950s London, within a community that was far more complex and nuanced than most historians and professional sentimentalists would have us believe. Damaged by war and ongoing shortages, this community was at once grateful and resentful. While they were glad to return to some of the everyday communality of the pre-war years, at the same time, not too many people complained when they were offered a home with an indoor toilet and a bathroom, even if it meant leaving familiar streets behind.

All over the UK as the rubble was cleared, established communities experienced tumultuous changes that continued for decades, and produced some weird mutations that defy the simplistic portraits of working-class life that are still embedded in media and academic narratives dominated by the middle classes. For instance, my part of East London featured trade unionists who were dedicated to improving the plight of their comrades, who would drunkenly sing 'The Internationale' on a Saturday night, but also had a nice little earner supplying hookey meat to the local butcher's.

This community believed in sticking together, and self-sacrifice in the name of the common good had seen them through extreme economic hardship and a world war. Yet, although none would think of themselves as a thief or receiver of stolen goods, everybody was at it; even those seeking the kind of modest respectable lifestyle promised by the Attlee government would have a dabble – after all, it's only a sausage.

There were so many gradations of skulduggery available to men and women who were still picking shrapnel out of their back garden flowerbeds into the 1960s. Some Argentinian beef or New Zealand lamb, a couple of school shirts or material to be turned into clothing or curtains could be purchased without fear of being apprehended or stigmatised.

White goods started appearing high on the list of desirable consumer durables but these had to be liberated from stores and warehouses rather than casually swiped from the docks. Graduates of dockside felony began earning more than mere beer money providing for a society where consumption now meant more than a bad cough.

By the 1960s, thieves, both part-time and professional, populated this working-class world of relative affluence, and some were connected to loose-knit networks of villains with aspirations that stretched beyond the post-war settlement of a home, a wage and retirement. Smart, stylish and very greedy, many of these professionals were also violent, willing to use weapons such as knives and razors as well as fists. Violent professionals often had links to pre-war territorial tensions and race-track conflicts, counting men who had made money and their reputations from the black-outs and shortages of the 1940s on their rosters. These men were joined by those possessing more cerebral skill sets, as well as enablers such as solicitors and accountants. Importantly, they resided in an underworld of criminal commitment and conspicuous consumption that was played out in venues across working-class London, and marked by an almost mystical criminal code that valorised the ability to stoically endure prison.

Patrolling the borders of these badlands were detectives, who concocted a heady, if at times toxic, cocktail of legally ambiguous entrepreneurship. By the time that a growing number of informants, grasses and supergrasses had exposed the criminal code as little more than a macho fairy tale, British society was undergoing permanent changes. Along with the decline in working-class jobs and the communities that had depended on them for their very existence, there was a shift to a more materialistic, Americanised society that fetishised business and all it could buy.

Once the police and security industry had rendered armed robbery a distinctively more perilous occupation, and the violent elite serving time in prison or perched on a barstool on the Costas were enthusiastically embracing the drug economy, trading had come to dominate both criminal and non-criminal economies alike. Today, whether at street level or in collaboration with partners on the other side of the globe, most acquisitive crime is based upon buying low and selling high. While theft and robbery will always have a part to play in criminal life, with the exception of increasingly rare fantasy heists, they tend to constitute temporary forays carried out in order to accrue investment capital.

When working-class jobs disappeared, the fabric of the old neighbourhoods was transformed, and life became harsher and more individualistic. The cheeky chappies with a ready smile and a carton of fire damaged woks, were replaced by dealers knocking out drugs to anyone seeking an alternative to cheap cider and daytime television. It was easy to get into business, you were self-employed and got to know who was who, and what was what, and just like during the era of amateur and opportunistic theft from warehouses and docks, as long as you kept to making a few quid from family and friends, it was safe and easy. However, the drug trade tantalisingly offered access to the status of businessman – a way of being sharp, resourceful and respected, but going professional upped the stakes, offering big rewards, along with heavy punishment for getting nicked. When I published my first book in 1988, the prison population of the UK was 47,271. Now in early 2021, it stands at over 80,000.

As villains have become more businesslike, so the glamorous conceits of the old underworld have faded away. On the face of it, modern youth gangs are similar to the Sabinis, the Krays and the other working-class gangsters who also began their careers protecting local streets from incursion by adjacent youth groups. However, many of the estates, housing projects and postcodes of 21st-century Britain have been monetised by the drug trade, which has injected an entrepreneurial edge into a traditional violent street life that has persisted for generations. While young men still fight territorial battles, now there is a desire to protect market share, providing the foundation blocks for many careers in crime. Which, along with the example of the night-time economy, is a reminder that no matter how complex crime networks become or how innovative the methodologies they employ, violence will always have a place in the criminal entrepreneur's toolbox.

Undoubtedly there are successful, powerful men who have made their money from crime and exist in the realm of corporate finance, police intelligence reports and rumour – lots of rumour. However, they are not my concern; my research has always been out in the open, never covert or undercover, and I have tended to work with the lower ranks, only concerning myself with household names as a means of providing a historical perspective.

When I started my research in the 1980s, crime in the East End of London was a normal part of everyday life, and the villains, who were the more committed practitioners, were part of an underworld, separate to the so-called 'straightgoers'. But now the rest of the UK has caught up and the so called 'entrepreneurial spirit' that has become so fetishised in British society has resulted in entrepreneurs becoming criminals, and criminals becoming entrepreneurs.[33]

During the 1980s, interactions between East Enders and detectives were often played out in pubs and clubs. Now the drinking culture of the CID, where alcohol was central to detective work, has gone, and modern policing frowns upon police officers consorting with criminals – that task is now a specialism that is highly controlled and subject to surveillance by managers. Consequently, sharp-eared officers nurturing 'friendships' with villains are ancient history in a profession that is now distinctly administrative and increasingly defined by technology rather than the hard-drinking values of cops 'doing the business'. This does not mean that corruption no longer occurs; it is simply less overt and when it does take place, it is as likely to include civilian members of the police organisation as it is high premium detectives. In the case of the latter, life-changing money is now on offer rather than the odd bottle of scotch, a spare avocado bathroom suite, £50 put behind the bar for the CID Christmas party or an all-inclusive week in Impetigo Bay.

A key change in policing took place in the early 1990s when the British government formally adopted the term 'organised crime' and moved towards specialised national squads to deal with an issue that had previously been regarded as a local problem, to be dealt with by local police who possessed local knowledge. These specialised squads have subsequently wedged villains into organised crime packages with all of

---

33   The criminal economy is now central to our way of life and, according to Antonio Maria Costa, head of the UN Office on Drugs and Crime, when the global financial system was in meltdown in 2008, 'Inter-bank loans were funded by money that originated from the drugs trade and other illegal activities . . . There were signs that some banks were rescued that way'. *Observer*, 13 December 2009

the associated 'underworld' language and assumptions that we have imported from the USA, such as, 'the soldier', 'the kingpin' and, of course, 'the mastermind'. All of which may be convenient for the criminal justice system and handy for gaining prosecutions but it is far from an accurate reflection of the chaotic, unstructured practices of the villains. Police and other government organisations operate in highly rigid hierarchies and assume that criminals do too, whereas the reality is, as we have seen, that they are constantly on the move, working within interchangeable networks in the overworld, where serious crime is a gateway drug to being a businessman.

More to the point, over the past 40 years, the expectations of the general population have changed, and few are still content with a basic, secure existence comprising shelter and a job; now everybody fancies a slice of the lush life, an ounce of this, a gram of that, 200 'Albanian Marlboro' and so much more. Consequently, large swathes of the population are forever doing the business, as the demand for illegal drugs, cheap cigarettes and alcohol, sexual services – or simply for somebody cheap to do the school run, the ironing and a little light dusting – propels illegal markets that are both flexible and unforgiving.

The old boys done bad can no longer manage all day drinking, and in the early evening we made our way out to the car park where some awaited cabs, and others lurched worryingly towards top-of-the-range saloons and SUVs. Except those who didn't. Norman, who slipped out of the car park in a shit-brown Toyota, had already quietly told me his story. Once known only half-jokingly as 'the dogkiller', after the fatal poisoning of a dog guarding a scrap metal yard followed by an unfortunate incident featuring a Rottweiler, Norman was now living with his elderly mother and reduced to claiming social security. Sixty years of ducking and diving, and at least two spells in prison had taken their toll; he looked tired, his sweater was old, the wool pilled and bobbled, and I was not the only person who noticed that Norman had not bought a drink that afternoon.

Unlike Danny, who had 'plenty of dough', kept a roll of ten pound notes in his pink Ralph Lauren shorts, drove a sinister looking SUV that appears to have been built to military specifications and latched on to me in the car park. Never mind the lorry loads of loot that passed through his hands over the past quarter of a century, sweaty half-pissed Danny was in my ear about the most recent extension to his bungalow. After a farewell geriatric play-fight of macho handshakes and Goodfella hugs, I cadged a lift to the railway station before settling back in a nearly empty train to ponder on the Dogkiller's future, as well as wondering what kind of 60-year-old man thinks that pink shorts are de rigueur for a November night in the suburbs.

When the deals are done and the crime fades away, all that is left is the money. The war against crime will never be won, and the best that we can hope for is to keep our noses above the toxic fumes of battle, and try to live with this ever mutating business without choking.

REFERENCES

The Business is based upon various research projects conducted over the past 40 years, and below I have cited these books and articles along with a number of Home Office publications that I co-authored. I have also cited the work of other writers whose work is relevant to these individual chapters.

Chapter 1
Dick Hobbs, (2013) *Lush Life*. Oxford University Press

Chapter 2
Dick Hobbs, (1988) *Doing the Business*. Oxford University Press
John McVicar (1979) *McVicar by Himself*. London: Arrow

Chapter 3
Dick Hobbs, (1988) *Doing the Business*. Oxford University Press

Chapter 4

Carl Chinn, (1991) *Better Betting with a Decent Feller*. Hemel Hempstead: Harvester Wheatsheaf

Frankie Fraser and James Morton, (1994) *Mad Frank*. London: Little Brown

Billy Hill, (1955) *Boss of Britain's Underworld*, London: Naldrett Press

Dick Hobbs, (2013) *Lush Life: Constructing Organised Crime in the UK*. Oxford University Press

Dick Hobbs, (2002) 'Obituary: John Gotti Mafia boss', *Independent*, 11 June 2002

James Morton, (1993) *Gangland: London's Underworld*. London: Warner Books

John Pearson, (1973) *The Profession of Violence*. London: Granada

John Pearson, (2001) *The Cult of Violence*. London: Orion

Raphael Samuel, (1981) *East End Underworld: The Life and Times of Arthur Harding*. London: Routledge & Kegan Paul

Heather Shore, (2012) 'Criminality and Englishness in the Aftermath: The Racecourse Wars of the 1920s'. In *Twentieth Century British History* 22 (4): pp. 474–97

Lucio Sponza, (1988) *Italian Immigrants in Nineteenth-century Britain*. Leicester University Press

Chapter 5

BBC Radio 4, 'Coupons and Nylons: The Underside of VE Day', presenter: Dick Hobbs, 8 May 1995

Frankie Fraser and James Morton, (1994) *Mad Frank*. London: Little Brown

Dick Hobbs, Obituary, Frankie Fraser. *Independent*, 28 November 2014

REFERENCES

Dick Hobbs, Obituary, Gerald McArthur, *Independent*,
17 September 1996
Dick Hobbs, Obituary, Charlie Richardson, *Independent*,
21 September 1996
Dick Hobbs, (2013) *Lush Life: Constructing Organised Crime in the UK*. Oxford University Press
Gerald McArthur, personal archive
Charlie Richardson, (1992) *My Manor*. London: Pan
Eddie Richardson, (2005) *The Last Word*. London: Headline Publishing

Chapter 6

John Bennett, (2016) *Krayology*. London: Mango Books
Dick Hobbs, (2013) *Lush Life*. Oxford University Press
Dick Hobbs, Obituary, Ron Kray, *Independent*, 18 March 1995
Dick Hobbs, Obituary, Charlie Kray, *Independent*,
5 April 2000
Dick Hobbs, Obituary, Reg Kray, *Independent*,
2 October 2000
Dick Hobbs, (2004) 'Kray, Charles James (1926–2000)' and 'Kray, Reginald (1933–2000)' and 'Kray, Ronald (1933–95)', in *Oxford National Dictionary of Biography*
Michael Levi (1981) *The Phantom Capitalists*. Abingdon: Routledge
John Pearson, (1973), *The Profession of Violence*. London: Granada
John Pearson, (2001) *The Cult of Violence*. London: Orion

Chapter 8

Duncan Campbell and Julia Hartley-Brewer, 'Torso murders case goes to appeal court', *Guardian*, 3 June 2000

Duncan Campbell, Obituary, Bert Wickstead, *Guardian*, 27 March 2001

Micky Fawcett, (2014) *Krayzy Days*. Brighton: Pen Press

Dick Hobbs, (2013) *Lush Life*. Oxford University Press

Leonard Read and James Morton, (1991) *Nipper*. London: McDonald

Bert Wickstead, (1985) *Gangbuster*. London: Futura

Chapter 8

Dick Hobbs, (2013) *Lush Life*. Oxford University Press

Chapter 9

Dick Hobbs, (2013) *Lush Life*. Oxford University Press

Chapter 10

Duncan Campbell, (1991) *That Was Business, This is Personal*. London: Mandarin

Dick Hobbs, (1995) *Bad Business*. Oxford University Press

Dick Hobbs, Obituary, George Chatham, *Independent*, 6 June 1997

Bruce Reynolds, (2000) *The Autobiography of a Thief*. London: Virgin

Peter Scott, (1995) *Gentleman Thief: Recollections of a Cat Burglar*. London: HarperCollins

Chapter 11

Dick Hobbs, (1995) *Bad Business*. Oxford University Press

Dick Hobbs, (1997) 'Professional Crime: Change Continuity and the Enduring Myth of the Underworld', in *Sociology*, Vol. 31 (1), Feb., pp. 57–72

Dick Hobbs, (2013) *Lush Life*. Oxford University Press

REFERENCES

Dick Hobbs, Obituary, Bertie Smalls, *Guardian*,
1 March 2008

Dick Hobbs, 'Bobby Cummines', in *Spitalfields Life*,
16 December 2015

Brian Cox, John Shirley and Martin Short, (1977) *The Fall of Scotland Yard*. London: Penguin

Bobby Cummines, (2015) *I Am Not a Gangster*. London: Ebury

Paul Lashmar, 'Old-style villain is revealed as UK's most wanted man', *Independent*, 22 October 2011

Paul Lashmar and Dick Hobbs, 'Diamonds, Gold and Crime Displacement: Hatton Garden, and the evolution of organised crime in the UK', *Trends in Organised Crime*, 21, pp.104–125 (2018)

Chapter 12

Dick Hobbs, (2013) *Lush Life*. Oxford University Press

Dick Hobbs, (2004) 'Violence and Organised Crime', in the *Handbook of Violence* (eds J. Hagan and W. Heitmeyer). Amsterdam: Kluwer

Dick Hobbs, (2001) 'The Firm: Organizational Logic and Criminal Culture on a Shifting Terrain', in *British Journal of Criminology*, 41/4: pp.549–560

Geoff Pearson and Dick Hobbs, 'Middle Market Drug Distribution', Home Office Research Study no. 227 (2001), London: Home Office

Chapter 13

Dick Hobbs, (1995) *Bad Business*. Oxford University Press

Dick Hobbs, (2013) *Lush Life*. Oxford University Press

Chapter 14

Dick Hobbs, (1995) *Bad Business.* Oxford University Press
Dick Hobbs, Phil Hadfield, Stuart Lister and Simon Winlow, (2003) *Bouncers.* Oxford University Press
Dick Hobbs and Steve Hall, 'Bouncers: The art and economics of intimidation', final report to the Economic and Social Research Council (2000)
Geoff Pearson and Dick Hobbs, (2001) *Middle Market Drug Distribution*, Home Office Research Study No 227, London: Home Office.
A.H. Wilson, (2002) *24 Hour Party People.* London: Channel 4 Books.

Chapter 15

Dick Hobbs, (1995) *Bad Business.* Oxford University Press.
Dick Hobbs, (2013) *Lush Life.* Oxford University Press.
Matrix Knowledge Group, 'The Illicit Drug Trade in the United Kingdom', Home Office Online Report (2007)
Geoff Pearson and Dick Hobbs, 'Middle Market Drug Distribution', Home Office Research Study no. 227 (2001), London: Home Office

Chapter 16

Dick Hobbs, (2013) *Lush Life.* Oxford University Press
Matrix Knowledge Group, 'The Illicit Drug Trade in the United Kingdom', Home Office Online Report (2007)
Geoff Pearson and Dick Hobbs, 'Middle Market Drug Distribution', Home Office Research Study no. 227 (2001), London: Home Office

REFERENCES

Chapter 17

Dick Hobbs, (1995) *Bad Business*. Oxford University Press
Dick Hobbs, (2013) *Lush Life*. Oxford University Press

Chapter 18

Jimmy Boyle, (1977) A Sense of Freedom. London: Pan
Dick Hobbs, (1995) *Bad Business*. Oxford University Press
Dick Hobbs, 'Going Down the Glocal: The Local Context
of Organised Crime', *The Howard Journal*, special issue on
Organised Crime, 37, 4. pp.407–422 (1998)
Dick Hobbs, (2013) *Lush Life*. Oxford University Press
Matrix Knowledge Group, 'The Illicit Drug Trade in the
United Kingdom', Home Office Online Report (2007)

Chapter 19

Dick Hobbs, (2013) *Lush Life*. Oxford University Press
Matrix Knowledge Group, 'The Illicit Drug Trade in the
United Kingdom', Home Office Online Report (2007)

Chapter 20

Dick Hobbs, (2013) *Lush Life*. Oxford University Press
Rob Hornsby and Dick Hobbs, 'A Zone of Ambiguity: The
Political Economy of Cigarette Bootlegging', *British Journal of
Criminology* (June 2007)

Chapter 21

Dick Hobbs, (2013) *Lush Life*. Oxford University Press.
Matrix Knowledge Group, 'The Illicit Drug Trade in the
United Kingdom', Home Office Online Report (2007)

Epilogue

Dick Hobbs, (1988) *Doing the Business: Entrepreneurship, Detectives and the Working Class in the East End of London.* Oxford University Press

Dick Hobbs, (1995) *Bad Business.* Oxford University Press

Dick Hobbs, (2013) *Lush Life.* Oxford University Press

ACKNOWLEDGEMENTS

Along the way I have worked with some fine people on projects that are referred to in *The Business,* and particular thanks are due to: Phil Hadfield, Stuart Lister, Simon Winlow, Steve Hall, Rob Hornsby, the staff at Matrix and Paul Lashmar.

Thanks also to Leslie Gardner at Artellus for doing the business, and to Ciara Lloyd, Liz Marvin and Justine Taylor at John Blake for enabling this book to become a reality. How Justine simultaneously coped with a global pandemic, home schooling and *The Business*, I do not know. I will always be grateful to Dave Hooper, Tony Goldman, the late Terry Morris, Betsy Stanko, and Nigel Fielding for opening some important doors. Big thanks to old friends including the late, great Geoff Pearson, who could do it all, and to Laurie Taylor, David Downes, Louise Westmarland, Trigger, Mike Levi, Robin Williams, Paul Crace, Adrian Maxwell, Snowy the Snout, Graham Hurley and Bob Lilly, none of whom took the academic malarkey too seriously, if at all. A special mention to the late Dave Robins who advised me to "Always keep the meter running".

In particular I am grateful to all those who talked to me about their skulduggery. Thank you for your time and trouble. Your time has been invaluable to me, and without your trouble, I would have had nothing to write about.

Dick Hobbs
London, May 2021